as it is

Volume 2

RANGJUNG YESHE BOOKS

Padmasambhava
Advice from the Lotus-Born
Dakini Teachings

Padmasambhava and Jamgön Kongtrül
Light of Wisdom, Vol I ✦ Light of Wisdom, Vol II

Yeshe Tsogyal
The Lotus-Born (Shambhala Publ.)

Gampopa
The Precious Garland of the Sublime Path

Tsele Natsok Rangdröl
The Heart of the Matter ✦ Mirror of Mindfulness
Empowerment ✦ Lamp of Mahamudra

Chokgyur Lingpa
Ocean of Amrita, Ngakso Drubchen

Mipham Rinpoche
Gateway to Knowledge, Vol I ✦ Vol II

Tulku Urgyen Rinpoche
As It Is, Vol I ✦ Vol II
Rainbow Painting
Repeating the Words of the Buddha

Ten Lamas
In Memory of Kyabje Tulku Urgyen Rinpoche

Khenchen Thrangu Rinpoche
Songs of Naropa ✦ King of Samadhi
Buddha Nature

Chökyi Nyima Rinpoche
Indisputable Truth
The Union of Mahamudra & Dzogchen
Bardo Guidebook ✦ Song of Karmapa

Tulku Thondup
Enlightened Living

Orgyen Tobgyal Rinpoche
Life & Teachings of Chokgyur Lingpa

Tsoknyi Rinpoche
Carefree Dignity

as it is

Volume 2

❖

Tulku Urgyen Rinpoche

RANGJUNG YESHE • *Boudhanath, Hong Kong & Esby* • 2000

RANGJUNG YESHE PUBLICATIONS
BELMONT COURT 6A, 10 KOTEWALL
HONG KONG

www.rangjung.com
RANGJUNG@EARTHLINK.NET

ADDRESS LETTERS TO:

RANGJUNG YESHE PUBLICATIONS
KA-NYING SHEDRUB LING MONASTERY
P.O. BOX 1200, KATHMANDU, NEPAL

PUBLICATION DATA:

TULKU URGYEN RINPOCHE (1920-1996).
INTRODUCTION BY TARIK RINPOCHE, TENGA RINPOCHE,
TARTHANG TULKU, THRANGU RINPOCHE, ORGYEN TOBGYAL
RINPOCHE. TRANSLATED FROM THE TIBETAN
BY ERIK PEMA KUNSANG (ERIK HEIN SCHMIDT).
COMPILED BY MARCIA BINDER SCHMIDT
AND EDITED WITH KERRY MORAN.
FIRST ED.
TITLE: AS IT IS, VOL. II
ISBN 962-7341-39-8 (PBK.)
1. MAHAYANA AND VAJRAYANA — TRADITION OF PITH INSTRUC-
TIONS. 2. BUDDHISM — TIBET. I. TITLE.

COVER PICTURE COURTESY OF SHECHEN ARCHIVES
COVER PHOTO: MATHIEU RICARD
PHOTO OF TULKU URGYEN RINPOCHE: UNKNOWN

Table of Contents

❖

Preface

The collection of teachings presented in *As It Is, Volume II*, is primarily selected from talks given by Kyabje Tulku Urgyen Rinpoche between 1994 and 1995. The emphasis in *Volume I* was on the development stage. The emphasis in *Volume II* is mainly on the completion stage.

In *Volume II* we attempted to show the intimate closeness and warmth that existed between Rinpoche and his students. We tried to authentically represent his style by showing his methods of interaction. We aspired to give readers a taste of what it was like to be in the presence of a master who was so playfully skillful, direct and inspiring.

Out of respect for the seal of secrecy that surrounds these teachings, it has been necessary to edit out some delicate points. If this has left any trace of confusion, please forgive the imposition. The transmission of Dzogchen cannot be received solely from books. Nor can it be extracted from the body of teachings from which it is the pinnacle, while discarding the rest. The work here underlines how essential it is to receive instructions of this sort in person from a qualified master and lineage holder of the Tibetan Buddhist tradition.

Volume I includes parts of interviews given by Rinpoche's sons after his passing. In *Volume II*, excerpts of statements from other great lamas are included as an introduction; we are very grateful to be able to reproduce these. Many sincere thanks go to all our Dharma friends who worked on *As It Is*: our editor, Kerry Moran, the proofreaders Lynn Schroeder and Michael Yockey, the transcriber, Dell O'Conner, the sundry taskmaster, Michael Tweed, and the printing sponsor, Richard Gere.

Please forgive any repetitions in this book; Rinpoche himself said that his talks were like the song of the sparrow, always the same! We regard *As It Is* as an offering to students of this tradition. At the same time, we hope that new students will get a feel for how to ask for and respond to mind teachings.

In conclusion, may whatever merit gained from being involved in a work such as this be of benefit to all beings in realizing the Great Perfection in actuality, and may it hasten the return of the reincarnation of our precious teacher, Kyabje Tulku Urgyen Rinpoche.

Marcia Binder Schmidt
Nagi Gompa, April 2000

Introduction

True Humility

⚜

Spoken by Tarik Rinpoche

Though there is not much I can say, I would like to say these few words. Tulku Urgyen Rinpoche and I came from the same area in Eastern Tibet, but we still seemed to live quite far from each other. In those days, we had no access to modern technology. Since there were no airplanes, no trains and no cars, everyone traveling had to either go by foot or on horseback. So, an area that today we consider easy to cover by modern transportation in those days seemed like a long, long distance away. Although we had of course heard about each other, it was not until I first arrived in the Kathmandu Valley that we began to have a connection.

When I came to Nepal, Tulku Urgyen was already living in Kathmandu. Knowing about him, I kept bothering him until he compassionately agreed to give me the transmission for the *One Hundred Empowerments of Chö*. In those days I was quite poor, and was unable to make any significant offering for this transmission. Since he was extremely kind-hearted and we came from the same homeland, I was fortunate to receive all the empowerments. From then on we have maintained a very pure samaya connection, without any damage or breach — intact, just like a delicate but unbroken eggshell. Because Tulku Urgyen was someone with great kindness and a strong sense of loyalty, he never changed his feelings for someone once he had gotten to know them well.

In terms of practice, between Sutra and Tantra, he was more learned in the tantric teachings, and among the Sarma and Nyingma traditions, he was more accomplished in the Nyingma practices. He was not someone you could freely ask about his personal realization. I never heard him mention that he had any special experiences or high level of realization. But, without a doubt, I feel that he was definitely an extraordinary practitioner. Anyone who met him could feel that he did not have any conceit, no ambitions of grandeur or fame, nor did he hold any resentment. He treated everyone graciously and cordially, and never turned his back on a friend.

Tulku Urgyen was also free of deceit and duplicity. If he said something, you could always trust that his words and his heart were in harmony. He did not act in a hypocritical way, saying one thing and doing another. In his relations with people, he was never dishonest or unreliable.

In terms of spiritual relationships, he was connected to the 16th Karmapa, one of the most important lamas in the great practice lineages. The Karmapa is on the same level as the Dalai Lama, the Panchen Rinpoche and Sakya Trichen. Tulku Urgyen is one of the Karmapa's gurus, as he offered him many empowerments and teachings from the *Chokling Tersar*.

Even though he had the status of someone whom the Karmapa venerated at the crown of his own head, Tulku Urgyen did not become full of self-importance or take advantage of this fame. When in a group of lamas or sitting in a large religious gathering he always refused to preside as the head, always insisting on taking a lower position. Taking the lower seat is a sign of having tamed one's own mind, and this is how he always acted. Otherwise, since he was the Karmapa's guru, it would have been perfectly fine to maintain a dignified presence, but because of being a *ngakpa*, a tantric practitioner, he would regard himself as lower than any other lama or even than an ordinary, fully ordained monk.

True humility is the sign of having gained experience and realization. Without experience and realization, we become involved in mundane attitudes — conceit towards people below, jealousy towards people above, and competitiveness towards our equals. This is unavoidable, because the five poisonous emotions of attachment, anger, dullness, pride and envy still remain alive within our stream of being. Even though someone may dress up as a renunciate or a yogi, these negative emotions still become evident from time to time. Tulku Urgyen, however, was not at all like that.

Our relationship was one of brothers; he treated me as an equal, just as if we had the same father and mother. When he shared his thoughts with me, there was never any discrepancy between his words and what he truly felt. This does not mean that other lamas are unreliable, but for me it was as if Tulku Urgyen was the only one I really felt I could confide and place my trust in. This may be because I am old-fashioned or that times have changed, but for me he was the main person I would rely on.

In all the Buddhist vehicles, it is taught that you should not regard your spiritual guide as an ordinary person. In Vajrayana practice, especially, everything depends on your guru; he is the basis for all accomplishment. So supplicate him sincerely, visualize him in the sky before you, mingle your mind with his mind indivisibly, and receive the four empowerments. By doing so you will soon have experience and realization and it will become possible for you to glimpse innate suchness — the Buddha within — in a single instant. This still holds true even when the guru is no longer within his body — if you supplicate him, you can still realize his nature. So, all of you disciples, please be very careful about keeping your samaya link with the guru.

In addition, remind yourself repeatedly of the words you personally heard him say and apply your mind to fully realizing their meaning. In short, in terms of learning, reflection and meditation, you should combine the words you have heard, reflect upon their meaning and then put them into practice. Doing so will fulfill your guru's wishes. This is called the offering of practice, which is far beyond lavish offerings of material things. Material offerings are good in their own way, of course, but there is nothing superior to this 'offering of practice'. Apply yourself in both word and deed with unwavering trust, and supplicate him one-pointedly. Please remember that this is what we all need.

Maybe I don't need to mention this, but still I feel that Tulku Urgyen's sons are remarkable people. They belong to the family line of Tsangsar, which is said to originate from divine beings. In this family line there have been a great number of accomplished masters, all of them extraordinary, respectable and noble-minded. I expect that Rinpoche's sons will live up to their heritage.

This is to all of you who are Tulku Urgyen Rinpoche's disciples: if you continue to keep your samaya connection with him throughout this life, the bardo and your next life, you will surely benefit. Follow the advice he gave you, and serve him in any way you can. There is nothing greater than that. By pleasing the guru you can remove obstacles. Displeasing and upsetting him is equal to committing the five most severe misdeeds. In this lies the foundation for attaining accomplishment. The guru is considered more important than both the yidam deity and the Dharma protectors. Devotion to the guru is the universal panacea.

Many of you disciples have heard Tulku Urgyen's words with your own ears. Please continue to follow his advice and keep your samaya connection. There is nothing better for this life, for the bardo, and for the future. Dedicate the merit you create and make pure aspirations that his wishes be fulfilled.

In order to show that everything is impermanent, even a sublime being like Buddha Shakyamuni, who was beyond birth and death, still passed away in Kushinagar, although this was only on the level of superficial reality. Similarly, Tulku Urgyen remains in dharmadhatu and is all set to come back. But a return is totally dependent upon the interest and inclinations of sentient beings. Do not think that a master who has left remains impassive; there are many other realms besides this one where beings can be benefited. To create a link for the future necessitates a vast amount of merit. So, do your best to create merit and fulfill his wishes. This is all I can say. Please, everyone, keep this in mind.

An Authentic Dzogchen Yogi

❖

Spoken by Tenga Rinpoche

I would like to briefly tell you about the fine qualities of Tulku Urgyen Rinpoche. About a century ago, a noble master who was the emanation of Prince Murub Tsenpo incarnated as a great tertön. His name was Chokgyur Lingpa and everyone, without dispute, accepted him. It is in the family line of this treasure revealer that Tulku Urgyen consciously chose to incarnate.

When young, Tulku Urgyen studied to perfection both the general and esoteric topics of knowledge. As he grew up, he sat at the feet of his sublime father as well as Rigpey Dorje, the 16th Karmapa, and received all the genuine instructions. Later he practiced extensively at the retreat center of Tsurphu, known as Pema Khyung Dzong or Dechen Chöling. Through this practice he realized the final of four visions of the Dzogchen teachings, the view known as 'exhaustion in dharmata'. Based on this realization, Rigpey Dorje, the 16th Karmapa, who could see the three times of past, present and future in actuality, as well as directly seeing the death and rebirth of all beings, and who is acclaimed by everyone in the snowy land of Tibet as an authentic and perfect being, then requested Chokgyur Lingpa's terma teachings from Tulku Urgyen. Thus, he accepted him as his root guru, the lord of the mandala.

Having accepted Tulku Urgyen as his root guru, the Karmapa received the ripening empowerments, the liberating instructions and the supportive reading transmissions for the profound Dzogchen teachings and the terma teachings of Chokgyur Lingpa, in their entirety, correctly and perfectly. It is for this reason that I feel that Tulku Urgyen definitely was both an authentic Dzogchen yogi who had reached the stage of exhaustion in dharmata, and an extraordinary and great master, fully qualified and perfect.

In recent years all the lineage-holders of the *Karma Kamtsang* — Shamar Rinpoche, Situ Rinpoche, Jamgön Rinpoche, Gyaltsab Rinpoche, as well as Dabzang Rinpoche and many others — accepted Tulku Urgyen as their root guru, supplicated him as the lord of the mandala, and received from him the complete terma teachings of Chokgyur Lingpa. From this perspective as well, I feel that he was without a doubt an accomplished Dzogchen master who had arrived at the stage of exhaustion in dharmata.

He spent his life in practice and retreat, living in later years at Nagi Gompa hermitage. Here, having reached the end of his practice, accomplished all his activities, and completed his life span, he displayed the temporary dissolving of his physical presence in order to inspire to practice we disciples who cling to permanence and hold on with attachment. Just like other noble beings and bodhisattvas, who never forsake the Buddhadharma and sentient beings, I believe that before long we will have the excellent fortune to behold the golden countenance of a sublime new tulku who will be enthroned to enact his eminent deeds of boundlessly turning the profound and vast wheels of the Dharma, his health and lifespan as indestructible as a diamond.

Tulku Urgyen Rinpoche bestowed immense kindness upon me, graciously extending his compassion by conferring the empowerments, instructions, and reading transmissions of the *Dzogchen Desum*, the *Three Sections of the Great Perfection*. Therefore, I consider him one of my special root gurus, one whose kindness is incomparable.

Rising to the Challenge

❖

Composed by Tarthang Tulku

One of the greatest masters of recent times was the treasure revealer Chokgyur Dechen Lingpa (1829-1870), considered an incarnation of the son of King Trisong Deutsen. The eminent lamas Jamgön Kongtrül and Jamyang Khyentse Wangpo greatly respected his wisdom and attainments, and, through them, his teachings had a wide impact. He revealed more than 250 of the texts contained in the *Rinchen Terdzö*, and he is honored not only in the Nyingma tradition, but also in the Karma Kagyü, Drukpa, Drigung, Taklung, and Sakya schools. Truly, in the times since Rigdzin Jigmey Lingpa, he is the greatest of Terma masters.

The lineage of Chokgyur Dechen Lingpa was passed on through his daughter, Semo Könchok Paldrön, and she in turn transmitted it to her four sons. One of her sons, Tsangsar Chimey Dorje, was the father of our beloved Tulku Urgyen.

Fully learned in the special traditions of Chokgyur Dechen Lingpa, Tulku Urgyen was also a great master of the Nyingma Kama and Terma, and was one of the most comprehensive lineage holders of our time. Like his student, teacher, and Dharma brother, the Sixteenth Karmapa, he received teachings from Karsey Kongtrül, the son of the Fifteenth Karmapa and an incarnation of Jamgön Kongtrül.

Tulku Urgyen demonstrated a devotion to Longchenpa, Chokgyur Lingpa, Jamyang Khyentse, and Jamgön Kongtrül that inspired all who knew him. In the 1950s he received teachings from my own root guru, the Second Jamyang Khyentse Chökyi Lodrö, journeying to Lhasa and Gangtok for this purpose. In addition to receiving initiations he had many close personal discussions with this great master. Jamyang

Khyentse Chökyi Lodrö, Dudjom Rinpoche, and Dilgo Khyentse all counted Tulku Urgyen among their advisers and spiritual friends.

Not only was Tulku Urgyen kind, wise, and compassionate, but he was humble and gentle as well. He was renowned as a yogi, and though he did not live the life of a mountain recluse like Milarepa, his mind exhibited all the qualities of such accomplished masters. With great modesty, Tulku Urgyen served the Sixteenth Karmapa as his assistant and counselor in both spiritual and practical affairs, and also gave him teachings on Atiyoga. A trusted confidante, he rendered indispensable assistance in such matters as the lengthy dispute over Swayambhu Temple. In fulfilling these responsibilities, he never once failed to follow through on a commitment.

Tulku Urgyen was not well known as a scholar, yet the depth of his actual understanding was unsurpassed, and many Nyingma and Kagyü masters stood in awe of his comprehensive knowledge. He had thoroughly studied and practiced the Atiyoga, and his teachings on Dzogchen transformed the lives of those he touched with gentle, penetrating clarity.

As a meditation teacher and a master of initiations, he was without peer. We are especially blessed in having received from him the profound teachings of the Chokling lineage, through which Avalokiteshvara and Guru Padmasambhava manifest in our lives. Direct and clear, these sadhanas make the complex teachings of the Vajrayana freshly available.

Besides his stature as a lineage holder and his prowess as a teacher, Tulku Urgyen was skilled in all the arts and crafts. He excelled in calligraphy, painting, sculpture, and the making of torma, and he had encyclopedic knowledge in many fields of human inquiry. He had a remarkable grasp of history, including Tibet's relations with China and Mongolia, the history of Kham, Nangchen, and Derge, and the biographies of great lineage holders.

Tulku Urgyen was very kind to my children and me. He and I traveled together extensively more than thirty years ago, and in later years I received from him several important teachings, including the hearing lineage of the *Gyü Chubdün* (the *Seventeen Dzogchen Tantras*) and the teachings of Chokgyur Dechen Lingpa. To have met and studied with this great lama, enjoyed his presence and received his compassionate guidance, is truly a great blessing. His loving gestures and marvelous heart brought us all boundless joy. Although others were much closer to him, I can say that his gentle nature, which became immediately apparent to all who met him, was truly unique.

Tulku Urgyen wore his knowledge and attainments lightly. Unlike some learned masters, who seem to lecture whenever they open their mouths, he spoke with such kindness and profound sensitivity that no one hesitated to ask him questions. He used his knowledge to touch the heart of everyone he met, making conversation with him a delight. He had the gift of making each person feel that he alone was the lama's favorite — so well did he manifest the beauty of compassion. His students responded with deep personal devotion and an eagerness to learn more. They were serious in their studies, and they often sought out the opportunity for long retreats.

In these times of the Kali Yuga, when great troubles have befallen Tibet, Tulku Urgyen rose to the challenge. Journeying to a new country, he established a foundation for the Dharma and made the special treasures of Dzogchen and the Chokling lineage widely available. He benefited the Sangha greatly, establishing centers, extending the teachings, and passing on his knowledge. Today there are more than thirty different monasteries in the Kathmandu Valley, and I personally trace much of this activity to the light that radiated from Nagi Gompa, where the presence of Tulku Urgyen, the teachings of Chokling, and the blessings of Guru Padmasambhava came together. Truly, whatever any lama could accomplish, Tulku Urgyen has brought to fruition.

Once while having the good fortune to stay at Nagi Gompa, I saw in a vision that through the blessings of Padmasambhava, the Dharma could one day spread out from this tiny valley, revitalized and newly powerful. Now that our beloved teacher is gone, I pray that his lasting influence will help this vision come to fruition.

Extraordinary Experience and Realization

❖

Spoken by Thrangu Rinpoche

Tulku Urgyen Rinpoche was someone with extraordinary experience and realization, a fact known throughout the world. This is not something I need to say. It is evident to everyone that he was unlike anyone else when it came to pointing out the nature of mind, and making sure that people both recognized it and had some actual experience. In this way he was extraordinary, and I feel it is all right if I don't talk too much about it. In a more general way, Tulku Urgyen was born into the family of Chokgyur Lingpa, a unique family line. In addition, he is the father of the present tulku of Chokgyur Lingpa, which is also something quite extraordinary.

Q: What does it mean when a lama remains in *tukdam*?

R: *Tukdam* comes about when someone has rested evenly in luminous wakefulness of samadhi during his life. The extent to which he remains in the after-death state of tukdam occurs to the same degree as his experience in samadhi. It is due to the strength of the samadhi that the body heat doesn't disappear, that the skin color doesn't fade, and that the body is able to remain in an upright sitting posture. Such visible signs occurring after death indicate that the person is in tukdam.

When the practitioner passes away, an experience occurs which we call the 'mingling of the mother and child luminosities', which means that the ground luminosity and the luminosity of that person's practice mingle indivisibly.

At that moment, the experience of luminous wakefulness is very strong. One simply remains in its composure naturally, meaning that high lamas or someone with deep experience and realization will naturally dissolve into or expand into this state of samadhi. When the ground luminosity dawns by itself, they recognize it, then remain in equanimity — that is called 'remaining in tukdam'.

Ordinary people also experience the ground luminosity, but because of not having trained in it during their life, they don't recognize this ground luminosity, and failing to recognize, they are therefore unable to remain in tukdam. On the other hand, great masters naturally mingle the mother and child luminosities. In the very moment the ground luminosity unfolds within their direct experience, they acknowledge this basic state and remain in samadhi. This is called 'remaining in tukdam'.

Q: What do such signs as a 'clear sky and dust-free earth' represent?

R: Tulku Urgyen Rinpoche was someone who kept a concealed profile, meaning that he didn't make a great display of himself. He concealed his qualities and hid what he actually was, often saying, "I'm nothing special, I'm not learned." Since he kept such a low profile, it could mean that, when he passed away, due to the power and strength of his extraordinary samadhi, the sign of a clear sky and dust-free earth naturally manifested. He probably concealed any other signs such as rainbows, rays of light, and so forth.

Q: What was the relationship between the 16th Karmapa and Tulku Urgyen Rinpoche?

R: The 16th incarnation in the line of the Gyalwang Karmapa regarded Tulku Urgyen's family line as very special and therefore received many of the empowerments for Chokgyur Lingpa's termas from Tulku Urgyen. Moreover, they were very close since His Holiness trusted Tulku Urgyen as his personal advisor in both spiritual and secular affairs. As we know, the Karmapa often showed how he held Tulku Urgyen in extremely high esteem.

A Jewel in the Crown Ornament

❖

Spoken by Orgyen Tobgyal Rinpoche

It is impossible for one person to truly judge another, so we can never really know how great a master Tulku Urgyen was. Only a buddha like Shakyamuni can fully know another being. However, during the twentieth century there have been a few masters who were unanimously accepted to be like the Buddha appearing in person. Along with the 16th Gyalwang Karmapa, Rangjung Rigpey Dorje, and Kyabje Dudjom Rinpoche, who was the emissary of Guru Padmasambhava, there has also been Kyabje Dilgo Khyentse Rinpoche. Within the contemporary Kagyü and Nyingma schools there has been no one more extraordinary and with so immense an impact on the Buddhadharma than them. Yet, these three all accepted Tulku Urgyen among their root gurus. If they respected Tulku Urgyen as their crown ornament, I, too, feel we should regard him as someone special.

Tulku Urgyen Rinpoche upheld both the teaching and family lineages of Chokgyur Lingpa. He kept this lineage of empowerment, instruction, and reading transmission alive, not only by practicing it himself, but also ensuring it will continue by passing it on to the Karmapa and Dudjom Rinpoche, as well as countless others. His activity on behalf of this Dharma lineage is an immense kindness that I regard as very special. Tulku Urgyen's family lineage comes through the daughter of Chokgyur Lingpa, Könchok Paldrön, and her son Chimey Dorje, who was Tulku Urgyen's father. Thus, he directly descended from the great tertön.

On one occasion Könchok Paldrön asked for advice from both Jamyang Khyentse and Jamgön Kongtrül as to whether it would be better to become a nun or get married. Both masters replied, "You should take a husband; in the future it is through your bloodline that someone will appear to benefit beings. This is very important."

Accordingly, she married a son of the Tsangsar family. The couple had many children, including Tulku Urgyen's uncle, the great master Samten Gyatso, who brought great benefit to the continuation of the Tersar teachings and was able to carry out great deeds. This lineage continues through Tulku Urgyen's many sons, who are all still alive and well. Although they have their individual titles and bear the responsibility to uphold their respective lineages, I hope that they will also personally practice and transmit the terma teachings of Chokgyur Lingpa, their father's own lineage.

Many people these days hold the opinion that Tulku Urgyen Rinpoche was just a Dzogchen yogi who only stayed up in his mountain hermitage, Nagi Gompa, and practiced one-pointedly — concluding that he was a good lama with high realization. Since he downplayed his talents, not many people seem to know the details of his qualities beyond these simple facts. But when I reflect on what I personally know, I feel that he was also a great scholar.

Tulku Urgyen was not someone famed for being learned. But if we begin to investigate in detail, starting from reading skills, we see he was a scholar, able to read many kinds of scripts, including even the rare *lantsa* and *wardu* variety. He was proficient in grammar, poetry, and the general sciences, so it is difficult to find anything about which he was ignorant. Concerning the inner knowledge of Buddhism, he had met many very educated and learned masters, and was especially well-versed in the *Ngakso*, the *Lamrim Yeshe Nyingpo*, and the *Guhyagarbha Tantra*.[1] He was a great calligrapher, very knowledgeable about many scripts that have been practically forgotten today. Not only was he proficient in *lantsa* and *wardu*, but in *uchen* and *umey* as well. Taking all this into consideration, I personally consider him very learned.

Tulku Urgyen Rinpoche was also a skilled craftsman. Because he could make original statues — unlike professional sculptors who usually just repeat themselves — his sculptures of deities often had much finer proportions. Some of these can be seen in the shrine rooms for the Dharma protectors at Ka-Nying Shedrub Ling. In the Nyingma *gönkhang* protectors' shrine, there is an extraordinary mask of Mahakala, while in the Kagyü temple there is a mask of *Bernakchen*, the Black-Cloaked One. When beholding these masks I felt that no ordinary artist could have created such works. And, if anyone wants to see what an expert tailor Tulku Urgyen was, I will be happy to show him or her the crown he made for the Chokling tulku. He re-created Chokgyur Lingpa's crown from memory, which was no small feat.

There is one strange thing that I would like to mention. The expressions of realization don't always appear so clearly. I often noticed that during Dilgo Khyentse Rinpoche's talks, or when he was writing, that everything he said would come out eloquently and unimpeded. But at other times the words seem hindered. It was the same with Tulku Urgyen; occasionally he had a very hard time reading and his eyesight turned so bad that an operation on his eyes was required.

When it came to mundane discussions he was extremely skillful. Even if people put their heads together, they are often still unable to decide what to do. But Rinpoche was always able to make a decision which was in harmony with both spiritual and social conventions; he always seemed to know what the best course of action would be, giving advice without hesitation. Often people would find that his solution was something they hadn't even thought of, and upon hearing it they felt, "Well of course!" His decision would put their minds at ease and they felt confident that this was the best solution. This is another example of the power of his intelligence.

There is a famous Kagyü saying, "Devotion is the head of meditation." Devotion is based upon one's guru, so to have the trust and devotion that one's guru is the Buddha in actuality is a most eminent method. To fulfill one's guru's wish to the letter and to serve him in whatever way possible is the proper way to apply the oral instructions.

In this regard, Tulku Urgyen's sense of trust, loyalty and samaya with other masters was constant. He regarded his own teachers as the Buddha in person. Once he had connected with a teacher through receiving empowerment or oral instructions, his trust was unwavering. If the opportunity came to carry out his guru's wish he was willing to give unstintingly of whatever wealth was in his possession, without any concern for personal hardship. If it came to it, I feel that he would even have been ready to sacrifice his own life without any hesitation or regret. Once Rinpoche took responsibility for a legal dispute on behalf of the Gyalwang Karmapa and it dragged on for so many years that it felt like half a lifetime. Though Rinpoche was successful in the end, it was only to his teacher's benefit and not to his own personal gain.

Tulku Urgyen Rinpoche was someone who could back up his words with action. In both spiritual and secular affairs, he wouldn't just talk about what needed to be done — he would go ahead and do it. Nor did he get involved in a lot of doubt and hesitation about the tasks at hand, worrying about whether something would be successful or not. He wouldn't get caught up in a web of concepts; instead he would make a decision free of doubt and never waver. That's the kind of man he was.

When speaking of the Buddhist scriptures — the Middle Way, Prajnaparamita and so forth — the 'exposition lineage' focuses on explaining the syntax and intent. But being learned is not just a matter of knowing the words and their meaning; there is also the transmission of the real meaning. Tulku Urgyen was a pandita in the true sense of the word.

At one time I went to see Tulku Urgyen to ask him to clarify a verse from the ninth chapter of Shantideva's *Bodhicharya Avatara* (*The Way of a Bodhisattva*):

> *When concreteness or inconcreteness*
> *Does not remain before the intellect,*
> *At that moment there is no other mental form,*
> *And so, there is utter peace without conceptions.*

I had studied it many times and asked many khenpos about it but still felt that none of them had given me an adequate explanation. I also asked Tulku Urgyen about certain points in the Prajnaparamita teachings in which the fact of emptiness is established; such as the statement that emptiness has no form, no sound and so forth. Only Tulku Urgyen was able to prove the reality of these statements in a reasonable way. His logic established emptiness in actuality for me, while the other scholars merely established emptiness in words.

At some point the reincarnation of Neten Chokling, Tulku Pema Wangyal, and a few of us went up to Nagi Gompa and spent a few days asking questions. During this time Tulku Urgyen clearly laid out the logic of establishing emptiness. Everyone was amazed at his clarity. Explaining how all sentient beings have buddha nature also proves that buddha nature is an intrinsic quality. This is especially done in the higher Middle Way School known as *Shentong*. In the biographies of many great lamas you find that they would bow down to and circumambulate even old dogs to show their respect for buddha nature, while saying, "I take refuge in the buddha nature."

Tulku Urgyen had confidence and utterly pure trust, based on the personal, direct understanding that buddha nature really is present in every sentient being. Just like oil is present in each and every sesame seed, any sentient being can realize the awakened state and thus has the basis for enlightenment. Therefore, Tulku Urgyen showed respect for every sentient being and didn't turn against anyone. He felt this not as mere platitude, but from the core of his heart.

Tulku Urgyen also showed vast insight about the meaning of the *Uttaratantra, Hevajra Tantra* and the *Profound Inner Meaning*, which are favored in the Kagyü lineage. Within the Nyingma school he was incredibly well-versed in both the root text of the *Lamrim Yeshe Nyingpo*, as well as Jamgön Kongtrül's commentary on it. He knew most of the root text by heart, and had repeatedly studied the commentaries by Rinchen Namgyal and Khenpo Jokyab. He was very knowledgeable in Vajrayana, having studied the *Guhyagarbha Tantra*, the *Secret Essence of the Magical Net*. In a discussion with Dilgo

Khyentse Rinpoche, it became apparent to me that Tulku Urgyen also had a complete grasp of the *Guhyagarbha Tantra*.

During the first *Ngakso* drubchen held at Ka-Nying Shedrub Ling, I had the chance to ask Tulku Urgyen questions about the tenfold meaning of mantra. He gave very clear explanations that made me appreciate his learnedness in the *Guhyagarbha Tantra*. He also had an in-depth knowledge of many other tantras. He was especially insightful when defining the kayas and wisdoms, and the 'chakras of syllable clouds', the sounds and meaning of mantra. In short, he fit exactly the title 'pandita of definitive meaning'.

Concerning tantric ceremonies, Tulku Urgyen Rinpoche was extremely competent in the mandalas for vast activities, knowing their proportions and the accompanying rituals of sacred dance and exorcism. He was a skilled torma maker as well as an expert *umdzey*, chant master. He had a remarkable grasp of architecture and all other necessary fields of knowledge connected to Tibetan Buddhist practice. While some *umdzeys* merely sing ceremonies from beginning to end, Tulku Urgyen's singing carried a certain blessing that could move the listener to devotion. When he gave an empowerment, even though the ritual may not have involved more than placing a vase on somebody's head, people would feel it was something really special. Even the way he looked at people would give them some understanding that was totally unlike an ordinary person.

When giving empowerment to a gathering of thousands of people, sitting on a throne made of brocade cushions, he never looked out of place. His air and bearing, impressive and dignified, never looked contrived. He was definitely extraordinary.

Rinpoche would always touch heads with whoever came into his presence, even the poorest Nepali worker, and ask, "How are you?" And you could see happiness on the person's face that far surpassed the joy of receiving thousands of rupees. There is no reason why someone should become so happy just by being asked how they are and touching foreheads, but people were so delighted. Many foreigners changed their whole perspective on life from only one meeting and felt extraordinarily blessed. Practitioners felt that they received blessings and even ordinary people still felt that something unusual had happened. Whoever came into his presence never felt tired, even after several hours had passed. That is totally unlike being in the presence of some politicians, when you can't wait to get away. Speaking for myself, I never tired of being with Tulku Urgyen — I only felt happy.

In all his conversations there was never any mention of prejudice. Whether you talked about religious or secular affairs, he always spoke honestly and clearly, never acting pretentiously or ever lying. He also had a sharp memory, and spoke of events long past as if they just happened yesterday. Nobody wanted to leave his presence; people always wanted to sit longer — they just wouldn't get out. I've heard that he scolded a few people, but I've never met anyone who actually got scolded. I never heard him say a harsh word. At the same time, anyone who lived near him or knew him for a long time felt timidity and a sense of awe.

His very presence was powerful. For instance, if you had to return to his room after having just left it, he would still pay you the same respect and you would still feel awestruck. Nor was he someone you felt you could talk nonsense in front of — you had to choose your words with sincerity.

The qualities of someone who has completely severed the ties of selfishness and pursues only the welfare of others may not necessarily be visible. But it is hard to find a more unselfish person than Tulku Urgyen. When focusing on benefiting others, our own aims automatically become fulfilled without having to deliberately try. Building a monastery is a very difficult task that sometimes seems insurmountable. But most people are not aware of how many temples Tulku Urgyen built. Nor does anybody know exactly how many years he stayed in retreat, which practices he did, nor the number of recitations he completed. People can vaguely say that he did it once or twice in Tibet and once in India but other than that no one knows. I figure he spent approximately half of his entire life doing intensive practice in retreat.

There are no accurate records of which empowerments, transmissions, and teachings he received. But he probably received most of the *Nyingma Kama* and *Terma*, all the Kagyü teachings, and the *Lamdrey* from the Sakya school as well as many other lineages. Every time you brought up a certain teaching and asked him about it, it seemed he held the transmission for it. He received an ocean of teachings. Tulku Urgyen's unique heart practice was the *Chetsün Nyingtig* and *Künzang Tuktig*, belonging to the Great Perfection itself. He is unanimously accepted by everyone as a great Dzogchen yogi.

It is not really up to me to speak about his attainment of great accomplishment, but in 1985, after a discussion with Dilgo Khyentse Rinpoche, His Holiness told me that Tulku Urgyen had reached the level of 'culmination of awareness'. When someone has arrived at the culmination of awareness there is nothing more to realize other than 'exhaustion in dharmata', so he was someone who achieved the final realization of the Great Perfection. In short, it is perfectly fine to regard him as a master who was both learned and accomplished.

From a personal point of view, I can say that I haven't met anyone superior to Tulku Urgyen. There has been no one who, in actuality, was better able to carry out the intent of Shantideva's *Bodhicharya Avatara* to the letter. Without any concern for personal hardship, he always aimed to do his utmost to benefit sentient beings. He was also extremely humble and self-effacing — totally in tune with Shantideva's bodhisattva ideal. He treated everyone, whether important or ordinary, with the same affection and attention, teaching everyone equally. In order to bring the highest benefit he always tried to communicate in the listener's own terms. And it was not only in his teaching, but also in all his conversations, that you would find the bodhisattva ideal of ocean-like activity clearly reflected. While I never saw him actually give away his head, arms or legs as you hear about in some of the bodhisattva stories, I feel absolutely certain that he was a great bodhisattva, able to do so.

In terms of Vajrayana, he had perfected the practices of both development and completion. I know he spent at least four three-year retreats doing sadhana and recitation. Later, he remained in what you could call life-retreat at his hermitage, Nagi Gompa. The scriptures mention something called the 'threefold gathering' and the 'threefold blazing forth', which is achieved upon having perfected the practices of the development and completion stages. I feel he possessed these in completeness.

Whether he was giving empowerment, instruction or reading transmission, he always gave his full attention, taking his utmost care to bring benefit to the recipients — particularly when giving the sublime Dzogchen teachings. He was unlike many teachers who, lacking substance, supposedly give teachings on Dzogchen while only teaching the words. When Tulku Urgyen imparted the pointing-out instruction, he would point out the real thing, nakedly and directly.

Once in Taiwan I witnessed Tulku Urgyen give the pointing-out instruction to a gathering of more than one thousand people. Despite the size of the group, he still gave the real thing nakedly and directly, leaving nothing out. This must exemplify what is called the 'expression of compassionate capacity', for he rose to the occasion out of the power of his realization. He said, "The oral instruction is like a candle: you can see only for as long as you're holding it; and when you put it down, you have no more light. But since all of you have taken the trouble to come here, expecting to hear me speak, I feel that I cannot refuse giving you the pointing-out instruction." Then he gave the instruction in coming face to face with your own nature, in a way that would have been unrivalled even if the great Khyentse, Kongtrül or Longchenpa were giving it. Yet I later met only a few people in that group who truly recognized their own nature.

Tulku Urgyen Rinpoche's way of giving a general outline of the ground, path and fruition of the Great Perfection was not extraordinary compared to that of other masters, but if you asked him about one single word, no matter how subtle or profound the connotation, his answer was just as subtle and profound. Both Dzongsar Khyentse and myself felt that compared to many months and years of studying books and going through analytical meditation, it was more beneficial to spend just a few hours asking questions of Tulku Urgyen and listening to his answers. I went to see him at Nagi Gompa many times and I received various empowerments, but I feel the actual teachings were revealed in ordinary discussion.

These days you find people who say, "I know the teachings but I don't like to practice sadhana in large gatherings. I don't feel like doing all that chanting." Honestly, there are people who have said this to me, and it surely proves their lack of realization. Anyone who truly understands the teachings, especially the Vajrayana, will also know that these teachings are implemented in group sadhana, training in development and completion, and chanting. That is the application of Vajrayana, and if someone talks but doesn't practice, then that person is definitely not learned.

Tulku Urgyen himself knew all about the encompassing activities of the Vajrayana and never belittled their application. He gave great attention to the performance of all the important rituals, including the drubchen ceremonies. In the first half of his life, in order to be of benefit to others, he learned these down to their minutest detail, never missing a single day. Nor did he ever belittle the consequence of any karmic action.

Without having to deliberately ask for donations, he managed to raise funds in an apparently effortless fashion. Tulku Urgyen was able to build all the temples and monasteries he intended. Yet all these projects were completed totally on the side; you never saw them as his main aim or occupation.

In the latter part of his life he basically abandoned all involvement in conceptual activities and didn't put any obvious effort into building. Yet temples still seemed to rise up continuously and many tasks were accomplished. He always spent the money that came during the day and when the sun went down he had nothing. He didn't keep a project schedule, nor have I ever seen or heard about him sending out any fund-raising letters, which are so plentiful these days. Even so, it seems he was able to build more temples than any other contemporary lama, no matter how much effort they put into it. So I feel confident that he accomplished his aims without hardship.

I feel certain that there is not the slightest difference between the state of mind of Tulku Urgyen and Samantabhadra. For those who regard him as the Vajradhara in person, the perfect root guru and the support for their supplications, he is definitely extraordinary.

While Tulku Urgyen Rinpoche was alive he had many disciples, some of them special. Among his sons, Chökyi Nyima Rinpoche, in particular, is a capable writer. Therefore, we should definitely write a biography of Tulku Urgyen in both Tibetan and English, starting with his birth and early years, when he was named Karma Urgyen Tsewang Chokdrub by the 15th Karmapa Khakyab Dorje and recognized as a tulku of Lachab Gompa, and continuing all the way to his passing. This biography, I feel, should be written without adding or subtracting a single thing. We cannot really write his inner life story because he never spoke of the visions or predictions he received, so there is nothing fabulous of that kind to put in writing. What we *can* write down is simply what he did, without any distortion. Some people may think that a life story with no extraordinary mystic events is unimportant, but please don't think that. Even the Buddha appeared in an ordinary human body and was seen as a human by others, so for most people a simple straightforward biography would be beneficial. Again, I feel that we should just write his story, without exaggerating or downplaying anything.

Rather than having several accounts of Tulku Urgyen's life story that conflict I would like to see a biography with straight talk that can be agreed upon by everyone. That includes the good with the bad, in ordinary, simple words. In this book I would like to see as many photos as possible. The basic text should first be done in Tibetan: later, this book could be translated into foreign languages. Nowadays we still have people connected to Tulku Urgyen who are old: they should be interviewed while they are alive. If this is done, in the future there will be something for people to read. I feel that such a project will be successful. So, let's try to accomplish this.

To summarize, Tulku Urgyen was an incredible master, both learned and accomplished. I have always felt confident about this, but until now I have never had the opportunity to go through his virtues explaining them one by one. Why didn't I talk about them before? It is because of the nasty times we live in, when everyone seems to be praising his or her own school or lineage. Even within the Nyingma School, there should not be any difference in prestige between the 108 major tertöns, since all termas come from Padmasambhava. But when I hear someone proclaim, "Our termas are better than theirs!" how can I start speaking of the greatness of Chokgyur Lingpa's termas, or his miraculous powers and great deeds? Even though this is true and it is appropriate to do so, I don't really feel like doing it.

So, really, there has not been any reason for someone like me to extol the virtues of Tulku Urgyen Rinpoche: rather, when the sun shines in the sky no one can deny its brilliant light. But now it is like the sun has set behind the western mountains. Therefore since the great masters of this time — the Karmapa of incomparable kindness, Kyabje Dudjom Rinpoche and Dilgo Khyentse Rinpoche — have all venerated Tulku Urgyen as one of their root gurus and a jewel in their crown ornament, there was absolutely no need for me to justify it. Teachings should always be given upon request, so since I was specifically asked, I have said what I personally know and have witnessed.

❖

as it is

Volume 2

1

The Inheritance

❖

We think, we remember, we plan — and the attention thus exerted moves towards an object and sticks to it. This mental movement is called thinking or conceptual mind. We have many different expressions in Tibetan to describe the functioning of this basic attitude of mind, of this extroverted consciousness unaware of its own nature. This ignorant mind grabs hold of objects, forms concepts about them, and gets involved and caught up in the concepts it has created. This is the nature of samsara, and it has been continuing through beginningless lifetimes up to the present moment.

All these involvements are merely fabricated creations; they are not the natural state. They are based on the concepts of subject and object, perceiver and perceived. This dualistic structure, together with the disturbing emotions and the karma that is produced through them, are the forces that drive us from one samsaric experience to another. Yet all the while, there is still the basic nature, which is not made out of anything whatsoever. It is totally unconstructed and empty, and at the same time it is aware: it has the quality of being able to cognize. This indivisible unity of being empty and cognizant is our original ground that is never lost.

What we are missing is the recognition that our natural state is the indivisible unity of emptiness and cognizance. We miss that recognition because our mind is always searching somewhere else. We do not acknowledge our actual cognizant presence, and instead are always pre-occupied by looking elsewhere, outside of ourselves. And we perpetuate this process continuously. Shantideva said, "Unless you know the secret key point, whatever you do will miss the mark." The secret key point of mind is that its nature is a self-existing, original wakefulness. To identify the key point we need to receive the pointing-out instruction, which tells and shows us that: "The nature of your mind is the buddha mind itself." Right now we are like the dim-witted person who lost himself in Asan Tol (in downtown Kathmandu), who runs around wailing, "I've lost myself! Where am I?" The pointing-out instruction is just like telling him, "You are *you*!" Through beginningless samsara, sentient beings have never found themselves until somebody says, "You are right here." This is a metaphor for introducing the secret key point of mind.

If it weren't for the buddhas' teachings, all sentient beings would be totally lost, because they need to be pointed towards that basic ground which is always present, but never acknowledged. That is the purpose of the pointing-out instruction, literally, the 'instruction bringing you face-to-face with your own essence'. This instruction is given impressive great names like Mahamudra, the Great Middle Way or the Great Perfection. All of these teachings point towards the same basic nature. They are the exact opposite of the conceptual thinking that holds a subject and object — the dualistic frame of mind that is unaware of its own nature.

It doesn't have to be this way. We *can* know our own nature. We can realize it by applying the pith instructions of Mahamudra, the Great Middle Way and the Great Perfection. Even though our nature is primordially enlightened, we are oblivious to that fact. Therefore we need to become re-enlightened. First we need to recognize; next, train in that recognition; and finally, attain stability. Once we are re-enlightened, we no longer need to wander in samsara.

The buddha nature is the very identity within which the body, speech, mind, qualities and activities of all buddhas are complete. It is out of the expression of these that the body, speech and mind of all beings appear. In fact, the body, speech and mind of any sentient being have the same origin as the body, speech and mind of the awakened ones. Body, speech and mind cannot come from earth, or stone, or matter. The unchanging quality is called the vajra body, the unceasing quality is called the vajra speech, and the undeluded quality is called vajra mind. The indivisible unity of the three is exactly what is meant by buddha nature.

Not recognizing in our own experience the unchanging quality of this buddha nature, we entered into the encasement of a physical body of flesh and blood. Our speech became wrapped within the movement of breath to become voice and words. It appears and disappears. Consciousness began to hold a perceiver as separate from the perceived. In other words, it became a fixation on duality, a stop-and-start process that arises and ceases each moment. Thoughts come continuously, one after the other, like an endless string. This endless string of thought has continued from beginningless time and just goes on and on. That is how the normal state of mind is. If we don't now recognize our own nature in this lifetime, we fail to capture our natural seat of unchanging, self-existing wakefulness. Instead, we chase after one perishing thought after the other, like chasing after each new bead on the string. This is how samsara becomes endless. While we are governed by this involvement in thought, we are truly helpless.

Who can stop samsara for us? There is nobody but ourselves. Even if all the sentient beings of the six realms were lined up and you cried, "Please, help me, so I can stop being overpowered by my own thinking!" — even then, not a single one of them could help. How sad that we are controlled by this involvement in thought, day and night, life after life! We could try to blow up a nuclear bomb to stop samsara, but it still wouldn't help. Nuclear bombs can destroy cities, even countries, but they cannot stop the mind from thinking. Unless we become free of conceptual thinking, there is absolutely no way to end samsara and truly awaken to enlightenment.

Great peace is when the conceptual thinking subsides, calms down. There is a way for that to happen. Thoughts are actually an expression of the buddha nature. They are expressions of our natural face. If we truly recognize buddha nature, in that very same moment, any thought will vanish by itself, leaving no trace. This is what brings an end to samsara. There is a supreme method to do this. Once we know that method, there is nothing superior we need to know. This way is already at hand in ourselves. It is not something that we need to get from someone else — it is not something we need to buy, bribe, or search for and finally achieve. Such effort is not necessary at all. Once you recognize your own natural face, you have already transcended the six realms of samsara.

What is the method? It is what one asks for when requesting a master to give instructions on how to recognize mind essence and train in it. Our mind essence is incredibly precious. It is the natural inheritance we possess right now. Receiving teachings on how to recognize the essence of mind and correctly apply them is called 'the Buddha being placed in the palm of your own hand'. That analogy means that at the moment of being introduced and recognizing, you don't have to seek for the awakened state somewhere else. Line up all the money, all the wealth in the whole world in one big heap and put it on one side. On the other side put the recognition of buddha nature, the nature of your own mind. What is most valuable? If you are going to somehow compare the two, I can promise you that recognizing mind essence, the 'amazing buddha within', is more valuable, a billion times more valuable.

If instead we continue to fool ourselves, we're simply doing what we have been doing for so long. How much trouble and misery have we gone through in samsara, among the six realms? Do we want to continue like that? How much more misery won't we go through again while traveling through the eighteen hells and the neighboring hells? Buddha taught that any sentient being has drunk more red-hot liquid metal in the hells than could fill up an entire ocean. That is an example of the suffering we have endured. It's only because we are dull ordinary beings that we have forgotten all about it. If we don't realize this natural state, there is no way to stop wandering about in the six realms of samsara. No one else is going to prevent you from rambling on, and it certainly won't stop by itself.

What is of true value? We need to think about this for ourselves. When we do business and make a profit, we rejoice. If we have a loss, we fall into despair. Let's compare our business capital to our buddha nature, which is like a wish-fulfilling jewel. If we don't use this wish-fulfilling jewel, endless samsara lies before us. Isn't it just incredibly stupid to throw away our fortune — and troublesome as well? We need to think about this. I am not reciting this from memory. It is not a lie either. This is the real, crucial point. If we didn't have a buddha nature, nobody could blame us. But we do have buddha nature, a buddha nature that is the identity of the three kayas of all buddhas. However, like Jamgön Kongtrül said:[2]

> *Although my mind is the Buddha, I don't recognize it.*
> *Although my thinking is dharmakaya, I don't realize it.*
> *Although nonfabrication is the innate, I fail to sustain it.*
> *Although naturalness is the basic state, I am not convinced.*
> *Guru, think of me. Quickly, look upon me with compassion!*
> *Bless me so that natural awareness is liberated into itself.*

We need to understand what mind essentially is. As I have often said, in this world, mind is the most important, for the simple reason that it is mind that understands and experiences. Besides mind, nothing else perceives anything. The five outer elements of earth, water, fire, wind and space — do they feel anything? In truth, there is nothing other than mind that experiences.

The whole universe is made out of the five major elements, which in themselves are insensate; they don't know anything. Likewise, the physical bodies of sentient beings are made out of the five minor elements. In their properties, the bones and flesh are the same as the element of earth. Blood and the other liquids resemble the element of water. The temperature of our body is essentially the same as fire. Our breath is wind, while the vacuities in the body, the different openings and hollow places and so on, are in essence the same as space. These five elements don't experience, they don't perceive anything whatsoever. Unless there is a mind in that body, the body itself doesn't feel anything.

The outer major elements and the inner minor elements are also similar in structure. Our body with its flesh and bones can be compared to the surface of this earth, with its soil and rocks. The greenery and shrubs growing on the hillside can be likened to our pores and small hairs. There are forests outside and we have hair growing on our head. Whenever you dig into the ground you usually find water, at one point or another. Similarly, if we ever make a hole in our body, some liquid will start pouring out. The heat of our body has the same property as heat found anywhere else outside. The wind that moves through our lungs is the same wind or air outside. The vacuities are the same as empty space. There is a very strong resemblance between inner and outer elements. In a sense, they are identical, in that the elements by themselves do not perceive.

We also have five senses, five sense doors — eyes, ears, nose, tongue and skin, with its ability to perceive texture through touch. However, these five senses really don't experience anything in themselves. If there is not a mind or consciousness connected with the five senses, the sense organs by themselves do not experience. A corpse has eyes, ears, nose, tongue and skin, but if you show something to a corpse, even if the eyes are open, it doesn't see anything; nor does it perceive sound. A corpse has no ability to smell or taste, and if you press the body it doesn't feel the touch either.

Then there are the five sense objects, the impressions we get of physical forms seen through the eyes, sounds heard through the ears, the different flavors we can taste through means of the tongue, the fragrances sensed through the nose, and the textures we can feel through the body. These objects of the five senses are also not cognizant. They don't experience anything at all. Unless there is a mind to perceive them, the objects by themselves don't perceive. A sentient being is basically made out of nothing other than mind. Apart from this mind, no thing in this world experiences anything at all. Without mind, this world would be utterly empty: there would be nothing known, nothing experienced. Matter would exist, of course, but matter doesn't know anything; it is totally empty of consciousness.

In this world, nothing is more essential than mind, except for one thing: the nature of this mind, buddha nature, *sugatagarbha*. All sentient beings have this nature, without a single exception. This buddha nature is present in everyone, from the dharmakaya buddha Samantabhadra down to the tiniest insect, even the smallest entities you can only see through a microscope. In all of these, the buddha nature is identical. There is no difference in size or quality — not at all. Buddha nature never differs in terms of quality or quantity. It is not like Samantabhadra has a large buddha nature and a small insect has a small one, or that the Buddha has a superior buddha nature and a fly an inferior one; there is no difference at all.

So, we need to distinguish between mind and mind essence. The mind essence of sentient beings and the awakened mind of the buddhas is the same. Buddhahood means to be totally stable in the state before dualistic thought occurs. A sentient being like ourselves, not realizing our essence, gets caught up in our own thinking and becomes bewildered. Still, the essence of our mind and the very essence of all awakened buddhas is primordially the same. Sentient beings and buddhas have an identical source, the buddha nature. Buddhas became awakened because of realizing their essence. Sentient beings became confused because of not realizing their essence. Thus there is one basis or ground, and two different paths.

Mind is that which thinks and remembers and plans all these different thoughts that we have. Thought in Tibetan is called *namtok*. 'Nam' means the object, what is thought of. 'Tok' means to make ideas and concepts about those objects. Namtok is something that mind churns out incessantly, day and night. A buddha is someone who recognizes the essence itself, and is awakened through that. A sentient being is someone who didn't, and who is confused by his or her own thinking. Someone who has failed to recognize the essence of mind is called a sentient being. Realizing the nature itself and becoming stable in that realization is called a buddha.

Isn't it true that this mind here thinks a lot? It remembers, it plans, it thinks, it worries. It has been doing so for countless lifetimes, day and night, without stop. Moment by moment, this mind is creating thoughts of one thing after another, and not just during this lifetime. Thinking takes place because of not seeing the essence of this mind itself. It thinks of something, makes thoughts and emotions about it — the process goes on and on. It is like beads on an endless string, life after life in an endless succession. This is called samsara.

It is the thinking that perpetuates samsara. Samsara will go on endlessly unless the thinking stops. As I mentioned many times before, mind is not a thing that has physical form, sound, smell, taste or texture. Mind is empty. Space is also empty. No matter where you go in space, there is no limit, no boundary, no edge. If you were to travel in a space ship in a single direction for a hundred billion years, you would not reach the end of space. Even if you could go all the way through the earth and come out the other side, you would not find the bottom of space. And were you to travel another hundred billion years, you still wouldn't find the bottom anywhere. It's the same with the other directions — you can travel forever, and you'll still never reach a place where space ends.

Now, how can something without limits have a center? It can't, can it? That is why it is taught that space has no center and no edge. The Buddha used space to point at how mind is. He said that mind is empty like space: that just as space has no limits in any direction, mind has no center or edge. As a matter of fact, wherever there is space, mind is present. And Buddha taught that throughout space, wherever space reaches, there are sentient beings. And wherever there are sentient beings there are disturbing emotions and the creation of karma. And wherever there is the creation of disturbing emotion and karma, there is also buddha nature. The awakened mind of the buddhas is all-pervasive. In short, the nature of this mind is empty in essence; it is like space. Because it has no form, no smell, no taste, sound or texture, it is completely empty. It always was, primordially. In being empty, mind seems like space. But there is a difference: space is not conscious; it doesn't feel pleasure or pain. Our mind is spacious, wide-open and empty, yet it still feels pleasure and pain. It is sometimes called the 'ever-knowing, ever-conscious mind'. Whatever is present is known by mind.

When this mind is put to work, it can invent any possible thing, even nuclear bombs. Mind creates all these amazing gadgets — voice recorders, airplanes that can fly through the sky. These inventions don't think, but they were created by the thinking mind. Sentient beings create the samsara that we have right now. The creation of samsara will not ultimately help us in any way.

Mind is invisible and intangible. That is why people don't know it. That is why they wonder, "Have I really recognized this nature of mind?" If it were a concrete thing, scientists would have figured it out a long time ago. But it isn't, so scientists don't necessarily know what mind is. If they did, all scientists would be enlightened! But have you ever heard of scientists becoming enlightened through science? Sure, they know a lot of other things. They can make telephones that let you instantly talk to anybody anywhere in the world. And they can make machinery that flies hundreds of people together through the sky. They can drive trains directly through mountains. All this is possible. If mind is put to work, it is an inexhaustible treasure; but that still doesn't mean enlightenment. When the mind is put to use for something and gets caught up in it, this does not lead to enlightenment. We need to know the essential nature of mind.

It is mind that right now thinks of all these different things. As long as thinking does not dissolve, we do not attain enlightenment. Being caught up in thoughts is exactly what is meant by spinning in samsara, just like a wheel in machinery. With wheels on a car, you can drive all over the world, right?

What is the way to dissolve thoughts, to totally clear them up and let them vanish? The Buddha had the technique on how to clear up thinking. That's what the pointing-out instruction from a qualified master is for. When you go to school, you have to repeat the ABC's back to the teacher so that he can be aware of whether you know the alphabet or not. Until one knows, one needs to be taught, to be shown. Until one fully knows mind essence, one needs a teacher. It's as simple as that.

Otherwise, our thinking spins like the wheels on a car. When the wheels on a car move, they drag the car around. Like the spinning wheels of a car, our thinking has never stopped, through so many lifetimes. Even when we try to stop it, it gets worse. Thinking is like the shadow of our own hand — just try and shake it off! You can order the thoughts to stop, but they won't listen. Wherever mind goes, thoughts follow, like the shadow of our body. But as long as this thinking is not exhausted, samsara does not stop. Samsara means spinning, circling, continuing to circle around. Apart from recognizing mind essence, there is no other way to stop the mind from thinking.

The operating system of this spinning around is called the twelve links of dependent origination, the head of which is ignorance, the lack of knowing. This ignorance of unknowing means not recognizing what our nature really is. Ignorance forces the five *skandhas* to be perpetuated — the physical forms, sensations, conceptions, formations and cognitions that make birth follow death, again and again. Mind doesn't die. When it remains ignorant of its own nature, again it perpetuates the arrangement of the five skandhas to create a new body in one of four ways — through a womb, as in the case of a human being; through instantaneous birth; through heat and moisture; or through an egg. These are the four different ways of taking rebirth in the three realms and among the six classes of beings.

Try and check how many sentient beings there are living on just one mountainside. See how many insects live in just one lake. They are all sentient beings. If you were to count the insects here on the slopes of the Shivapuri Mountain behind my hermitage, you would probably find that they outnumber the number of human beings in the whole world. Human bodies are very few compared to the amount of other sentient beings. Even though we happen to be human, if in this life we don't attain realization by recognizing our own nature, we will continue again in some other state within samsara. The Buddha taught that if we were to collect the blood that has spilled from each death we have experienced, there would be more blood than the ocean could hold; not from the deaths of all sentient beings, but merely from one sentient being. That is how many lives we have had before.

If we continue to spin around in the realms of samsara, will this process somehow stop by itself? Not at all! Right now we have attained what is described as a precious human body. We're at a point that is like being at the fork in the road: one road leads higher, the other one lower. We are right at that point now. If we recognize and realize our buddha nature, we can go upwards to enlightenment. If we are careless and ignore it, we don't have to try to go deeper in samsara — it happens automatically. Negative karma doesn't require much effort. The normal mind thinks mainly in terms of being against something, being attached to something, or being simply dull and not caring about anything. This automatically creates negative karma, further perpetuating samsara.

True virtue, real goodness, is created through recognizing our buddha nature, our natural state. Recognizing our own nature is itself the path of enlightenment. Not recognizing buddha nature is itself the path of samsara. There are these two roads. The basis for these two is the same: it is buddha nature. There are two choices, two paths. One is the path of knowing, the wakefulness that knows its own nature. One is the path of unknowing, of not recognizing our own nature, and being caught up in what is being thought of, through the consciousness connecting with sense objects via the senses. This process continuously puts the wheel of samsara in motion. That is why a famous statement goes:

> To recognize is the path of nirvana;
> Not to recognize is the path of samsara.

When ordinary people see an object, a rosary for instance, they think, "This is a rosary." Next they wonder, "Are there a hundred beads? Where is it made? Maybe in China, or maybe India, I don't know." It will be one thought after the other. This conceptualizing an object is namtok. The object is the rosary and all the ideas we have about it are the concepts. "It is yellow, it is Indian, maybe it is Chinese, I like it, it is quite neat." One thought is continued after the other. For the ordinary person there is the object observed, the rosary. The subject is the mind, that which knows. A yogi practitioner, on the other hand, does not dwell on the object but recognizes the nature of the subject.

There is knowing. The mind of any sentient being is both empty and cognizant, and it is the cognizance that can recognize its own nature. In the very moment of recognizing, you see the empty essence. This empty essence is called the dharmakaya of the buddhas. The cognizance is called the sambhogakaya of the buddhas. These two are actually indivisible, and this indivisibility is nirmanakaya. This indivisibility of emptiness and cognizance is a natural quality, just like water's liquidity or the heat of a flame. They are a union. You cannot take the heat away from a flame. Moreover, the recognizing of one's natural face is called svabhavikakaya. This is to be face to face with the three kayas of the buddhas, and we cannot find anything superior to that in the entire world.

Recognize your mind, and in the absence of any concrete thing, rest loosely. After a while we again get caught up in thoughts. But, by recognizing again and again, we grow more and more used to the natural state. It's like learning something by heart — after a while, you don't need to think about it. Through this process, our thought involvement grows weaker and weaker. The gap between thoughts begins to last longer and longer. At a certain point, for half an hour there will be a stretch of no conceptual thought whatsoever, without having to suppress the thinking.

The essence of mind that is primordially empty and rootless is unlike holding the *idea* of emptiness in mind, and it is not the same as the sustained attempt to feel empty. Neither of these helps much. By growing used to this natural, original emptiness again and again, we become accustomed to it. Then there will be a stretch throughout the whole day from morning to evening, which is only empty awareness untainted by notions of perceived objects or the perceiving mind. This corresponds to having attained the bodhisattva levels, the *bhumis*. When there is never a break throughout day and night, that is called buddhahood, true and complete enlightenment.

From the perspective of mind essence, the interruptions of thoughts are like clouds in the sky. The empty essence itself is like the space of the sky. Our cognizance is like sunshine. The sky itself never changes whether it's sunny or cloudy. Similarly, when you realize the awakened state of the buddhas, all cloud-like thoughts have vanished. But the qualities of wisdom, meaning original wakefulness, are fully developed, fully present, even now, when thoughts are present. We need to train in slowly growing more and more used to the recognition of mind essence. This will dissolve our negative karma and disturbing emotions. In this recognition it is impossible to be tainted by karma and emotions, just like you cannot paint mid-air.

I would like to give you a famous quote from the *Hevajra Tantra*:

> *All sentient beings are buddhas,*
> *But they are covered by temporary obscurations.*

This temporary obscuration is our own thinking. If we didn't already have the buddha nature, meaning a nature that is identical to that of all awakened ones, no matter how much we try we would never be enlightened. The Buddha used the example of churning milk into butter. Sentient beings contain within themselves the butter-yielding milk, in the sense of this basic material of enlightenment. It is not like being water — you can churn water for a billion years and still you will never get butter out of it. All sentient beings have the essence of buddhahood within themselves. But if you ignore this most precious essence inside yourself, you will continue spinning around in the three painful realms of samsara.

Samsara is painful because of being impermanent. There is the unavoidable pain of death, for example. There is nothing in the world you can do to avoid dying. If we never died, it would be just fine! Or if the mind died when the body dies, well, that wouldn't be so bad either. But actually what happens is the body dies at the end of every life, and the mind experiences this and continues on. We just keep on experiencing. Even when we lie down to take a rest, we keep on dreaming the whole night long. It's like that; it just goes on and on. Recognizing that the essence of mind is empty cognizance and realizing that will enable us to cross the bardo.

Having received the pointing-out instruction, we need to resolve upon it — not merely recognize, but also to make up our mind that this is how to solve the basic problem of samsara. To have that kind of trust and also the diligence to practice is like the famous proverb that 'the son of a rich father naturally receives his inheritance'. Where the father is rich and has a son, there is no question that the son will inherit the wealth. We missed the chance to be primordially enlightened like all the buddhas, bodhisattvas, dakas and dakinis and Dharma protectors with the eye of wisdom. Nevertheless, if we recognize our nature and train in that diligently, we have the chance to be re-enlightened, just like the son of a rich father taking hold of his inheritance.

STUDENT: What does 'constructed' mean?

RINPOCHE: A state of mind that is constructed means that you have to think about something in order for that moment to be. Unconstructed means it doesn't require any thought whatsoever. That is the difference. The moment of nowness or evenness that is mentioned — is that constructed or unconstructed?

STUDENT: I guess that then it would be unconstructed.

RINPOCHE: This moment of openness, does it have different parts to it, like past, present and future?

STUDENT: I don't know. I would like you to tell me that.

RINPOCHE: To hold a notion in mind of anything that is past or still is present or is about to come, is to be tainted by conceptual frame of mind. But there is also the possibility of being untainted by any concept of past, present and future. If you don't conceptualize this present moment of wakefulness, there are no three times. In short, were it not for this present wakefulness, this body would be a corpse. And were this present wakefulness to pursue anything, that is called thinking mind. In other words, don't pursue anything.

To be involved in thinking is the dualistic frame of mind. To be un-involved in thinking is self-existing wakefulness. Sometimes it is said that the mind is similar to space, because you cannot say that space arrived, space left, or space came from somewhere or goes in any direction. The dualistic frame of mind, on the other hand, does come and go. It is like a cloud; it is formed and dissolves again. The term 'view' refers to our basic state, which is unchanging like space. This type of view is unobscured by thought. However, our thinking can obscure the view. It happens when we start to formulate a concept about how it is. The view, meaning the basic state, is like space. It totally defies any conceptual formulations such as having it or not having it, getting it or losing it.

STUDENT: What is meditation in this context?

RINPOCHE: Teachers say, "Now meditate," then one sits down and one may think that one should imagine emptiness. That is not what is meant. What is meant is don't wander, don't wander. Hearing the word *meditate*, it sounds like one has to do something. But there is not even as much as a dust mote to do as an act of meditation. It's just like space here — a totally inconcrete openness. Try to imagine that, imagine space. Can you imagine space? You can imagine it is empty, but that is a thought. Does that thought help anything? To meditate on a thing means bringing that to mind, but can you bring space to mind? Okay, space is empty. To keep that in mind is another thought. But without thinking anything, meditate on space. Can you? Isn't it better to leave it unimagined? Unmeditated? That is why it is said:

> The supreme meditation is to not meditate.
> The supreme training is to keep nothing in mind.

There is no need to meditate upon space. It is much better to let it remain without imagining! This message 'meditate, meditate', really fools people, it does fool us. When we hear that we think, "There must be something to do, to keep in mind." Ultimately, to not meditate is the supreme meditation.

While resting free of anything to imagine, like space, do not be distracted for even one instant. The one who trains like that can truly be called a 'space yogi'. A yogi is an individual who connects with that which is naturally so. Space means that which always is. Remain without imagining anything at all, not meditating on anything. Once you start to meditate *on* space, it becomes an imitation. Simply allow the space to not wander. Remain undistracted. There is no impetus for any thoughts to reoccur. A thought is a mental way of formulating something — in other words, our attention formulates a thought. The thought doesn't come from anywhere else. If we don't think, where would a thought come from? In the basic space that is unimaginable, remain undistractedly. Let your indescribable awareness remain undistracted in the naked state of basic space. It doesn't have to be imagined, because this basic space that is utterly naked is our own nature already. You don't have to imagine that this is so.

Imagine space! It is not an object of thought. Give up thinking and what is thought of, both the present and what is about to come. Past has already gone. Now abandon the present and what is about to come. Then what is left?

Bringing something to mind is like thinking of the shape of a buddha. First, imagine the face, next, the arms. When the arms appear, the face is gone. Now we imagine the legs, and the arms are gone, then we have to start all over again. It is quite difficult. Without imagining anything, that is the supreme meditation. As far as I am concerned, development stage is kind of hard. Completion stage is incredibly easy!

People try to make me do physical exercise daily. And maybe it is good, but it is not so easy. Development stage is like doing exercise. When you move your body, it becomes flexible, pliable. By exercising the imagination, it becomes pliable and some benefit results. It is not useless. The three aspects of deity, mantra and samadhi are not useless, definitely not. But in the moment of recognizing buddha nature, these three — deity, mantra and samadhi — are automatically and completely present, without any effort.

In Tibetan Buddhism we need to train in the stages of development and completion. Here is a simple way to practice: Imagine the physical presence of the deity. Develop the pure notion, "I am the deity, my voice has the nature of mantra, my state of mind is samadhi." To remind yourself of that is the development stage. When you say, "I am," it is only mind formulating a concept. A concept does not refer back to any concrete entity that exists like a lump somewhere. When you recognize the identity of that which thinks 'I' — at that moment of seeing, the thought has dissolved, it has vanished, and you have arrived at the completion stage.

2

Blessings and Enlightenment

✿

STUDENT: Could Rinpoche explain exactly what 'blessing' is?

RINPOCHE: What people usually consider blessings are what I would call 'superficial blessings'. Often when you have something you want to get rid of, you might ask, "Please bless me to be free from what I don't like." This can be sickness or pain or an attack by evil spirits. It can also be as mundane as one's business not going so well, and so on. People ask for protection cords to wear around their necks, sacred medicine to eat, maybe a ritual to be performed. When they are cured, when the evil spirits have been repelled, the business is going well again, or whatever, they'll say, "I got the blessings." These are known as conventional blessings. On the other hand, true blessings are the oral instructions on how to become enlightened in a single lifetime, which you can receive from a qualified master.

Consider, please, that the body we have right now is a precious human body. In this world there are countless sentient beings. Among all of them the best form to have is this precious human body. It is very hard to obtain this again and again. Only if you have created sufficient merit in past lives can you be born in this body that we now have. It is impossible to obtain a precious human body through demerit, through unwholesome karmic actions. It is only through incredibly great positive karma that we can arrive in a human body. Having been born as a human is like arriving on an island of jewels. But if we don't take any of them, if we just keep our hands crossed over our chest and go home, then what? Having been born as a human, it is important to make it meaningful. How do you make it meaningful? By practicing a spiritual path. Unless you do that your life is that of an ordinary human.

An ordinary human is a being who has a human body and looks human. If that life is not combined with a spiritual path, its aims are actually no different from those of an animal. Among all human beings, we now have a precious human body. We can listen to teachings when they are being explained; we can also put them into practice. Wasting a precious human body is a great loss. There couldn't possibly be any greater failure.

Truly and honestly, I would definitely encourage you to practice the Dharma. To practice the Dharma means, chiefly, to nurture the qualities of trust, diligence and insight. Trust is to have confidence in the teachings and the ones who taught them — in the Buddha and in the Sangha, the upholders of the teachings. Diligence is that which carries you through to completion. Otherwise, in any job you do, is it ever completed if you begin and don't finish? Insight is the outcome of listening to teachings, thinking about them and applying them. When you hear something and you gain confidence in that, then you have insight, which is the knowledge resulting from learning. Thinking it over is the knowledge from reflection. Finally, there is the knowledge acquired through meditation practice which means personal experience through training.

Trust is indispensable, and to mistrust is a great shortcoming. One might be quite insensitive, like someone who sees buddhas and bodhisattvas flying in the sky and says, "They are just showing off." Or if you see a creature lying with its stomach open and the entrails falling out, you might just shrug and say, "It's his own karma — after all, everybody dies." If one has no compassion and no trust, it is very hard to penetrate to the heart of the Dharma.

Develop appreciation from the core of your heart, even towards four lines of the Buddha's teachings. Think, "How wonderful! This is incredibly precious!" When you regard others, always try to regard them like this: "They are my own parents, yet they suffer. What can I do? I will make it my responsibility to help them." In this way, train in compassion towards all sentient beings — not merely as a platitude, but from the core of your heart. Compassion and devotion should not be a mere show, but sincere. Trust in the teachings of the Buddha means pure appreciation. Honestly, it is completely amazing that through a few words of teaching, we can make a difference. When we truly apply the teachings, it can change the causes for rebirth into the lower realms. In other words, the Dharma can overturn the depths of samsara. This is the level at which trust arises, and this is the kind of trust that is necessary.

It is also possible to fake faith and devotion and insincerely mutter platitudes like "How wonderful." These empty words do no one any good. We need to have trust that is so penetrating that tears come to our eyes, the hairs on the body stand on end, and simply remaining passive seems difficult for us. Words alone will not help. When thinking of other beings, we should try to have genuine compassion. Reflect that they are our parents, and that they simply don't know what to do. Because they have no idea about the ultimate truth, the true state of samadhi, they create immense pain and suffering for themselves. They wander about from one life to another in samsaric states that are like links in an endless chain. When one truly and sincerely feels like that, tears come to one's eyes. This overwhelming emotion is the kind of compassion that is necessary.

The individual whose stream of being is filled with overwhelming compassion for sentient beings and devotion to the enlightened ones will, without any doubt, receive the blessings of all buddhas and bodhisattvas. To superficially act as if one pities sentient beings and respects enlightened ones and merely pay lip service to this is not enough to receive the blessings. It has to be a hundred percent sincerity. Some signs of receiving the blessings within one's stream of being are that you no longer have to try to feel compassion; the feeling arises spontaneously. Nor do you have to deliberately try to be respectful; it also comes naturally. Those are the signs. To trust the consequence of karma is the actual accomplishment of Dharma practice.

Authentic accomplishment means to be compassionate and devoted. You may hear that someone is clairvoyant — that he makes precise divinations, or can do small miracles, or read other people's minds. This kind of thing is not a true accomplishment, not at all. It is nothing special. Many ordinary people get certain abilities from spirits. It's not that rare for this to happen. They may not have any trust in the enlightened ones, or any compassion towards sentient beings. They may lack trust in the karmic consequence of their actions. Yet such people still have the reputation of having blessings and powers of accomplishment. And still their mind-stream may remain like solid stone, insensitive towards others, uncompassionate, with no true appreciation for the sacred teachings. They may be attached to nothing other than samsaric states. From the moment they wake up until the moment they fall asleep, they try to get the better of their enemies and help only their own friends. This is described as being 'blessed by formless spirits'.

In contrast, you may not have much knowledge of the Dharma; but if you have trust in the Three Jewels and kindness towards other beings, while acutely understanding that in this life nothing lasts forever, you have already received the blessings of the Three Jewels. What it really comes down to is, have we or have we not received their blessings? Otherwise, merely to know a lot of teachings usually results in nothing but conceit, of thinking, "I have practiced so much, so many years of shamatha and samadhi." If people who have a lot of practice behind them become only more miserly and stingy, it is proof that the teachings have not taken effect and that they have no blessings.

STUDENT: What exactly is 'enlightenment'?

RINPOCHE: There are different levels of enlightenment. There is the enlightenment of an arhat, of a mahabodhisattva, and the complete and perfect enlightenment of a buddha. The 'five paths' and the 'ten bhumis' are progressive stages that gradually lead to complete and perfect enlightenment. The way to complete and perfect enlightenment is by unifying means and knowledge, which are great compassion and insight into emptiness. When emptiness and compassion are indivisible, then that itself is the true path to the complete and perfect enlightenment of a buddha.

Now, compassion is immensely profound, because it's a fact that we are related to all other beings. Not only in a general way but also deeply, in that there is not a single sentient being who, at one point or another through our innumerable past lives, hasn't been our own mother. We are thus connected by a link of great love. But, at the same time, by not knowing how to avoid the causes for suffering and further rebirth in samsara, all sentient beings are on a totally mistaken path. When you take this universal pain to heart in a genuine way, there is no way you can turn your back on all suffering beings and feel that it is enough to attain enlightenment just for yourself.

Compassion is thus extremely important in practicing the path. At the time of complete enlightenment it is out of compassion that the activity for the welfare of others takes place. Through having realized dharmakaya for the benefit of oneself, and by clearly seeing the state of other beings and what is needed, a buddha manifests continuous activity for the benefit of others. He doesn't just sit back and relax. All this skillful activity springs out of compassion.

The great master, Karmapa Rangjung Dorje, expressed another reason for compassion — in the sense of compassion being love:

In the moment of love, our empty essence nakedly dawns.

True love can be either devotion to enlightened beings or compassion for unenlightened beings. In the moment when you totally give up any selfish attachment and the mind is filled only with devotion or compassion, there is no concept that can make the realization of emptiness stray into some sidetrack. That's the ultimate safeguard — to experience the realization of emptiness suffused with compassion. That's why the Sutra system of Buddhism says that the true path of enlightenment is the unity of compassion and insight into emptiness.

Compassion comes from clearly seeing the state of how others are. Shifting your attention away from being concerned with merely yourself, you begin to tune into how other beings feel. Soon you realize that their aims and what they actually manage to achieve are in total contradiction. Everyone wants to be happy and free, but the involvement pursued through thought, word and deed for the most part creates further pain, further entanglement. When one really sees this clearly, the sense of compassion becomes overwhelming. The insight into emptiness in the moment of overwhelming compassion is totally free from any sidetrack, so that you can realize the primordially free, primordially pure essence, the buddha nature present in everyone. That's why compassion is so important in the Sutra system. To unify means and knowledge, compassion and emptiness, is the very essence, the very heart of the general teachings of Buddhism.

Vajrayana tells us that the nature of mind of all beings is covered by two obscurations. One is called 'the emotional obscuration' — desire, anger, and dullness. The second, the 'cognitive obscuration', is the subtle holding onto subject, object and interaction, in which awareness strays into dualistic clinging. These two types of obscuration need to be dissolved and purified. This is accomplished by gathering the two accumulations — the accumulation of merit and the accumulation of wisdom, the training in original wakefulness. By gathering the two accumulations we unfold the two types of supreme knowledge — the knowledge that perceives whatever possibly exists and the knowledge that perceives the nature *as it is*. By unfolding the two types of supreme knowledge we realize the two kayas, dharmakaya and rupakaya. 'Rupakaya' means 'form body' and has two aspects: sambhogakaya, which is the form of rainbow light, and nirmanakaya, which can take the physical form of flesh and blood. This is a summary of the Vajrayana path. To practice this and attain enlightenment is the real blessing.

The complete and perfect enlightenment of a buddha is endowed with inconceivable great qualities of love and compassion, of wisdom-knowledge, of continuous activity, and of the capacity to save and liberate others. The awakened state of mind is not like dead space, insensitive and unfeeling. In space there is nothing that feels — there are no qualities present, no wisdom, and no compassion. Even though space doesn't suffer, neither is there any wisdom. Space doesn't go to hell by doing evil, nor does it get liberated. It's simply empty, a void. If the awakened state were like that, there would be no point in pursuing it, because it would lead nowhere. But, in fact, it isn't like that. The awakened state of mind is cognizant as well as empty. Mind is not made of anything whatsoever: there is no material substance, no concreteness to it in any way. However, when completely and perfectly awakened, tremendous qualities are already present. The wisdom that perceives whatever exists and the original wakefulness that sees the nature exactly *as it is*, as well as compassion, the capacity to act for the welfare of others — all these qualities are fully present, unlike dead space. We don't awaken unless the two obscurations that prevent us from being fully awakened are removed. The way to remove them is by perfecting the two accumulations.

Our basic nature is in no way different from that of a buddha. It's like pure space, which, whether it is obscured by clouds or is a cloudless and clear sky, remains the same in its basic, essential nature. But if you pretend that your nature is already enlightened and don't progress along the path of removing the obscurations, then your enlightened nature doesn't become realized. Therefore, we must truly consider what is actual, what the facts are. Do we have obscurations or not? If you see that there still are obscurations, there is no way to avoid having to remove them by gathering the two accumulations.

If our nature wasn't already enlightened, we couldn't awaken to it no matter how hard we tried. Buddha nature cannot be fabricated. Our nature is primordially enlightened, but at present our ordinary body, speech and discursive thinking obscures it. The nature of our mind, buddha nature, is like space itself, but it is space obscured by clouds. The whole point of Dharma practice is to remove the clouds and allow the actualization of what already is — the awakened state of mind, the buddha nature. The nature of our mind is primordially pure, primordially enlightened. The way to remove our two obscurations is to train in conditioned virtue and the unconditioned training in original wake-fulness — the two accumulations.

We awaken to enlightenment by recognizing and fully realizing the primordially pure essence already present as our nature. That's how to be an awakened buddha. Even though the enlightened state is actually already present, imagining or forming a thought-construct of enlight-enment doesn't make you enlightened. It's the same as when you are really hungry and you look at a plate of food and try to imagine what it tastes like. Does it work to then imagine, "Mmmmm, I'm eating the food, I'm no longer hungry." You can think this for a very long time — forever, in fact — but it still doesn't dispel your hunger. Once you actu-ally put the food in your mouth, it tastes delicious, and your hunger is satiated. It's the same with experience. Experience only occurs in a di-rect way, in practical reality, not through a theory about taste. If your meditation practice is merely an exercise in imagining and keeping something in mind, it is only a theory, and not direct experience.

You often hear the teaching that all things are empty and devoid of self-entity, that there is no personal identity in the individual, and that all phenomena are devoid of any self-nature. Simply hearing this, or even intellectually understanding it, doesn't make much of a difference. The only way to actualize it is by recognizing our nature, the self-exist-ing wakefulness that is naturally empty. It's by experiencing natural emptiness that we become free, not by imagining emptiness.

We may understand that mind in itself is without visible form, sound, taste, smell or texture. But understanding this is not the real thing — it's only an *idea* about how it really is. This is not enough. If it was, you could simply say, "I am a buddha," and you would be a bud-dha. But, honestly, it doesn't happen that way.

The awakened state, our self-existing wakefulness, does not need to be fabricated or altered in any way at all. It is natural emptiness. *Empty* means free of visible form, sound, smell, taste or texture. The *-ness* is the knowing, cognizant quality. We need to see that this is so — that it is not only empty, but also naturally cognizant. And we need to not only see this and experience it, but also to grow used to it. Growing accustomed to this clears away the obscurations, the negative deeds and past karma, and destroys delusion at its root. That is how to become enlightened, and that is the root of blessings. Simply understanding how enlightenment is doesn't truly enlighten you.

To reach enlightenment, you need to directly experience the emptiness of mind. Empty means not arising, not dwelling, not ceasing. Like the space here all around us — does this space come from somewhere? Does it stay at some location? Does it go anywhere? It's just like that. In the same way, the empty essence of mind is beyond all limited mental constructs, yet it naturally has the ability to know. Absorb this, and you have to agree with what the Buddha taught: the nature of mind is an unconfined empty cognizance. This is obvious, and why? Empty means there is no thing to see. Yet there is a knowing, an awake quality that sees that there is no thing to see, which we call cognizance. These two are not confined to one or the other; while being empty you can still cognize; while cognizing mind essence is still empty. If it were confined to one or the other, it would be either a void state or a conscious entity. But it is not one or the other — it is a natural unity of both. The nature of mind is truly an unconfined empty cognizance. The quality of empty essence is what we call dharmakaya, the cognizant nature is sambhogakaya and the unconfined capacity is nirmanakaya.

If our basic state were restricted to being empty, it would be like being knocked out, oblivious, unconscious. There would be no experience of anything; we would be incapable of seeing, of hearing, of knowing. But we know for certain that we are capable, that our capacity is not blocked but unconfined. While perceiving, mind essence is empty. While empty, we perceive. While hearing, the mind is empty; while being empty, we can still hear.

In short, mind is the indivisible unity of empty cognizance. You can look for your mind for a billion years, and you will never find any concrete, material thing. It is empty, devoid of tangibility. Doesn't concrete or material mean that there should be an entity to see, hear, smell, taste or somehow take hold of? You won't find such a thing, not even if you looked for a billion years. This is because mind is empty.

Cognizant nature means we can know *anything*, whatever there is. It is only the minds of sentient beings that can know. The outer elements like water, earth, fire, and wind — they don't know anything. Also the flesh, the blood, the air in the body, and the cavities in the body — they don't know anything either. Similarly, the sights, the sounds, the smells, the tastes, the textures by themselves don't know anything. 'Knowing' means to feel pleasure or pain. Do earth, fire, water, and wind feel anything? What about the body, the flesh and blood, breath and heat — do these feel anything? This is why mind is the most important. Only mind can know.

Many people say, "If mind is empty, there would not be any *thing* that can know." Don't ever think that mind is only empty; it is empty *cognizance*. In this world, apart from mind, what can know? What is there that knows? Without mind, everything would be utterly dead. What is it that creates nuclear bombs? It is the mind of sentient beings. We need to know, and know exactly, the basic nature of this mind.

The way to be enlightened is to train in recognizing mind essence and become stable in this recognition. It is not by doing any other thing at all. Unless you recognize this nature of mind, you cannot go beyond the six classes of beings. Being unaware of how to know the nature of mind is the definition of 'sentient being'. Once we know how, without too much hardship we can progress through the stages called shravaka and bodhisattva and eventually become a buddha. Otherwise, as an ordinary being, we are not much different from a cow — we eat and we sleep, simply that, nothing more.

The path to enlightenment is based directly on this mind. As a famous statement goes: "Outside of mind, there is no other buddha." This refers to the original fresh state of mind essence — not to the outdated state of being already involved in thought! This original fresh state is self-manifest and unceasingly self-liberated. Because it is unmade, there is absolutely no need to create it at all. That is why we call it the 'original fresh state'. In terms of practical experience, our recognition of it may not last very long right now — perhaps only a few seconds. This is because since beginningless lifetimes this originally fresh state has been caught up in thinking. If the moment of recognition lasts only a short while, we need to repeat it many times.

In accordance with your master's pith instruction, apply the shepherd of mindfulness. Without this 'reminding', there is no way for a beginner to recognize. It is like the electric light here in my room; we need to flip the switch for the light to come on. Would the light come on by itself otherwise? The act of flipping the switch is the same as mindfulness. In the very moment of recognizing, you arrive at unconfined empty cognizance without having to do anything further than that. Don't think the nature of mind is something amazing. Don't think that it needs to be extraordinary. Don't correct the immediate wakefulness. This recognition is not an act of meditating; it has not even as much as a hair tip of effort in it. If we think "Empty, empty," this only becomes a meditation. In other words it is an imitation, a fabrication of emptiness. Instead of doing this, we simply need to acknowledge the naturally empty, rootless and groundless state.

Before we begin this type of training, we need to have settled the question of whether mind is empty. This is the first step, and it is extremely important to do this, so that later on we will not be hesitant, thinking "Maybe it is empty, but on the other hand, maybe not." The Buddha taught that mind is definitely empty.

Next we need to settle with certainty that mind is also naturally cognizant. If it was only empty, like space, how could there be any wisdom, any wakefulness? How could there be any compassion? How could there be any activity? How could there be any ability to assist other beings? Where would those qualities come from? These are all qualities of this natural cognizance. If this capacity is blocked, it is the same as being mindless. If your aim is only to become mindless, just have somebody regularly hit you hard on the head and knock you out so that you don't know anything. When you are unconscious, you don't see anything, unless you wake up. This temporary receding of cognizance is called the 'obstruction of capacity'. The natural capacity, however, is unconfined.

Another word for capacity could be energy. When physicists speak of empty matter they say it is empty, and yet there is energy. It's similar to when Westerners say, "There is nothing to see, but still there is energy there, an ability." This ability to know is what we call capacity, in Tibetan *tukje*. The same word can also mean to be kind. When we ask someone, "Please be kind"; we are actually asking them to activate the loving aspect of their capacity! In terms of the three kayas, it is the third of these three: empty essence, cognizant nature and unconfined capacity. That threefold nature is our most precious asset.

Do you understand that mind is both empty and cognizant? Don't hold onto this understanding. Don't attach a name to it, telling yourself "There it is, now I've got it" — that is merely to add more thinking. Don't hold onto it. Attaching names is clinging. The awakened mind of a buddha does not cling. When reflections appear in a mirror, the mirror does not attach names to these; it does not cling. The mind of a sentient being fixates, and then clings. Do you understand that we need to train in such absence of clinging?

Now I will show you how to train. You are working, and in the middle of working, you remember to recognize mind essence. Then you continue working busily, and again you recognize mind essence. This is called sustaining the practice. In the beginning, we cannot sustain the practice continuously throughout the day. So we carry on doing our normal work, and again at a certain point we remember. This is called 'reminding'. Once you have reminded yourself, simply let be in that. This is how one trains in order to become adept.

Unless we train like this, we will never be able to overcome our attachment, our anger, and our delusion. The moment of recognizing mind essence — that itself is the three kayas of the awakened state. The three poisons have no power at that moment; they have lost. When we get fully used to recognizing the nature of mind, the three poisons have no foothold any longer; they cannot do any damage. On the way to reaching buddhahood, the three poisons don't immediately disappear, but they do get weaker and weaker. If a recognition lasts unbroken from morning to evening, that is called the bodhisattva bhumi. If that wakefulness remains unbroken throughout day and night, forever unceasing, then the three poisons are totally obliterated. At this point, while the body is that of a human being, your mind is that of a true buddha.

STUDENT: What does it really mean to be a yogi?

RINPOCHE: We can all agree that mind is empty cognizance; to understand this is not that complicated or beyond us, not at all. If our minds were only empty like space, we wouldn't see, hear, smell, taste or touch anything. Can you deny that you see, hear, smell, taste or feel textures? It is undeniable. Mind essence is not confined to only being either empty or cognizant. These two are indivisible.

These two aspects, being empty and being cognizant, are one taste. As Padmasambhava said, "One taste of empty cognizance suffused with knowing." That is the key phrase. It is not more empty than cognizant, not more cognizant than empty. They are of one taste, meaning indivisible. The crucial difference lies in whether or not there is a knowing that recognizes this. For an ordinary sentient being, mind is also one taste of empty cognizance, but it is suffused with unknowing. This is because the awake quality focuses outwardly, latching onto whatever is experienced. Then the attention gets caught up in the three poisons: "How nice, I like that," or "How ugly, I hate it." The three poisons — aggression, attachment and dullness — become almost continuous.

The practice of a true yogi is to recognize the state free of the three poisons and remain continuously in this through the training of being undistracted. First, recognize; next, train; finally, attain stability. The degree of nondistraction is exactly what defines the stages towards complete enlightenment. Complete nondistraction is like a cloudless, clear sky that is free of any darkness whatsoever, suffused with sunshine. The single sphere of dharmakaya, *rigpa,* is utterly and completely undistracted. For a yogi, the vital difference lies between distraction and nondistraction.

Right now it is not morning or afternoon, but noon. At this time of day you cannot really separate the empty space from the sunlight, so this image for complete enlightenment is the indivisibility of space and daylight. Sentient beings are no further away from buddhas than this shaded area is from being sunlit. It is very close. It is only a matter of recognizing or not recognizing.

What we should be introduced to and recognize is the state of non-meditation. By training, this nonmeditation becomes stabilized, fully perfected. This state is called the 'dharmakaya throne of nonmeditation'. One does not reach the state of nonmeditation by meditating. The seed, the root cause, cannot be something different from the result. If you plant a medicinal plant, it will not at a later point become a poisonous plant, and if you plant a poisonous plant, it will not somehow become a medicinal plant. What we train in from the very beginning — what we recognize — should be, in essence, the same as that of complete enlightenment. You never hear the term 'dharmakaya throne of meditation'. It is always the dharmakaya throne of nonmeditation. What we should recognize to begin with, what we should train in as the path, is the state of nonmeditation. The way of training is nondistraction. Nondistraction makes the whole difference. Distraction destroys everything.

The dharmakaya throne of nonmeditation describes the fruition of the Mahamudra path. In Dzogchen it is called the 'exhaustion of conceptual mind and phenomena'. Conceptual mind means the perceiving mind that fixates. Phenomena mean the perceived objects — the five elements and all the different entities in our life. We need to go beyond perceiver and perceived. When nothing is held in mind as solid, the five elements and five sense objects and so forth are all seen as what they actually are, an insubstantial, empty, nonexistent presence. They are like rainbows, insubstantial yet *seemingly* there. The yogi who fully realizes this state is not harmed by the five elements. A true yogi can move through solid matter, does not sink into water, is not burnt by fire and is not obstructed by wind. That is the sign of having fully realized this fact. We should train in the state of rigpa that is originally pure. Although the essence is primordially enlightened, the yogi has to be re-enlightened. We have fallen into delusion. Attaining stability in nondelusion is called re-enlightenment.

The first thing we are introduced to in Dzogchen is the state of nonmeditation — of insight free of concepts, free of the concept of looker and a thing looked at. If you begin with an entity to meditate on, any result obtained through this meditation would be similarly conceptual. If this was the case, from where would the compassion of the buddhas ever appear? A yogi should be like a swan, a creature that can separate water and milk when drinking. The yogi should be able to separate the milk of inherent wakefulness from the water of ignorance.

Saraha said, "Give up the thinker and what is thought of." That is the actual way of benefiting beings. But giving up everything doesn't include giving up recognizing. Give up doing, but don't give up nondoing. If you give up recognizing, it becomes a state of indifference. Give up conceptual experience, but don't give up nonconceptual wakefulness. Rigpa is like your naked body, and dualistic mind is like clothing. Throw away all clothing and remain naked. Strip off all dualistic thinking and remain as the naked, thoughtfree state of dharmadhatu. While wearing clothes, you are not naked, right? Similarly, while having thought, there is no naked rigpa. Once you undress, it is possible to be naked. The naked body cannot be thrown away; it is your own body. Without imagining, without thinking of anything, awareness is primordially empty and rootless. Whoever sees this is a true yogi. Yoga means to bring the natural state into actual experience. The one who does that can be called a yogi. If view, meditation and conduct are mixed with concepts, such a person is not a Dzogchen yogi. Once you have recognized the natural state — in other words, once it is an actuality in your living experience — people can truly say, "the yogi arrived," when you walk into a room! Your body is still that of a human being, but your mind is Mahamudra.

3

Iron Rod Technique

❖

STUDENT: When I recognize rigpa, all thinking dissolves, but the appearances of sights, sounds, and so on do not disappear. What is the difference between experience and thought?

RINPOCHE: There is no need to block experience. Simply avoid fixating on the experience and labeling it. It is very hard to avoid experiencing. In fact, if you really want to avoid experience, you'll need to have someone knock you out with an iron bar! If you want to totally stop encountering anything, and experience no mind, perceive no appearances, have your friend give you a hard whack over the head. Then you will succeed — at least for a while. When both thinking and perception cease, there is the state we call 'utter oblivion', which is mindless and without thought. That state resembles the original cause of ignorance. When both the thinking and the perceived are halted, your samsaric state is only put on pause, on hold.

The true way is to be 'untainted by the perceiving mind and unspoiled by fixating on the perceived objects', but that doesn't mean that the wakefulness is somehow interrupted — not at all. If your training is for the purpose of bringing thinking and experience to a halt, you must have somebody knock you out. If you prefer, you could also do it by yourself. You don't need to have somebody else knock you out. Every time you wake up, take hold of the iron bar, if that's your training, and knock yourself out. You could get quite good at it after a while! This is quite easy to accomplish. As soon as you regain your senses and start to have one thought, immediately hit yourself in the head! Your meditation aid would be the iron bar. If you want to bring both sensations and thoughts to a halt, use the iron bar. This will help you to reach the ultimate stupidity! This was the pointing-out instruction for the stupid state of complete oblivion.

Experience, such as a physical sensation, and the thought about that experience occur in combination. For example, if somebody puts a needle to your skin, the thought, "it hurts," arises, triggered by that sensation. Physical sensation can be present anywhere on the body. When you touch yourself with a needle, don't you know it immediately? It is quite easy to point out what the sensation is, just take a needle and prick yourself. Do not use a knife — that's a little too risky! You won't die from a needle. But put a needle in a corpse and it won't feel anything. There won't be any reaction, will there? Right now there is a mind in this body, so if you want to be completely free from physical sensation, you need to die. A corpse doesn't feel anything. That was about sensory experience.

In the moment of recognizing mind essence, sensation does take place, but it's an empty sensation. This means that the impressions of your five senses are vividly experienced; yet they are indivisible from emptiness. Sights are empty sights; sounds are empty resonance. While seeing the empty essence, any object of the five senses arises as emptiness. They don't get interrupted; they are still felt, still fully experienced. Whatever occurs to your eyes is called empty sights. Whatever occurs to your ears is empty sounds. For your tongue, empty taste. For your nose, it is empty smell. You don't become totally vacant, a void; there is still sensation; there is still experience. If you want to be totally free of sensation, just turn into a corpse! On the other hand, one can experience sensation and not hold onto that; that's perfectly fine. The vital point is this: it is impossible to fixate while seeing the essence. At the same time, there is a knowing of whatever takes place. Whatever is seen is empty sights, whatever is heard is empty sounds — at that moment there is no fixating.

While not seeing the essence, the empty quality is missing, isn't it? In the moment of seeing the empty essence, there is no attachment, no clinging, and no fixation; yet there is knowing. The five senses are wide open; everything is vividly clear. Here is a profound statement:

Utterly awake, with the five senses wide open.
Utterly open, with unfixating awareness.

This complete openness, called *zangtal* in Tibetan, means not attached to anything, not fixating on anything. This is precisely the opposite of an ordinary person's frame of mind that clings to and fixates on everything. The openness of rigpa, the openness of a yogi, does not fixate on anything; it does not hold anything. We need to grow used to this type of openness. Your five senses are wide open, wide awake and yet thoughtfree. Remain in that state, utterly open. This openness is like a windowpane of clear glass. It doesn't obstruct the view of anything from outside; it is totally transparent. This transparency is the same as not holding onto anything, not fixating on anything — an openness that has no division between outside and inside. Like the windowpane, there is nothing blocking the view of what is outside and what is within. It is unlike this wall that is neither transparent nor open. We could use the wall as the symbol of being mindless, struck with the iron bar. That's really mindless!

Right now, my visual experience is unblocked, unobstructed. It occurs through the eyes — I can see every face individually; none are mixed together, each is distinct and clear. I don't attach words to whatever I'm seeing, or fixate on any of the details. The field of experience is unblocked and vividly clear. Similarly, the moment you recognize mind essence, there is a sense of being wide awake. When not fixating on what is experienced, experience in itself doesn't harm anything. Fixating means to attach concepts to each detail — "This is this, that is that" and so forth. Here is a quote from Longchenpa's *Dharmadhatu Kosha*:

When sentient beings look away from themselves, everything seems solid and concrete.

When the yogi recognizes the utterly free state of rigpa,
He knows that it is open like space,
And the appearances of this world are a marvelous show.

Appearances all seem to be real, but actually they have no reality, just like a mirage, a reflection, a rainbow. You may know about certain psychedelic drugs. What happens when you see hallucinations? If you want to know exactly what the nature of experience is, ask a drug taker. Once the effect of the drug wears off, where are the hallucinations? It is like that. Everything is like that. It is exactly like right now!

In his writings Longchenpa often mentions that all these experiences, whatever we perceive, seem like they are here, they seem real, but actually they aren't. Sentient beings hold the strong belief that things are real. Last night you probably had all sorts of different dreams. Where exactly did the dreams go the moment you woke up? Where are they right now? Where do dreams come from, and exactly where do they go? Find out where your dreams go. Find out whether they are real or whether they are illusory. All the different kinds of daytime experiences are displays of mind; they are made by mind.

This is why miracles are possible. When the display of deluded mind vanishes at the moment of enlightenment, one realizes that ordinary appearances are merely illusion. The realized yogi is not burned by fire. He can walk on water and traverse solid matter. An ordinary person like us is certain to get burned by fire, blown away by the wind, and drowned in water. How does a yogi manage to experience these in a different way? Because buddha mind doesn't hold onto anything, appearances can't cause any harm. That is why we are told again and again: don't grasp at anything, don't fixate on anything. Simply recognize the state of rigpa and become stable in it. Dzogchen training is all about exactly this. The ability to perform miracles doesn't happen by glimpsing the awakened state just once or twice. It happens only when you attain stability in rigpa, in the essence of mind. Stability in rigpa is the reason all the great masters of India and Tibet were unable to be harmed by fire, crushed by mountains or drowned by water.

This is not the case of merely a few masters — there were many, many accomplished beings. There is a song by the Tibetan Master Götsangpa:[3]

> *All these appearances are deceptive trickery.*
> *This relative reality is like a magical show.*
> *The rock behind my back is transparent.*

A yogi like Götsangpa could traverse freely through solid rock, like the mountain behind my hermitage. Why, because he attained stability in rigpa. It wasn't that he was so strong that he could force his way through the mountain. It is because in actuality all appearances are a magical trickery. In Götsangpa's experience, all fixation was brought to exhaustion.

Relative reality is truly like a magical show. Are you familiar with magic? In India there were magicians who, by means of mantra and special substances, could bring forth a palace and invite kings with their entire entourage to enter and stay there, in this magical palace that is 'experienced without truly existing'. There's a story that a magician once invited the Buddha with his following of five hundred Arhats into such a palace, and served them magical food. The Buddha acted as if he didn't know and ate the food. The magician thought, "I managed to fool him." At the end the Buddha dedicated the merit, still acting as if he didn't know, and left with his entourage. The magician then tried to dissolve his magical creation, but the Buddha had put a spell on it so that it just remained there. He got very upset and went to find the Buddha. The magician said, "I'm so sorry I tried to trick you. Please forgive me and allow it to vanish." Buddha then snapped his fingers and the whole magical show collapsed.

There is no reality to a magical apparition, not even as much as a hair tip. It is created only by the application of mantra and special substance. You can conjure something forth to be seen, while in fact it has no existence. That is the metaphor for how everything is — the world and all the beings in it. Samsara, nirvana, the path — everything is like a magician's creation. There are traditionally eight analogies for illusion, including magic, reflection, a rainbow, a dream, and a mirage. All these are examples for that which is perceived to be, but which in fact doesn't really exist. They are like a magical show brought forth by a magician. All appearances, whatever we perceive, are like that — insubstantial and devoid of true existence. The more stable we become in rigpa, the more the four elements outside are seen as they are: visible yet nonexistent, like a rainbow in the sky. Before, one was simply deluded by these non-existent appearances. Through becoming stable in rigpa, we realize that whatever we perceive is delusion created by ourselves. It is personal de-luded experience. It is like Tilopa's statement to Naropa:

> *Son, you are not bound by the perceived, but by clinging.*
> *So cut your clinging, Naropa.*

When, through your master's pith instruction, you realize from within that clinging is rootless and baseless, then whatever you perceive can neither harm nor help in any way at all. Whatever you experience is your individual perception, and all individual perception is empty. Right now we may think, "I perceive this piece of wood here, so how can that be empty?" Because it can be burnt and utterly destroyed, it is empty of inherent existence — not only at some future point in time, but already. At a certain point seven fires will consume the entire uni-verse, as thoroughly as a piece of paper destroyed in a flame. That which is left behind, the empty space, cannot be destroyed. The fact that the universe first is formed, then remains and eventually disinte-grates is proof that it is in fact empty. The Buddha stated:

> *Form is emptiness and emptiness also is form.*
> *Form is no other than emptiness; emptiness is no other than form.*

Whatever you perceive are empty forms. Try to understand this, slowly and carefully. If a thing were not empty it would be indestructi-ble. It could not be destroyed by fire. But once you burn a piece of wood and blow away the ashes, there is not even an atom left behind. The mind is emptiness because you can't even burn it; can you? Can you flush mind away? Can you somehow bury it underground?

Only buddha nature is true in actuality. Here is a celebrated quote:

> It's said that everything is empty,
> But the way of the Buddha is not to be empty of the kayas and
> wisdoms.

Emptiness of mind is indestructible; it cannot be burnt by fire, it cannot be washed away by water, it cannot be buried beneath earth. Everything else, even the most solid of mountains in this world, will utterly disintegrate in the huge flames of the last fire of the *kalpa*, after which the fire simply vanishes in itself. The billionfold universe will vanish without leaving a single atom behind. Doesn't that prove that everything is empty? But the emptiness of mind cannot be destroyed by fire; it cannot be blown away. You can't do away with it; it is like space. Can you burn space? Can you blow space away? Can you wash space away, or bury it under the ground? Buddha nature is like that.

Everything perceived is empty, but the actuality of buddha nature transcends both being empty and not empty. Please understand this remarkable fact. In the moment of recognizing buddha nature, you don't need to do a lot — simply recognize the identity of that which wants 'to do', that which thinks. When recognizing, one immediately sees that there is no basis or root of anything there. This baseless, rootless essence is not some concept. Having a concept of something non-conceptual doesn't help anything. A thought-construct of emptiness is not useful. We need the natural emptiness. The moment you recognize mind essence, it is already seen. Isn't that quite easy? If the Buddha had said that there was some 'thing' to see and you somehow miss it, you would be in trouble. But there is no 'thing' to see; it is emptiness. This is what we need to see. When seeing that, nothing is missing, nothing is left out that you still haven't seen. In the moment of recognizing the essence, there is no thought; it is free. It is not an entity that slowly comes into you like being possessed by a spirit. In the *very moment* of recognizing, in that same instant, the empty essence is seen. By merely seeing the empty essence, no thought remains — it is liberated, free. This is quite easy, isn't it? There is nothing you have to carry on your back, nothing you need to make up, nothing you need to accomplish, nothing you need to imagine. Isn't that wonderfully simple and easy?

"Seeing no thing is the supreme sight." When looking at objects you don't see mind, but they are all experienced by mind. It is mind that sees objects. When it comes to recognizing the empty essence of mind, there is no need to chase after it as if it was an object, because it is mind which *experiences* objects. At that moment of recognizing, objects are of no consequence; they do not affect the essence. Objects themselves don't experience. Earth doesn't see water, water doesn't see fire, fire doesn't see wind, and so on. Only mind can experience. While being empty, it is not stuck here; any experience can unfold.

There is no need to hold onto being the experiencer of a particular experience. The moment you leave everything wide open, free from clinging and fixation, you discover that the concepts of perceiver and perceived naturally subside. The fuel of further samsara is exactly these dualistic concepts. When the perceiver and perceived naturally vanish, what is there to keep samsara alive? Train in this. It is like crossing a hundred rivers over one bridge! It is like cutting a tree's eighty-four thousand branches and leaves by a single slash to its main root; all eighty-four thousand branches will wither simultaneously. If you cut the root of just this dualistic mind, you simultaneously cut through the eighty-four thousand kinds of disturbing emotions. This is what to train in, just this. Can you trust this? Can you feel confident in this now?

STUDENT: Yes.

RINPOCHE: What is the use of just being empty and void? Do you think that is useful?

STUDENT: No.

RINPOCHE: The empty quality of the essence is dharmakaya, the cognizant quality is sambhogakaya and the unity of being empty and cognizant is called nirmanakaya. The moment you recognize mind essence, you are face to face with the three kayas. When you do not recognize, you experience the three poisons. To cut through the three poisons, recognize mind essence. "Knowing one frees all." The moment you recognize this unity of being empty and cognizant, all the eighty-four thousand kinds of disturbing emotions are simultaneously liberated.

"Knowing one frees all" — knowing this one essence liberates all states of dualistic mind. But it is also possible to "know a hundred while missing one". Or, as is often said: "Not knowing the thatness of mind, whatever you do is upside down." The thatness of mind is the moment when you recognize that there is nothing to see, it is empty. Yet there is knowing. This means experience is empty, and, while being empty, there is still an experience that is totally wide open, unimpeded. This is the 'thatness' of mind, the reality of mind. Without knowing this reality, whatever you do is upside down. All accomplishment comes through recognizing this actuality, the thatness of mind. Without recognizing this, whatever we do is upside down.

Rigpa is like a mirror that can reflect anything. When an image is reflected in a mirror, the mirror does not go after the reflection; it does not pursue it or attempt to manipulate it in any way. We beings, on the other hand, go after the objects; we pursue whatever is experienced. Rigpa is like the mirror. The mirror has the capacity to reflect, and any possible thing can be reflected in the mirror. Our essence is empty, our nature is cognizant, and our capacity is unconfined. It is in this unconfined capacity that anything can arise, like a reflection in a mirror. If it were not for this, we would merely be oblivious, insensate, unknowing. If you want to be oblivious, try knocking yourself out with the iron rod technique!

You can scan every single thing in this whole world and still not find an instruction superior to the one showing you how to recognize the nature of mind. I am telling you how it is. It is the path all past buddhas have traversed. Whoever awakens right now follows this path; all future buddhas will awaken only by following this path. It is also called the great Dharmakaya Mother, Prajnaparamita. This is not some sort of literal old lady. The Dharmakaya Mother is unconfined empty cognizance.

You need to grow used to this state through training. The training is simply recognizing, not a willed act of meditating. In the moment of recognizing, it is seen. In the moment of seeing, it is free. That freedom doesn't necessarily last long. The fact that there is no 'thing' to be seen is clearly seen *as it is*. It is not hidden; it is an actuality. Short moments, but repeated many times. You need to train like that. Once you are fully trained, you don't need to think twice. You don't need to think about doing something you've learned by heart, do you? For you to chant OM MANI PADME HUNG: do you need to think about it? Each time you say OM, do you have to think about what comes after that? Sure, one has to have the initial thought, "Now I will chant OM MANI PADME HUNG." In the same way, we need to first remind ourselves to recognize mind essence. But you don't have to worry about what comes after OM, and then after MA, do you? When you say OM MANI PADME HUNG, OM MANI PADME HUNG, do you need to think twice at all? This is called having trained. It is like that. The foremost level of training is to recognize, naturally, from the moment you wake up in the morning until you fall asleep, without deliberately meditating at all, and yet being totally undistracted.

Recognize unconfined empty cognizance. Be wide awake. Remain undistracted, with no 'thing' to meditate upon. What would it be like to remain in that uninterruptedly throughout the day? If it occurs spontaneously and unceasingly throughout day and night, how would that be? The knowledge that knows all, the loving compassion, the activity of enlightened deeds — these qualities unfold spontaneously, without having to be produced through meditation.

STUDENT: It seems that hope and fear are unavoidable for practitioners. Those of us on the path fear that we waste a lot of time; we hope to spend it wisely and attain accomplishment. On the other hand, we are taught that when sustaining the view, hope and fear ruins it. How do we overcome this hope and fear?

RINPOCHE: There are two aspects here, the view and the conduct. You need to distinguish between them. These are two different aspects which you cannot — and should not — simply fuse into one. If you lose the view in the conduct, it means you are always accepting and rejecting. You may incessantly entertain thoughts of something that needs to be attained and of something that needs to be left behind. That is called losing the view in the conduct.

On the other hand, if you lose the conduct in the view, you think that there is nothing to accept or reject — that whatever you do doesn't matter, and that there is no good and no evil. That is an even greater mistake. One's behavior has to be in harmony with worldly values as well. However, Dharma mixed with worldly work is not the perfect Dharma, I'm sorry to say. Dharma and worldly aims are a contradiction, so keep those two things separate and distinct in your mind. There is always a little unwholesomeness involved in worldly work. Evil deeds are an obstacle for the spiritual path. To practice Dharma, you need to give up evil deeds. Our body and speech are the servants of the mind that is the maker of these deeds. Whenever the mind is caught up in the three poisons, our actions are evil deeds. We don't need to burden ourselves by creating negative deeds.

The view should be free of the three poisons. In the mind of an ordinary person, there is nothing but the three poisons — there is only hope and fear. It's impossible to do worldly activities without hope and fear. You cannot do anything in this life without accepting and rejecting. Trying to go beyond this becomes a huge problem. So you cannot practice the Dharma without hope and fear, without accepting and rejecting. This doesn't mean that one has to be like an ordinary person whose view is only the three poisons which, by the way, is the definition of an ordinary person, and whose behavior is to carry out the three poisons. That is not what is meant. The mind-stream of an ordinary person is called 'black diffusion', which means there is nothing other than an unbroken, incessant flow of negative thought patterns, throughout day and night. For ordinary people, the view is missing. In terms of the view, there is nothing to accept or reject. However, if one doesn't accept what is good and reject evil — if one doesn't accept the Dharma or reject mundane aims — one simply goes on living a worldly life. In short, you need to distinguish between view and conduct. The view is free from hope and fear. The conduct is with hope and fear.

When it comes to training in the view itself, then it's definitely true that hope and fear, accepting and rejecting, need to be left behind. There is no equality until one leaves behind the impulse to accept and reject. These are simply two ways of grasping, and they are both conceptual thoughts. To act, to carry out the conduct, you must accept and reject; there is no other way. We need to practice the Dharma, and we don't need to create evil deeds, although these often occur automatically. Ordinary people are under the influence of thinking. The root of negative deeds is thinking, thought. The thoughts of a sentient being are not spiritual; they are only anger, desire and close-mindedness. They are either attracted towards an object by desire, set against it through aggression, or ignorant of it in terms of dullness. In other words, there is nothing but the three poisons.

You need to give up negative actions. You need to apply the Dharma. So, it is impossible to practice the Dharma in one's life without hope and fear, without accepting and rejecting. It is only in terms of the view that there is nothing to accept or reject through hope or fear. Both hope and fear are thoughts. The view is free of these, but the conduct is not. The whole purpose of the four mind-changings, for instance, is to accept and reject. Accept what should be adopted, which is the path of Dharma. Reject what should be left behind, which is the mundane patterns of life. In order to become a spiritual practitioner, one surely needs to accept and reject, and that is based on hope and fear. There is nothing wrong with that. It is in the view that there should be no accepting and rejecting. Guru Rinpoche said:

> *Do not lose the view in the conduct;*
> *If you lose the view in the conduct, you will never have the chance to*
>   *be liberated.*
> *Do not lose the conduct in the view.*
> *If you lose the conduct in the view, you stray into black diffusion.*

To lose the conduct in the view means that the view, which is emptiness, is superimposed upon all one's actions. One might say, "Good is empty, evil is also empty, everything is emptiness, so what does it matter." Then one becomes uncaring and frivolous and doesn't discriminate between help and harm, good and evil. That is called losing the conduct in the view. Please be careful to avoid this mistake!

The other extreme is to lose the view in the conduct, to only think in terms of good and evil, what is virtuous and unvirtuous. Guru Rinpoche also said, "If you lose the view in the conduct, you will never have the chance to be liberated." It is through the view that one is liberated. If you lose the view in the conduct, you will never have the opportunity to be free. If you lose the conduct in the view, then you ignore the difference between good and evil. It's very important to keep view and conduct distinct. Please discriminate carefully between these two!

Guru Rinpoche also said, "Though the view should be as vast as the sky, keep your conduct as fine as barley flour." Don't confuse one with the other. When training in the view, you can be as unbiased, as impartial, as vast, immense, and unlimited as the sky. Your behavior, on the other hand, should be as careful as possible in discriminating what is beneficial or harmful, what is good or evil. One can combine the view and conduct, but don't mix them or lose one in the other. That is very important.

'View like the sky' means that nothing is held onto in any way whatsoever. You are not stuck anywhere at all. In other words, there is no discrimination as to what to accept and what to reject; no line is drawn separating one thing from the other. 'Conduct as fine as barley flour' means that there is good and evil, and one needs to differentiate between the two. Give up negative deeds; practice the Dharma. In your behavior, in your conduct, it *is* necessary to accept and reject.

4

Shamatha and Vipashyana

✦

STUDENT: A little while ago you told me to train while not meditating. I've done that for the last week, and it appears to me that my distraction has increased. What should I do now?

RINPOCHE: The traditional phrase is: *cultivate shamatha; train in vipashyana*. Buddhism never says that shamatha and vipashyana are superfluous, should be ignored or totally set aside. Nor would I ever teach that. But there are times, when I seemingly put down shamatha a little bit. There is a reason for that, and that reason is found only in a particular context.

The context of the general teachings is one of talking to a sentient being who is experiencing uninterrupted bewilderment — one thought or emotion after another like the surface of the ocean in turmoil, without any recognition of mind essence. This confusion is continuous, without almost any break, life after life. To tell such a person that shamatha is unnecessary is definitely not the correct way of teaching, because his mind is like a drunken elephant or a crazy monkey; it simply won't stay quiet. Such a mind has grown used to the habit of following after what is thought of, without any insight whatsoever. Shamatha is a skillful means to deal with this state. Once confused thoughts have subsided to some extent, it is easier to recognize the clear insight of emptiness. It is therefore never taught that shamatha and vipashyana are unnecessary.

Teaching styles are adapted to the two basic types of mentality: one oriented towards perceived objects, the other towards the knowing mind. The first mentality pursues sights, sounds, smells, tastes, textures and mental objects, and is unstable in buddha nature. This is the situation with the 'threefold bewilderment' — the bewilderment of object, sense faculty and sense perception which causes rebirth in an ordinary body. Due to this deep-seated habit of getting caught up in one thought after another, we traverse through endless samsara. To stabilize such a mind, the first teachings need to show that person how to calm down, how to attain or resolve upon some steadfast quality within the turmoil. It's like the example of muddy water: unless and until the water is clear, you can't see the reflection of your face. Likewise, instructions on shamatha are essential for the individual who gets carried away by thoughts.

Thoughts come out of our empty cognizance. They don't come only from the empty quality. Space doesn't have any thoughts, nor do the four elements. Sights, sounds, and other sensations do not think. The five sense-doors do not think. Thoughts are in the mind, and this mind, as I have mentioned so often, is the unity of being empty and cognizant. If it were only empty, there would be no way thoughts could arise. Thoughts come only from the empty cognizance.

The general vehicles hold that the method of shamatha is necessary in order to abide peacefully. To counteract our tendency to constantly fabricate, the buddhas taught us how to rely on a support. By getting accustomed to this support, our attention becomes stabilized, able to remain steady. At this point it is much easier to have pointed out that the attention's nature is empty cognizance. But please remember that merely abiding, merely resting in the stability of shamatha practice, does not guarantee the recognition of the naked state of self-existing wakefulness.

Generally speaking, mind has many different characteristics: some good, some bad, some calm, some untamable. Some people grasp with desire, some are more aggressive; there are so many different kinds of worldly attitudes. If you want your mind to become quiet and still, by training long enough it *will* become quiet and still. It will indeed — but that is not a liberated state.

The process of becoming quiet is like a person learning how to sit down instead of roaming about bewildered and confused. Still, looking at him from a distance while he sits doesn't necessarily give any knowledge of his true character. And, as you know, people do have different personalities. One person may be very gentle, disciplined, a very kind person — while he is just sitting there, you won't know that. Another one may be very crude, short-tempered and violent, but you won't know that either. These characteristics only show themselves once his thoughts begin to move again. When thoughts move, we usually become caught up in delusion. At the same time, our nature is primordially free of the obscuration of emotions and thoughts. Thoughts and emotions are only temporary. The actual 'character' of mind is one of self-existing wakefulness, the state realized by all buddhas.

The instructions of Dzogchen, Mahamudra and the Middle Way all explain how whatever thought arises is free of form, sound, taste, touch, and so on. All movement is empty, empty movement. Though an emotion is empty, it still seems to arise. Because our nature is empty cognizance, thought movement *can* occur. To get carried away by a thought is the state of a sentient being. Rather than that, recognize your basic state as being the essence, nature and capacity that are the three kayas of the buddhas. Remain in uncontrived naturalness for short moments, repeated many times. You *can* become accustomed to this. The short moment *can* grow longer. In one instant of remaining in unfabricated naturalness, a kalpa of negative karma is purified. An instant of naturalness transforms a kalpa of negative karma.

You need to simply *allow* the moment of uncontrived naturalness. Instead of meditating upon it, meaning focusing upon it, simply allow it to naturally be. As you train like that — and the words for training and meditating sound the same in Tibetan, so to play on that word — it is more a matter of familiarization than meditation. The more you grow familiar with mind essence, and the less you deliberately meditate upon it, the easier it becomes to recognize, and the simpler to sustain.

The glimpse of recognizing mind essence that in the beginning lasted only for a few seconds gradually becomes half a minute, then a minute, then half an hour, then hours, until eventually it is uninterrupted throughout the whole day. You need that kind of training. I mention this because, if the goal of the main training is to construct a state in which thoughts have subsided and which feels very clear and quiet, that is still a training in which a particular state is deliberately kept. Such a state is the outcome of a mental effort, a pursuit. Therefore it is neither the ultimate nor the original natural state.

The naked essence of mind is not known in shamatha, because the mind is occupied with abiding in stillness; it remains unseen. All one is doing is simply not following the movement of thought. But being deluded by thought movement is not the only delusion; one can also be deluded by abiding in quietude. The preoccupation with being calm blocks recognition of self-existing wakefulness, and also blocks the knowing of the three kayas of the awakened state. This calm is simply one of no thought, of the attention abiding in itself while still not knowing itself.

The root of samsara is thought. The 'owner' of samsara is thought. Nevertheless, the very essence of thought is dharmakaya, isn't it? We need to train in recognizing this essence of thought — the 'four parts without the three'. Training in this is not an act of meditating on something, but a 'getting used to'. Yet, it is not like memorizing either, as in learning verses by heart.

Meditation generally means paying attention. But in this case, we need to train in being free of the watcher and what is watched. In shamatha there is an observer and an object observed. So, honestly, shamatha is also a training in blocking off emptiness. Shamatha makes the mind used to and occupied with being quiet. Something is always maintained. That kind of state is a product of a technique. One applies a lot of effort to fabricating a certain mind-made state. And any state that is a product of training is not liberation. Simply being able to remain quiet does not cause confusion to collapse.

The ocean may look totally still if you could somehow force the waves to subside, but inside the water, all sorts of sediment is still floating around. It may be free of waves, but it is not free of debris. In the same way, during a sustained state of stillness, the habitual tendencies for the eighty innate thought states, the fifty-one mental events, and all the virtuous and unvirtuous emotions are all latently present. They may not be obvious; they may not be active; but still, they are not liberated.

What I am criticizing here is the idea that the stillness of mind free of thought is ultimately preferable or a goal in itself. The Buddha's teaching is that it isn't; stillness in itself is *not* liberation. By pursuing it, one can attain long, long stretches of complete tranquility, but this is not the same as true liberation.

The awakened state of rigpa, on the other hand, is wide open. Nothing is fixated upon, like the ocean in which no sediment remains. When you mix earth into water, it makes the water dirty. In the same way, you don't attain enlightenment by shamatha alone. You need the vipashyana, the quality of clear seeing, which is inherent in the emptiness beyond conceptual mind.

At all levels of Buddhist practice, these two have to go together: stillness and insight, shamatha and vipashyana. In beginning shamatha practice, one may use either a pebble or the breath as the object of attention, but in this case there is always duality: the split between the object of attention, and the attentive mindfulness itself — that which keeps an eye on that from which one should not be distracted. In Dzogchen, on the other hand, one is introduced to the naked state of dharmakaya from the very beginning. In the Dzogchen context it is sometimes said that stillness is not absolutely necessary. This is only meant for the person of the highest capacity; it is not meant for everybody. It is not a general Dzogchen teaching to dispense with shamatha, not at all. In Dzogchen, Mahamudra and the Middle Way, it is never taught that you don't need shamatha; it is only the above-mentioned shortcoming of shamatha that needs to be avoided.

So, you begin with shamatha and continue until you are able to remain acceptably steady. At this point it is much easier to see your naked essence. It's like wanting to see your face reflected in a pool of water — it doesn't help to continuously stir the surface of the water. Rather, you need to allow it to become still and placid. In order to gain the insight of vipashyana it is first necessary to allow the mind to settle so that your essence can be seen clearly. In the general system of Buddhism, this is indispensable.

As you progress further through the vehicles, you uncover more depth to the meanings of shamatha and vipashyana. There is, for instance, the ordinary and extraordinary shamatha and vipashyana. Ultimately it is said that "buddha mind is the unity of shamatha and vipashyana," but that kind of shamatha and vipashyana is not the ordinary, conceptual type of induced stillness followed by an achieved insight. The name used at that point is the 'shamatha and vipashyana that delights the tathagatas'. In other words, they are pleased with that kind because it is flawless. Similar words, different meanings: the ordinary and extraordinary shamatha and vipashyana are as different as sky and earth.

Once more, don't think that shamatha and vipashyana are unnecessary. In rigpa, the intrinsic steadiness is shamatha and the awake quality is vipashyana. The steadiness free of thought is the ultimate shamatha. Being free of thought while recognizing your essence is the indivisible unity of shamatha and vipashyana that delights the tathagatas.

Dzogchen as well uses the words shamatha and vipashyana, but at that point, they do not refer to an outcome of practice. The *Treasury of Dharmadhatu* by Longchenpa says:

> *The original nature, totally free of all thoughts, is the ultimate*
> *   shamatha.*
> *Natural cognizance, spontaneously present like the radiance of the sun,*
> *Is the vipashyana that is utterly uncontrived and naturally present.*

From this Dzogchen perspective, shamatha is the unchanging quality of innate steadiness, while the natural sense of being awake is the vipashyana aspect. Neither of these are produced or fabricated in any way. Saying that shamatha is not needed refers to the stillness of mind-made fabrication. When I told you before to not meditate, it was to not meditate in the sense of mind-made meditation. It was that kind of shamatha I told you to stop.

Clear seeing, vipashyana, is your empty cognizance, your naked awareness beyond waxing and waning. This sentence has incredible meaning. In Dzogchen it refers to the true recognition of rigpa, while in Mahamudra, it is called the innate suchness. This is when the *real* is recognized. It can be called many things, but in short it is the seeing of mind essence simultaneously with looking. "Seen the moment you look. Free the moment it's seen." There is not a single thought that can stick to that state. However, after a bit of time you discover that you are again looking at something seen. That is when thought has arrived. Then you need to apply 'remindfulness', and once again, immediately, the looker is dropped. Relax into uncontrived naturalness!

(Rinpoche remains in rigpa as a direct transmission, and then continues to speak.)

When remaining without doing anything whatsoever, there is total letting go. In the same moment there is also a sense of being wide awake; there is an awake quality that is unproduced.

Simultaneous with the disappearance of thought, there is an awake quality that is like the radiant flame of a candle, which exists all by itself. That awake quality doesn't need to be supported through meditation, because it is not something that is cultivated. Since it's recognition only lasts for a short while, it is necessary to remind yourself again. But honestly, how far away is it to get to that moment? When you put your finger out in the air to touch space, how far do you need to move your hand forward before you connect with space? In the same way, the very moment you recognize mind essence, it is seen the very moment you look. It is not that at some later point you will see it; or that you have to continuously look, look, look for it. There are not two different things going on here.

The recognition of emptiness is accomplished the moment you look. "Seeing no 'thing' is the supreme sight." When seeing emptiness, you don't need to do anything whatsoever to it. The key word here is uncontrived, which means you don't have to alter it in any way; just leave it as it naturally is. At that moment, you are totally out of a job; there is nothing you need to do to it. In other words, no act of meditating is necessary at this point. That is what I meant by "don't meditate". Because at that moment whatever you do to try to keep, or prolong the natural state only envelops it in more activity and complexity, which is not really what we need. We have been doing that non-stop anyway, for countless lifetimes.

The perfect dharmakaya is when thought has been allowed to subside. Ordinary beings have fallen under the influence of thought. It is a matter of either recognizing or not. In Dzogchen, the essence is seen the moment you look. Yet, dharmata is not a thing to be seen. If it were, it would be a product of mind.

(Once again Rinpoche gives direct pointing-out by example of remaining in rigpa.)

Sentient beings hold on to this moment. In the present moment, the past has ceased, and the future has not arrived. Be free of the three times, then there is nothing except being empty. Trekchö is like cutting through a string; there is no thought conceptualizing past, future or present. Free of the thoughts of the three times, your present, fresh wakefulness is rigpa.

The shamatha I told you to be free of, in the sense of not meditating, is mind-made peace. It is extremely good that you have dropped it. Mind-made peace is not the perfect path to liberation. Existence and peace, samsara and nirvana — we need to be free of both of these. *That* is the perfect state of enlightenment.

The natural state of totally naked awareness has the quality of being unimpeded; that is true freedom. Recognize the moment of totally open and unimpeded awareness, which does not hold or dwell on anything whatsoever. This is not the mere absence of thought activity, as in induced serenity. That is one major difference. That is also the main reason why shamatha is not by itself the true path of liberation; it needs to be conjoined with the clear seeing of vipashyana on every level, all the way to complete enlightenment.

The ultimate achievement through shamatha practice, with partial but not the full and clear seeing of vipashyana, which is the recognition of mind essence, is to attain the nirvana of an arhat, but not the non-dwelling true and complete enlightenment of a buddha. We should always aspire towards the complete enlightenment that dwells neither in samsara nor in nirvana.

It is also possible to have a sustained meditative state of serenity and yet not be liberated. Here is a story about that. Once I was with my father at a benefactor's house. The man who brought in the tea was a meditator. While carrying the tea in through the door, he somehow suddenly froze, the teakettle lifted in mid-air. One of the boys wanted to call him, but my father said, "No let him be — if he drops the pot of boiling tea it would make a mess; simply leave him be." He stood there for hours, and as the sun was about to set, my father gently called his name into his ear. He slowly regained his senses. Someone said, "What happened?" He replied, "What do you mean what happened? I am bringing the tea." They told him, "That was this morning, now it is afternoon." He said, "No, no, it is right now, I just came in with it." He was interviewed more about what he experienced, and he said "I didn't experience anything at all — it was totally vacant, with nothing to express or explain, just totally quiet." When he was told that so many hours had gone by, he was quite surprised, because to him it didn't feel as if any time had passed.

The key point in this context is 'don't meditate'. That doesn't mean you have to frown upon all the years of training you have put into meditation. That training was beneficial in that there are far fewer thoughts. However, it is not beneficial to continuously pursue a special, thoughtfree mental state. Rather, simply allow yourself to be in naturalness free of any fabrication. This uncontrived naturalness is its own remedy to thoughts or emotions.

Mind is something amazing: it is said to be like a wish-fulfilling treasury, a treasure-chest of any possible thing. Whatever you put mind to; it can produce that. The true way to go beyond stillness is, whenever you experience the quietude of an absence of thoughts and emotions, recognize the experiencer — what it is that feels the quietness, what it is that abides. At that moment it becomes transparent; in other words, the fixation on stillness disintegrates.

When shamatha is destroyed or disintegrates, then there is true emptiness, an uncultivated emptiness, a natural emptiness. This primordial emptiness is dharmakaya indivisible from sambhogakaya and nirmanakaya. It is the nature of the three kayas — one instant of the essence of mind. Shamatha taints the three kayas with work. The three kayas in themselves are totally effortless.

Our aspiration should be, "Not bewildered in samsaric existence, nor dwelling in the quiescent peace of nirvana, may we liberate all beings." Through recognizing mind essence we are of course free from disturbing emotions that create further samsara. But attaining the peace of no disturbing emotions is not enough to be beyond nirvana. So form the resolve to go beyond both.

There is one way to make one hundred percent sure that your spiritual practice goes in the right direction, and that is simply the three excellences. Always remember, no matter what level of practice you are doing, to start with refuge and bodhichitta. It doesn't matter how much you are able to practice while being totally free of concepts; just train to the best of your ability for the main part of the session. Always complete by dedicating the merit to all sentient beings and make pure aspirations. Embracing your spiritual practice with these three ensures that you are proceeding in the right direction.

Otherwise, one can easily be 'meditating' in a way that doesn't necessarily lead near true liberation. There are certain states within samsara called the formless realms. Many people regard the causes for the formless realms as being the true meditation practice. Cultivating these, however, will lead to nothing but a prolonged visit to such a state. Whenever something is deliberately kept in mind, it becomes easier as one goes along because the mind assumes the habit of doing so. Eventually one comes to believe that it is totally effortless.

One could exert sustained effort on dwelling on the idea of emptiness, or just dwelling on feeling clear and quiet. One then "attains" such a state, but because this state is a product, it eventually wears off. Fading from a formless god realm, you awaken after a long, beautiful stay in that meditation realm, and discover that your body died at some point, way back in the past. You now realize, "I am dead, I am not liberated in spite of everything, and all of this meditation was for nothing." At that moment the resentment you feel due to the futility of your efforts becomes a direct cause for rebirth in one of the lower realms. Thus, it makes a tremendous difference what you currently identify as being the meditation state, and with which motivation you practice.

For many people, shamatha can be a way of preparing for the formless realms. It can also simply be quieting down the mind, or imagining a state of emptiness. One repeatedly tries to quiet the mind, to calm down and keep the idea of emptiness in a sustained way, without the real knowing of what it is that sustains. What we need is to combine shamatha with the clear seeing of mind essence itself. In this context such seeing is called vipashyana, and it is totally beyond anything that dwells and anything to be dwelled upon. That is the moment when shamatha and vipashyana are a unity. Understanding this point is extremely important.

The Buddha himself described the path as a progression through stages of meditation practice:

> *Just like the steps of a staircase,*
> *You should train step by step*
> *And endeavor in my profound teachings.*
> *Without jumping over any steps, proceed gradually to the end.*

> *Just as a small child*
> *Gradually develops its body and strength,*
> *My teachings are also in this way —*
> *From the beginning steps of entering*

Up until the complete perfection.

Some teachers have explained that the phrase 'complete perfection' here means the Great Perfection, the Dzogchen teachings. This quote also means that the teachings are dependent upon the recipients. Because people are of different types, and can be of sharp, mediocre, or lesser capacity, a buddha wanting to benefit them has to teach according to their own level. A teacher may want to teach Dzogchen to everyone, but that is only possible if every single person is of the highest capacity. That would be wonderful, but not realistic. Even a fully enlightened buddha cannot avoid having to teach nine gradual vehicles. It doesn't help to give the teachings on a level that people are not actually at. In the same way, you don't give low teachings to someone of higher capacity. That is why it is indispensable to have nine different levels of vehicles.

Amazing: this unmade, present wakefulness
Is the true Samantabhadra
From which you have never been apart for even an instant.
While recognizing, let be in naturalness.

This is a very important verse, and I will discuss it line by line. It begins with the exclamation *ema*, which means amazing. The first line is: "This unmade, present wakefulness." The word for 'present wakefulness' here is the same as the word for consciousness or mind; it is simply what experiences right now. *(Rinpoche snaps his fingers.)* You hear that sound, right? There is no question about that. There is a hearing of sound. That is because there is present wakefulness in these bodies. There is a mind in the body right now, and that is why it is possible to hear through our ears. When mind, the wakeful quality, leaves your body — in other words, when it becomes a corpse — I can snap my fingers a hundred times in front of your ears but there still won't be any hearing. There is no consciousness that hears, no cognition of sound, because mind has departed. That which experiences is not the body, it is that which is *in* the body right now, which is in this moment, right now — not in the past and not in the future, but just in this present moment.

When somebody snaps his fingers like I just did, an immediacy of hearing readily takes place. That is only possible because of present wakefulness. Nothing else can hear sound. The ears by themselves cannot hear, as in the case of a corpse. The five elements and so forth don't hear; the sense organs by themselves don't hear; it is only mind that hears. This unmade, present wakefulness — unmade means natural — should be left as it naturally is.

I have often — maybe too often! — given a very simple example for naturalness. When wood grows as a tree in the mountain, it is natural; but if it is cut down and shaped into a table, it is not the natural form of wood anymore. The word 'unmade' here means that you are to leave your present moment of wakefulness exactly *as it is*, without doing anything to it. There is nothing adopted or avoided, nothing to be held, accepted or rejected, nothing to be examined at all. Without any hope or fear whatsoever, simply allow present wakefulness to be *as it is*. That is the first line: "This unmade present wakefulness."

The second line is: "Is the true Samantabhadra." Samantabhadra is the full mastery of the nature that is present throughout all samsaric and nirvanic states; it is your buddha nature, which is all-encompassing but fully realized. The true Samantabhadra is the realization of your own present wakefulness.

The third sentence is: "From which you have never been apart for even an instant." At no point of time, ever, has your nature been lost. Mind and its essence are never separate, like the example of the sun and its rays not being separate. This is called *rangjung yeshe*, self-existing wakefulness. The buddha nature is like the sun; the rays of light are like the thoughts of sentient beings' mind.

Mind and its essence are not separate, just like the sun and its rays are not separate. Coemergent wisdom and coemergent ignorance are also as inseparable as fire and smoke. We have never been separate from this essence for even a moment. Our true nature is Samantabhadra — the nature pervading both nirvana and samsara. Even though it's always been present, this alone doesn't help, because it hasn't been recognized. We need to recognize it.

The fourth sentence is: "While recognizing, let be in naturalness." You need to go beyond dualistic intelligence. Go beyond viewer and what is viewed; go beyond duality. Right now our intelligence is an act of thinking *of* something. This moment of original, self-existing wakefulness is thoughtfree. We need to recognize this, train in it and attain stability in the recognition. Recognizing is like the example of an infant, who grows up into a man of twenty-five years old. From infancy, the training is to recognize and continue recognizing until full mastery.

Whether you are Buddha Samantabhadra or a tiny insect, there is no difference in the quality or size of the buddha nature itself. Here's what makes the difference: in the case of a sentient being there is no knowing of itself, and therefore the cognizant quality grasps at what is experienced. In other words, out of ignorance emerges a bewilderment that is endlessly repeated.

The paths and levels towards enlightenment describe degrees of stability in recognition. We need to recognize empty cognizance — what this present moment of unmade wakefulness really is. Allow that to simply be *as it is*, let be in naturalness. That is the whole teaching in a nutshell. Having recognized this, train in it through uncontrived naturalness. Finally attain stability. To repeat these four lines:

> *Amazing: this unmade, present wakefulness*
> *Is the true Samantabhadra*
> *From which you have never been apart for even an instant.*
> *While recognizing, let be in naturalness.*

Every sentient being is cognizant. Cognizance is incessant, as is our nature. It is the nature of mind to cognize. Wakefulness is present always, at any moment. If the present moment of wakefulness is left without altering it, that is the very essence of naked mind. The past has ceased, the future has not come and the present is not conceptualized in any way whatsoever. The present moment of unfabricated wakefulness is seen the moment we look. Sometimes it is called present mind, ordinary mind, naked mind. Ordinary mind meant that it is neither worsened nor improved. Ordinary means that unceasing wakefulness is present in all beings from Samantabhadra down to the tiniest insect. This unceasing wakefulness is the true Samantabhadra.

Usually we contrive our present wakefulness through hope and fear, accepting and rejecting. At this moment, after having recognized its nature, however, you don't need to do anything more to it. It is not something that has to be kept or maintained in any way whatsoever, because it is *naturally so* by itself. If we simply leave it *as it is* without doing anything to it, it is beyond improvement or ruin.

Honestly, it's not like there is a good buddha nature in Samantabhadra and a bad one in an insect. The minds of every single one of us possess the same quality of buddha nature. It is so close and easy that we don't believe it. It is so close and it is so easy that most people find it impossible to trust that simply letting be is sufficient! But the difference between samsara and nirvana is simply a matter of either recognizing or not recognizing. The very moment you recognize, there is nothing simpler than that. In the moment of seeing mind essence, it is already recognized; there is nothing more that needs to be done. At that very moment it is not necessary to meditate even a speck. Shamatha needs to be meditated, cultivated. This emptiness does not possess an atom of anything to meditate on.

After recognizing, of course, we lose the continuity. We get distracted. Losing the continuity, becoming distracted, is itself the state of delusion. Meditating on buddha nature as if it were an object is the work of conceptual mind. This conceptual mind is exactly what keeps us spinning through samsara.

'The immediacy of your present wakefulness' means no longer thinking of the past, and not planning the future. The past thought has gone, and the future thought hasn't come yet. Although a gap may appear in the present, sentient beings continuously close it up; we reconnect to thoughts, instead of allowing a gap that is free of concepts. Instead of hurrying to do that, simply let be in present wakefulness. Naked ordinary mind, *what naturally is*, is present. You don't have to do anything to bring it forth. That going beyond thoughts of the three times is the essential meaning of the 'three gates of emancipation' mentioned in the Sutras.

There is no need to do anything to your present wakefulness at that moment; it is already *as it is*. That is the true meaning of naked ordinary mind, *tamal kyi shepa*, a famous term in Tibetan. Ordinary mind means not tampered with. There is no 'thing' there which needs to be accepted or rejected; it is simply *as it is*. The word 'ordinary mind' is the most immediate and closest way to describe how the nature of mind is. No matter what terminology is being utilized within The Middle Way, Mahamudra or Dzogchen, naked ordinary mind is the simplest term. It is the most immediate way to describe how our nature really is. It means that nothing needs to be accepted or rejected; it is already perfect *as it is*.

Do not project outwardly, do not withdraw inwardly, don't place your wakefulness anywhere in between. Whether the attention is directed outside or inside, it's not necessary to place it in a forced state of calm. We need to be free of the thoughts of the three times. There is nothing easier than this. It is like pointing at space: how much do you need to do before you point at space? It's like that. That is the moment in which no doing is required whatsoever. 'Mind essence is originally empty and rootless'. To know that is sufficient in itself. Of course you can know your own mind!

To 'cultivate shamatha and to train in vipashyana' is like learning the alphabet. If we do not learn it we will never be able to read or write. Once meditation has dissolved into the expanse of your basic nature, then it is 'easier to see and easier to maintain'. 'Easier to see' means that recognizing is simple. 'Easier to maintain' means to be proficient in naturalness. Without projecting, without focusing, without thought, get accustomed to the continuity.

To make it extremely short: "Never meditate, yet never lose it." It is not an act of meditating like shamatha. But if you forget and get distracted, you fall back into confusion. Never meditate, and never be distracted. When you forget, apply mindfulness. Without this watchfulness, the old pattern takes over again. The old habit of not seeing mind essence and being continuously caught up in thought is called 'black diffusion'. Without the watchfulness, without reminding, there is nothing to remind us to recognize mind essence.

5

Transmuting Emotions

Whether the emotion is desire, anger, jealousy, pride or dullness, the principle of liberation for each of the five poisons is exactly the same. The nature of mind in all these situations is always unconfined empty cognizance. If the cognizance were confined, then all its qualities would be obstructed. Confinement is similar to unconsciousness, to being hit on the head with an iron rod — all that happens is that you black out and are unaware of anything. The moment of recognizing your mind is not an unconscious state, yet it is impossible for any normal disturbing emotion to remain within it. Once again, please understand that there is no difference between how any of the five poisons vanish. When you recognize the indivisible empty cognizance, the emotion dissolves. What is left over is original wakefulness. Here is a quotation from Padmasambhava's *Lamrim Yeshe Nyingpo*:

> *When the thought of attachment towards a desired object occurs,* ༔
> *Do not suppress or encourage, but release into naked, aware emptiness.* ༔
> *Without clinging to bliss, experience is awakened from within.* ༔
> *That is called discriminating wisdom.* ༔

When your mind is moved by desire, don't cling to pleasure, but simply recognize its empty essence. Remain in naked awareness. The view is self-existing wakefulness. Self-existing means empty, while wakefulness is the cognizant quality. This self-existing wakefulness that is present in all beings is exactly what all the great masters in the past have pointed out. Recognizing it is the basis of the path. Knowing it frees desire and all the other emotions.

This is not the same as trying to avoid feeling desire, which wouldn't be so easy, because disturbing emotions do arise and move through our minds. The other vehicles have techniques to suppress emotions. These may help you to temporarily suppress desire, but you still don't see its root, its basic nature. For example, in the Theravada system you visualize the person to whom you are attracted as being a skeleton or rotten corpse. You try not to feel attraction through this negative image. This technique works on a temporary basis, but it's like trying to dam up a river filled with dirty water. The dirt doesn't disappear; it simply gets held back for a while. It's not purified, because when the water is allowed to flow again, it is still impure. In the Dzogchen way, to recognize mind essence is to meet the indivisible three kayas face to face. The essential point is to know how to recognize empty awareness. The essence of the five poisons is the five wisdoms. The methods that suppress the poisons do not reveal the wisdoms. Just like darkness cannot remain when the sun rises, none of the disturbing emotions can endure within the recognition of mind essence. That is the moment of realizing original wakefulness, and it is the same for each of the five poisons.

We need to discontinue ordinary notions that solidify reality. The only way to truly do that is by recognizing that the very nature of bliss is empty, without any concrete substance whatsoever. That recognition can utterly purify the grasping at bliss, the craving for pleasure. If one hasn't recognized the nature of mind, at least one can practice the three pure notions of deity, mantra and samadhi. To truly perfect the training, however, you must recognize that the nature of mind is empty cognizance. This is the case whether there is desire, anger, jealousy, pride, dullness, greed, or ignorance. In any of the five, six or seven disturbing emotions, the empty cognizance is not something into which we have to transmute the emotion. The essence of the emotion is *already* this indivisible empty cognizance. Its empty aspect is dharmakaya, its cogni-

zant aspect is sambhogakaya, and the indivisibility of these two is nirmanakaya. When recognizing the nature of the three kayas, you don't
need to change the essence of the poison into what its very nature already is. When not recognizing, as for ordinary beings, the expression
of the essence unfolds as the five poisons. Recognition of the essence in
actuality causes the disturbing emotion to simply vanish. This is the real
path.

The root of samsaric worldliness is uninhibited involvement in the
three poisons. The root of buddhahood is to face the three kayas. Suc-
cinctly put: Knowing the three kayas as our nature, we are enlightened.
Being overpowered by the three poisons, we roam in samsara.

Desire is nothing but your mind feeling attraction; anger is nothing
but your feeling of aversion. There isn't anyone without this. All sentient beings, even insects, dogs, pigs and so forth, have desire; they all
want to experience pleasure. Desire creates samsara; this is why the
Buddha taught, first of all, that his followers should become monks and
nuns. Desire is a massive preoccupation that makes one unable to practice the Dharma. Through samsaric desire one makes children — without any children, samsara would be emptied. First, you find a partner;
next, you make children. Then the children need food, a place to live,
and clothing. They get sick, they need some kind of education — and
you have this constant source of worry and distraction. On the other
hand, if you are a monk or nun you don't have children, and when you
don't have children you don't create further samsaric anxiety in that
way. Therefore you have the free time to practice the Dharma whole-
heartedly. The intent of what the Buddha taught in the *Pratimoksha
Sutra* and other texts like that is to help followers avoid a lot of distractions. Abstaining, and thus not being distracted from spiritual practice,
is an external way of dealing with desire. Simply avoiding negative actions and doing the ten virtuous actions will of course lead to a higher
rebirth, but it doesn't guarantee liberation from samsara. Higher
teachings are therefore necessary, so Buddha taught Mahayana, the
vehicle for bodhisattvas, and especially the Vajrayana.

Vajrayana is the swift path because it teaches how the five poisons can be purified into the five wisdoms. The essence of the five poisons is space and wisdom. Space and wisdom is another way of saying unconfined empty cognizance, which is the nature of the three kayas. When recognizing that the essence of an emotion, in this case desire, is empty cognizance, we don't need to transform it. It is not that the emotion has to be transformed into empty cognizance; in essence it is *already* empty cognizance. An emotion is merely a motion of mind not knowing itself.

All three levels of Buddhist teaching, all three yanas, describe methods of dealing with emotions: abandoning the emotions, transforming them, and recognizing their essence. It is never taught on any level that one can be an enlightened buddha while remaining involved in disturbing emotions, never. But the way in which the different levels deal with emotions is different.

Emotions are often compared by analogy to a poisonous plant. In Tibet there is an incredibly toxic root called *tsenduk*; you don't have to eat much of it before you die. At the same time, this plant can also be used as medicine. It is the strongest poison, but it is also one of the strongest healing medicines. Using *tsenduk* as a metaphor for emotions, a Hinayana practitioner is like someone who understands that the plant is dangerously poisonous and should not be allowed to grow further. He will put a big stone atop the shoot to block it off so it will not harm anyone. A Mahayana practitioner will see that the root is still there and can continue to grow. He will therefore pull up the shoot by the root, so there is no longer any cause for it to grow forth. But a Vajrayana practitioner is someone who acknowledges the plant's usefulness as medicine. Rather than blocking it or uprooting it, in both cases leaving it behind, he skillfully utilizes it as medicine and is able to cure disease. These three levels are called abandoning, changing and recognizing.

The third approach, recognizing, is based on the ability to recognize the nature of mind whenever you become involved in disturbing emotions, and on the fact that the very essence within that emotion is basically pure. When their essence is recognized, the five poisons turn into the five wisdoms. To recognize the empty cognizance in the moment of dullness is called dharmadhatu wisdom. To recognize the pure nature in the moment of anger is called mirror-like wisdom, and so forth. In this way, the basically pure nature of any emotional state is recognized as one of the aspects of original wakefulness known as the five wisdoms.

Any emotional state is in essence pure from the very beginning. In the moment you remember to recognize, you don't need to suppress the emotion. Nor do you need to throw it away, or uproot it. It can be utilized as the path. Of course, the negative emotion itself is impure, but the vital difference of its effect depends upon how it is viewed. In Vajrayana, to recognize rigpa is the single antidote. The basis of negative emotions is thought. The essence of thought is dharmakaya. What you need to recognize is this dharmakaya rigpa.

To repeat, in essence the five poisons are the five wisdoms. One needs to know what is, *as it is*. To be able to transform poison into medicine, you definitely need pith instructions. Through the pith instructions, the suffering of a sentient being can be transformed into wisdom. The Ati Yoga path means to possess the panacea, the universal remedy that can cure all diseases. Our basic state consisting of essence, nature and capacity is the identity of the three kayas — when it is recognized!

The essence of the three poisons is empty and insubstantial. As a matter of fact, all objects — earth, water, fire, wind, space — are all empty, and they always were. At present they may seem to be solid substance, but every single thing that appears to be solid can be totally destroyed, burnt and scattered, and then there is the space again. Everything is formed out of emptiness, and everything dissolves into emptiness.

The nature of the minds of all beings is the identity of the three kayas, when recognized. When it is not recognized, they are carried away by the three poisons. The first cause is ignorance. From that, endless samsara has unfurled. Without applying any of the vehicles of skillful means, samsara will certainly continue. Because of that, when the ordinary act of engaging desire is not embraced by any method, it just perpetuates unwholesome karma and obscurations, and samsara continues. Nobody has to teach a dog or a pig how to copulate; they all know that very well. It is only human beings that seem to have to be taught. But all animals, even the tiniest insects, seem to know it spontaneously.

Vajrayana is very precious because it brings us closer to the nature of mind. The ultimate value is to recognize this natural emptiness. Some people may deny the existence of the deities, but actually, they are the qualities of spontaneous presence that are intrinsic to the primordial purity of our nature. This is why the deities appear when engaging in Tögal practice, or in the bardo state after passing away. They don't come out of nothing. According to Ati Yoga, they are a part of your own nature. Maha and Anu Yoga teach that they abide in the body, and that in this way your body is the mandala of the victorious ones, the buddhas which at the moment of death appear out of the body.

The statement "Everything perceived is emptiness" also means that *all* perceptions are empty, not just bliss. Being impermanent is, as well, a sign of emptiness. The perceived is impermanent, but the nature of the perceiving mind, self-existing wakefulness is not impermanent at all. Our mind is empty in essence and cognizant by nature. It is indivisible empty cognizance, not subject to impermanence. Understand the difference between the perceiver and the perceived, the experience and emptiness. The essence of mind is not something that can vanish. The qualities of buddha nature are always complete. Samsara, on the other hand, can be destroyed because it is impermanent.

The elements and the entire world are in essence empty space. Space itself cannot be changed or destroyed in any way whatsoever. The four other elements are appearances, and appearances can be destroyed. The perceiver of these appearances is mind, which in essence is empty cognizance, the identity of three kayas. This essence is not governed by karma and disturbing emotions. Let me restate the verse I mentioned before:

It's said that everything is empty,

But the way of the Buddha is not to be empty of the kayas and wisdoms.

If our nature were empty of kayas and wisdoms, the attainment of enlightenment would be nothing but a void. The perceived is impermanent, but the perceiver, which in essence is empty cognizance, the kayas and wisdoms, is not impermanent. Otherwise what would be the use of pursuing buddhahood, if it was impermanent and would only be lost again?

The world and beings are emptiness; that we can say for sure. At some point the whole universe will be destroyed. Everything is destroyed in the great fire at the end of the kalpa, and there remains not even as much as one atom. The bodies of sentient beings, their voices, everything will vanish. But space itself cannot be altered or destroyed in any way whatsoever. However, space has no innate qualities, feels no pleasure or pain, nothing. The essence of mind of all sentient beings *does* have many intrinsic qualities. Thoughts can vanish, of course. But the essence of mind that is the three kayas is not something that can disappear. When a sentient being dies, the consciousness is left behind to continue. In that situation the consciousness is called the bardo consciousness, which is comprised of the skandhas. It has no physical form-aggregate, but the other aggregates still remain.

The five aggregates need to be transformed into the five buddhas. The skandha of form should change into the buddha Vairochana. This is only possible when one has awakened, when one has realized the nature of the three kayas. As a matter of fact, the only way to be enlightened is by recognizing *rangjung yeshe*, self-existing wakefulness. Otherwise, as with any other sentient being, there is no real path of enlightenment. This recognition is like one bridge that simultaneously crosses over a hundred rivers. Without recognizing, even if you had the tongue to chant the whole *Tripitaka* a million times in one day, you still wouldn't become enlightened.

STUDENT: How do we make offerings to the buddhas and the protectors of the Dharma? How should we do this, and who are they, and where do they come from?

RINPOCHE: There are different ways to make offerings, depending on who the guests are. We usually speak of four types of guests. The first is the respected guests, the Three Jewels. Below them there are the qualified guests, the protectors and guardians of the Dharma. Below them are the pitiful guests, all sentient beings. The lowest ones are the obstructing guests, the spirits who make obstacles and our karmic creditors.

These four types are treated in different ways. When for instance giving a drink to the Three Jewels and the Dharma protectors, you imagine that what you raise up in your hand is an immense ocean of sense pleasures. One doesn't throw it on the ground; it is given in a respectful way because they are the guests possessing great qualities. When giving to sentient beings or to karmic creditors, one does not pay great respect. To the sentient beings one gives straightforwardly, at an even level, but the offering to obstructers and creditors is thrown down on the ground. There is also a particular way to hold what is being given. When the offering is being given to ones higher than oneself, one holds the bottom of the vessel. If it is to someone equal, one holds it in the middle. The offerings to those below oneself are held at the top, even putting one finger in the vessel, and then throwing it outside.

Where are these beings? Wisdom beings dwell indivisible from the Akanishtha realm of dharmadhatu: in other words they are immaterial, unmanifest. When they manifest, they appear by the mere thought of the one who calls upon them, in an instant. You don't have to think they are in a particular place and need to travel from a certain direction to arrive before you to receive the offering. They simply appear by your mere thought. You don't have to imagine all the details of how they look like. It's the same as when you invite somebody over. You don't have to imagine that they have clothes on; they just come wearing their particular dress. It is like that.

There are different ways to invite beings, as well. For the wisdom beings, one says, "Please approach." For protectors or beings on the same level, one says, "Assemble here." And to the low ones, one says, "Come right here and take this!" There are different attitudes also. For instance, in the Vajra Kilaya petition to the protectors, you say: "From the Akanishtha palace of dharmadhatu, Vajra Kilaya with your retinue of boundless protectors, please approach." Where are these deities, the wisdom protectors? They are dwelling in the dharmakaya buddha field, at a level which is totally unmanifest.

Of course there are different details in the different invocations to protectors. Sometimes a liturgy may say, "From the eastern direction of the dharmakaya buddha field, or from the western direction of Akanishtha, please approach!" — summoning them from different directions. Occasionally there are references to actual places. For example, Rahula and Ekajati are sometimes invoked from a certain geographical place, or sometimes simply "From your natural abode." That natural abode actually refers to the cognizant nature indivisible from the empty essence. One always invokes the wisdom protectors from the cognizant nature.

Sometimes protectors have many names and different titles that have to be mentioned, and all these are read like a roll call, a long list of who they are. "The Great Slayer of Tsang, the Great Dralha of such-and-such" — you may repeat a lot of epithets and titles. You often find this in the rituals for protectors.

STUDENT: What is the importance of aspirations?

RINPOCHE: To make noble wishes and aspirations in combination with our good actions is incredibly important. Otherwise the result of positive karma will not ripen in the right direction. Whenever one does virtuous acts, one should always form the wish: "May this be used towards complete enlightenment. May I become the great guide, like the captain of a ship that can sail all sentient beings across to the other shore. May I quickly attain complete enlightenment, and having attained the state of a buddha, may I guide all sentient beings to liberation and the awakened state itself." That kind of aspiration is incredibly precious and makes the difference between whether good karma ripens as fleeting pleasure, or whether it is used to lead towards liberation and enlightenment.

Take the example of the many human beings in this world. A human rebirth is the result of wholesome karmic actions, but very few humans have the interest in spiritual practice. This is because most did not combine their good actions with noble wishes and aspirations. On the other hand, some people travel to Nepal from far-away countries. They are not forced to come to Nagi Gompa in particular, or even to the East. Why did they spend all this money and travel this long, long distance with so many difficulties? It is because their past good karma was combined with pure aspirations. It is the force of those aspirations that bring them all this way to receive teachings. Otherwise, there would be no point in coming here — it's just a big hassle. So you see the difference between the incredibly enormous number of human beings in this world, and the tiny handful who actually use this human existence to pursue the spiritual path. It's said the latter are as few as stars in the morning sky.

Pure aspirations are very precious, and very rare. It is of course best if you can spend all your time, day and night, in the continuous recognition of buddha nature. Through that you would certainly attain true and complete enlightenment in one lifetime, but it is not so easy to do. If you are not able to practice like that, at least combine all of your good efforts, meaning all Dharma practice, with pure aspirations. If you do this, you can be assured that at least in the following lives you will reconnect with the Dharma and be able to practice further and further. Sooner or later, you can attain complete enlightenment. This is really important.

One should never, as some people do, just be interested in the Dharma for a little while, and then when nothing special happens right away, just give it up. Some people are interested, give it up, do a little practice, and give it up again. Instead, carry on all the time at a steady pace. Have this determination: "I will never give up spiritual practice! I may not progress very quickly, but I will never turn back!"

The objects of refuge, the Three Jewels, will never fail you. If you place your trust in Buddha, Dharma and Sangha, I can promise you that you will never be deceived, not in this life, not in the bardo, and not in future lives.

The Buddha is the completely awakened one, while the Dharma is the scriptures of teachings, of what is being taught. The real Sangha are the noble beings on the ten bhumis, the bodhisattvas, including the arhats who have attained liberation. There is also the 'resembling sangha', anyone who cuts their hair and wears the red shawl and red skirt. Although they may not be enlightened or have any exceptional qualities, because of their resemblance to the Sangha, there are still blessings in paying respect to such people. The noble Sangha, on the other hand, is extremely important; they can uphold and continue the lineage of the buddhas by transmitting the teachings. If a couple has no children, the family line dies out. Without the noble Sangha, the family line of the buddhas would die out.

I'm going to tease you a little. The Buddha said: "As long as the mind continues to get involved there is no end to the number of vehicles." Mental involvement is thoughts, so as long as one continues to have thoughts, there will always be questions. Then there is no end to the answers, the vehicles of the teachings. Practicing is most important. Know the 'one thing that liberates everything', which is the practice of mind essence. This is the most important thing.

6

Buddha Offsprings

❖

To extend the moment of recognizing buddha nature, we simply need to grow more used to it. This growing used to does not involve *doing* anything to keep a state between two thoughts. Recognition of buddha nature is not a 'thing' that we can hold onto and maintain. The only way to allow that gap to continue is through uncontrived naturalness. That is the whole meaning of 'short moments, many times'. If we try to prolong the moment, it only results in a state of conceptual mind. Short moments are free of conceptual mind. By repeating these many times, we get used to it — we get the habit, we become more and more accustomed to it.

Rangjung yeshe means self-existing wakefulness. The word rangjung, self-existing, means it is not the outcome of effort, not that we try to do something and all of a sudden there is this self-existing wakefulness. The word wakefulness, yeshe, refers to the original state of being awake which is never lost, never distracted. It does not appear or disappear. It is exactly the same basic state whether you are a buddha, who has realized it, or a sentient being, who has not. Regardless of our recognition or lack of recognition, it is always present as our basic nature. It is not an entity that is made.

As a sentient being, buddha nature becomes overtaken by hope and fear. The state of mind is distracted, contrived, disturbed. In the state of buddhahood, the unmade, unfabricated nature is self-existing, but in this case the wakefulness is undistracted. Sentient beings have fallen into distraction and are overtaken by conceptual thought. We have gotten used to this 'negative meditation' of distraction, not knowing that we are distracted or that we are fabricating. We have done this in life after life. You can know what these words mean once you have been introduced to the basic nature by a master — once you have recognized the uncontrived naturalness of your mind.

Uncontrived naturalness is not something that one *does,* even though it sounds like you *do* remain in naturalness, and you *avoid* fabricating. When we hear these words, our own habit and obscurations make it sound like keeping the natural state is something we should *do* — but actually, it is the opposite of doing. One does not do anything.

By repeatedly letting be in the state of uncontrived naturalness, it becomes automatic. Don't think that there is a long moment between two thoughts that you need to somehow nail down and own. That would not be automatic; it would be fabricated. Rather than improving upon the recognition of buddha nature, simply remain completely at ease. It is a matter of self-existing wakefulness getting used to itself. Do not try to keep the state of naturalness. The state will be self-kept as the natural outcome of your growing familiarity with it. Do not fall into distraction. Short moments, repeated many times.

Because of our habit developed from countless past lives to always *do* something, the moment of nondoing, when we let be, doesn't last long. In other words, there is no real stability. It almost immediately slips away. That is just how it is, and there is not much that we can do about that initially. That is why we practice recognizing for short moments, repeated many times.

If we do not repeat the recognition of mind essence, we never grow used to it. 'Short moments' ensures that it is the real, authentic natural-ness. For a beginner, recognition of the authentic state does not last longer than a short moment. 'Many times' means that we need to grow more and more familiar with this state. This is the key point in how to practice according to Longchen Rabjam. The essence of all his *Seven Treasuries* can be captured in this phrase: "short moments, many times."

Rather than sitting for long periods only a few times a day, it's better to do short moments throughout the day, repeated again and again. If we try to sustain the natural state for long stretches, we inevitably slip into the conceptual frame of mind. Feelings like, "I must *do* this, I must *keep* natural, now I *must not* fabricate" — these kind of ideas are always mixed with a conceptual attitude.

Space is the example for mind essence, because space is unmade. But mind essence is not totally like space, in that space cannot think. Space has no knowing. Our mind is cognizant emptiness — empty like space, but with a natural knowing. That union of cognizance and emptiness is seen when recognizing. It is immediate, like the example I mentioned of pointing into mid-air. You do not have to wait to raise your arm for your finger to touch space — you are already touching space, all the time. You do not have to move your hand forward; the contact is already occurring, and has been your entire life. All you have to do is recognize that it is taking place. It's the same with mind essence. First of all, remember to recognize mind essence according to your master's pith instruction. At that point, at that very first moment, you *see* that there is nothing to see. Unfortunately, we usually do not trust this. That is why this short moment lacks stability. Instead we create doubts through conceptual thoughts, wondering, "Is this it?" or "Maybe not?"

When short moments are repeated many times, the recognition becomes automatic. It becomes stable in itself. Any act of meditating is conceptual involvement: this is exactly what we are training in *not* doing. To be relaxed and let go in the moment of recognizing — that is the most important thing. Then, when the recognition slips away, we can simply repeat it again.

What we are trying to train in is not constructed in any way; it is not *made* through practice. By training in this way, our awareness of the natural state becomes uninterrupted. Usually, our innate state of self-existing wakefulness is interrupted by distraction. Dualistic mind is like the electric current up here at Nagi Gompa — it is not continuous; it is interrupted repeatedly by power cutoffs, load-shedding, and so on. But rigpa is continuous, like the flow of a river. Rigpa's self-existing nature is like a natural jewel. Rigpa is also like the glass window here, which does not obstruct the light in any way, but is totally open and transparent. Normal, thinking mind is obstructed. When one thought disappears, whatever you thought of vanishes. It is interrupted each and every moment.

While we are in actuality not separated from rigpa for even one instant, it's the lack of knowing that makes the division between realizing this or remaining in ignorance of it. We can speak of two aspects here: intrinsic wakefulness and intrinsic ignorance. Rigpa is the essence of mind, and thus is intrinsic to mind. Everything else — every samsaric state — is superfluous, extraneous. The realized state of any buddha is like the front of your hand. When self-existing wakefulness is fully actualized, you can see the three times as clearly as the lines on your palm. Samsara is like the backside of your hand, not evident at all. Being ignorant or being awake is like two sides of the same hand — they are not that separate from each other. Sentient beings and buddhas do not have two minds; they are two sides of the same hand. They share the exact same mind, only one is knowing and the other is ignorant. When there is knowing, all the intrinsic qualities of the buddhas are fully present. It's like when the sun shines, or when the light is turned on — suddenly there is no darkness, and we can see everything clearly. When as sentient beings we are involved in ignorance and conceptual thinking, the original state kind of slips. At that moment, the lack of knowing one's own nature and the subsequent conceptual thinking obscure this basic state of original wakefulness. Being ignorant means that we do not know that much. Even if we try, we are not able to know what is going to happen tomorrow. Nor do we know what is happening in other places. Buddhas, on the other hand, have complete clairvoyance.

In the beginning, one tries to approach the natural state by settling the mind. Otherwise, our strong negative habit of involvement in thinking of this and that keeps the attention very busy, and a multitude of different thoughts arise. The starting point is therefore letting go, relaxing, and settling completely. This is nevertheless a mental activity, because this settling of thoughts is the attempt to keep quiet and remain in one particular state. Among the thoughts that arise, remain and disappear, one tries to keep the quality of relaxing and remaining. That requires effort, and thus is not the effortless natural state.

Our basic state does not require our making anything in order to be *as it is*. The act of trying to keep mental calm and quiet is not the natural state; it is trying to create a state of stillness. At the same time it is helpful, because when the mind becomes more quiet and settled, it's easier to recognize what is it that feels quiet, what is it that keeps still. When recognizing the insubstantial nature of the abider, one becomes free of abiding. That is the vipashyana aspect. The stillness quality of shamatha is important in that you become more stable, and the movements of mind become less and less. Through training in it, it becomes easier to recognize and easier to maintain.

When your mind, your attention, is not so busy, you can see that it is not an entity. That seeing is the vipashyana aspect. Vipashyana means seeing clearly. You see clearly that there is no entity that abides in stillness. Unlike shamatha, the vipashyana quality does not require any effort. It is the awake and knowing aspect of your mind, which is utterly transparent and endowed with abundant great qualities. Rigpa is free of originating, abiding and disappearing. Trying to keep the mind still is work. Shamatha keeps the mind employed. Since it is mental doing that keeps us wandering in samsara, mind needs to be unoccupied. Leave the mind unemployed. In its essence, mind is unborn, non-dwelling and non-disappearing.

We need to be introduced to, recognize, and then train in self-existing empty cognizance. In other words, it is not a product. We do not have to make our mind essence empty — it is already empty. We do not have to make our nature cognizant — it is already cognizant. These two qualities, which are indivisible, are self-existing. They have been so always; they are not something new. Empty cognizance is an original state that is never lost. It merely needs to be known. We need the knowledge of self-existing empty cognizance — the *knowing itself* to be empty and cognizant. Otherwise, we experience only the state of a normal sentient being; also empty and cognizant, also self-existing, but with no knowing that this is so. As sentient beings, we are ignorant of how the nature of our mind really is, of the actual empty cognizance. Because of this, we again and again become involved in the mind's grasping outwardly at sense objects through the sense openings, and through that link creating thoughts and emotions. In this way, we perpetuate samsaric existence. We are bewildered by not knowing. It is like we are caught up in the illusory display of a magician.

The yogi does not need to continue creating more of this samsaric delusion. In one instant he recognizes the three kayas: the empty quality as dharmakaya, the cognizant quality as sambhogakaya and the unconfined quality as nirmanakaya. The bottom line of being introduced to mind essence is to recognize that it is empty, cognizant, self-existing, suffused with knowing. That is the true training in recognizing the nature of mind. Mind that is empty and cognizant suffused with unknowing continues to wander in samsara.

The key point, after being introduced and recognizing, is to not *do* anything to the natural state. We do not have to try to improve upon this empty cognizance, or try to correct it in any particular way that requires effort on our part. In fact, we do not need to do anything to make our mind empty and cognizant. It does not require any job whatsoever. This nondoing itself is the training, and it is the opposite of our usual habit. Simply train in not correcting this empty cognizance, which is our natural state. That is the way to experience. And this is exactly what sentient beings don't do. Instead, they always obscure themselves. They always try to change the natural state or create an altered state, and they do this through hope and fear, accepting and rejecting.

The difference between buddhas and sentient beings is that sentient beings are busy fabricating. Our self-existing wakefulness becomes altered and contrived. It has become fabricated. And as long as it continues to be so, that is how long we will wander in samsara. Instead, we need to recognize the nature of mind. Right now I am explaining this to you so you can get the idea, the understanding, of how this is. The next step is for you to experience. It is not enough to intellectually understand how the nature is: you need to actually taste it, and finally realize it. Train till it becomes uninterrupted!

One is introduced to the empty quality. That which recognizes the empty quality is self-cognizant wakefulness. This uncontrived wakefulness is the knowing. Each individual has this potential. Your essence is empty and your nature is cognizant, in the same way that the nature of fire is hot. The essence of mind is empty, while its nature is capable of knowing; its nature is naturally cognizant. These two aspects are unified as empty cognizance. It is very important to comprehend this point. Otherwise we may think that the enlightened state is a thing we need to manufacture and achieve — that maybe a teacher gives it to us, or perhaps we produce it through many years of practice. It is not like that. The heart of the matter is simply one of being either distracted or undistracted from knowing your present wakefulness. Distracted is a sentient being; undistracted is a buddha. Undistracted is recognizing the essence. There is no effort in the actual recognizing of the essence; it is effortless.

Sunlit space is a really good analogy for how our basic state actually is. Space is empty, and not made by anyone. At the same time, the sun is always up there shining in the sky. We may not be able to see it directly from where we are, but although it may look to us like the sun is gone away, it has not left space. The sun does not go to a place where there is no space; it never leaves the expanse of the sky. Sun and sky are inseparable. This is a very good picture of the three kayas, our basic condition. The empty quality of space is the example for dharmakaya; the sunlight is sambhogakaya; and the indivisibility of these two is nirmanakaya. The three kayas remain as the essence of your mind. This is the three kayas that we are never separate from. When recognizing this to be *as it is* — that is the svabhavikakaya, the essence-body. This knowledge is the distinguishing characteristic of all buddhas who have attained the three kayas. Just like darkness cannot remain when there is sunlight, or a hair cannot remain in the fire, karma and disturbing emotions cannot remain when there is recognition of mind essence. These are all examples of how the recognition of self-existing wakefulness is. The natural state is within us; it is simply a matter of recognizing it.

Sentient beings follow thoughts and pursue outer objects. Their inner perceiving minds become lost in the outer perceived objects. In between subject and object, they have the five senses. When we die and shed our bodies we experience the bardo. Due to the power of the habitual tendencies of our five senses, it's as though we have a body with five senses. Because of the force of this conceptual mind, we then take birth in one of the six realms of samsara.

We create future states of samsara through pursuing solidified objects into the four places of rebirth, where the perceiving mind becomes the traveler, journeying from one life to another. It is a process that perpetuates itself. The four types of rebirth are instantaneous birth, womb birth, birth from an egg, and birth from heat and moisture.

Without appearing to have any mother or father, when conditions like moisture and heat come together, insects of all different kinds come about. When I was a child, I lived near a pond where monks and nuns would throw in their cut-off hair following the three-year retreat. I went there a few weeks after and looked. The hair was full of worms of different sizes and kinds. At that time I thought they were growing out of the hair, but actually they come through the combination of heat and moisture, one of the four types of rebirth. In this way, there are innumerable sentient beings. And each of these worms and insects, which are beyond number, has buddha nature as well. They have mind. They feel pain; they feel pleasure; and if they could somehow receive teachings and practice and perfect the training, they would become buddhas. But if not, if their empty cognizance is filled with unknowing, they continue on and on in samsaric existence because of negative deeds. Samsara is truly endless.

In short, within the essence of our mind are the three kayas of self-existing wakefulness. This can be obvious when we are not under the power of conceptual thinking. Buddhas and bodhisattvas have cut the thought, cut the conceptual thinking, at its very arising and attained stability. It is like the line from the *Treasury of Dharmadhatu*:

The original essence is like the radiant sun,
Naturally luminous and primordially unformed.

Our original essence is not obscured in any way whatsoever. All samsaric states come about through the mental constructs of grasping and fixating. Caught up in dualistic grasping at the perceived and fixating on the perceiver, we become sentient beings. It is through grasping at outer objects that we have been born in one of the six classes of sentient beings. Fixating mind is conceptual thinking. Right now, by practicing, by allowing the mind to be uncontrived and unaltered, by not being conceptual, by not hoping or fearing, we arrive at the original essence, the starting point. To be unmoved from the natural luminosity is to be without thoughts. The wisdom of equality is our natural luminosity, the original wakefulness that is free of accepting and rejecting, hope and fear. It is not all right to let simplicity be fettered by complexity. Please understand this vital point, even though I am meandering a little back and forth here.

We must start the training of recognizing mind essence, a training that is not exactly the same as keeping the mind still and quiet. To practice the emptiness of shamatha requires effort. It is a training in trying to remedy the restlessness of mental movement. Ultimately, phenomena have no arising, dwelling or ceasing. The practice of shamatha is to try to keep dwelling on something, and it is possible to achieve some type of accomplishment in that. Unless one has had the proper guidance, one may very well congratulate oneself at this point, saying something like, "Wow, I can stay still for long, long periods of time. I have no thoughts, no disturbing emotions. I even have clairvoyant powers; I can see what will happen tomorrow, and what is happening in other places. Now I've really got it!" Shamatha can yield a shallow degree of clairvoyance and super-knowledge. At that point one may think oneself to be an incredibly great practitioner, and believe that one has reached quite a high level. Maybe one thinks, "There is nobody who has reached as high a state as I have." One might even have the thought "I'm enlightened!"

Infatuation with temporary attainments is not true realization, because the keeping of stillness is not the natural state *as it is*. Our original state is that which is beyond arising, dwelling and ceasing. You cannot say that our buddha nature, which is a self-existing, empty cognizance suffused with knowing, arises from anywhere. You cannot say it remains anywhere. You cannot say it ceases, or that it disappear into any place whatsoever. However, at the same time, it *appears* as if it does. It seems as if somehow our buddha nature came into this body. It also appears as if it is dwelling in this body — even though you cannot put a finger on where in the body the buddha nature is. You cannot say it is in the brain, the heart or the fingertips. It feels like there is sensation wherever you touch. There is a quality of knowing, but you cannot totally pinpoint it. Likewise, you cannot say that it ceases to be, even though it looks like it does cease when we die. One tantra says, "Although the essence of all buddhas is beyond arising, dwelling and ceasing, it acts as if it arises, dwells and ceases."

If you have a particular question you can ask it now.

STUDENT: Could you please explain about the dividing-line between samsara or nirvana, because isn't that exactly where we find ourselves right now?

RINPOCHE: Briefly, samsara is the six classes of beings; nirvana is all the buddhas and the buddhafields. One state is suffering; the other is free of suffering. The buddha nature is equally present throughout both of these two states. The pure buddha nature is how the three kayas are present. The vajra body is the unchanging aspect, the vajra speech is the unobstructed aspect, and the vajra mind is the undeluded quality. In the state of suffering, these three vajras are experienced as the three poisons.

In actuality, the victorious ones' three kayas permeate all of samsara and nirvana. They are complete in our buddha nature. The ordinary body, speech and mind of sentient beings are the expressions or reflections of the unchanging body, the unobstructed speech and undeluded mind. They came about as the expression of the victorious ones, just like the light radiating from the sun. Sentient beings are never, for even a single instant, separate from the buddhas.

Yet sentient beings flounder around in samsaric existence because of being confused. It basically comes down to confused sentient beings or unconfused buddhas. If we sleep, we dream. If we are not asleep, we will not dream. As sentient beings, we have not cut the great sleep. Since the buddhas never fell asleep, they are not dreaming. They are undeluded and awake. We are deluded, and while asleep we dream the myriad dreams of conceptual thinking.

Buddha nature, also known as the three kayas, pervades both samsara and nirvana, buddhas and beings. Dharmakaya is like space, sambhogakaya is like sunlight, and nirmanakaya is like a rainbow — the one dependent upon the other. These three examples are all based on one single aspect: space. Without space, how could the sun shine? Without the sun, how could there be a rainbow? The three kayas can be regarded as external, but the internal three kayas are when we recognize mind essence. We don't ever see it as a 'thing'. Nobody can ever see his or her mind, because mind is not a thing to be seen, which is the dharmakaya quality. That empty, insubstantial essence we have is also cognizant: that is the sambhogakaya quality. The two of these are indivisible, which is nirmanakaya. Thus, these three are a single unity. In the minds of sentient beings, the three kayas are complete, even though they do not know it.

The dividing-line between samsara and nirvana is basically between knowing and not knowing. When there is knowing, it is nirvana; when not knowing, it is samsara. What is it that is to be known? The knowing is to know that our nature is the unity of empty cognizance, that the three kayas of the buddhas are not outside, but complete within the essence of mind — your *own* mind. Recognizing and knowing this is nirvana. Not knowing how to recognize that the three kayas of buddhahood are present in oneself is unknowing, which is samsara.

For instance, when we see a beautiful object through our eyes, we like it, don't we? If we see an ugly object, isn't it true that we dislike it? And when a thing is neutral, we do not care about it; we feel indifferent. That is how dualistic mind works. Similarly, if we hear a sweet sound, we like it. This liking is desire, attachment. If it is a harsh sound, we dislike it. That is anger, aversion. Any sound in between which we do not care about, we just basically ignore. This is dullness. Ignorant sentient beings are always caught up in the three poisons.

Instead of perpetuating the three poisons, recognize your own mind. Knowing mind essence is also called rigpa. Right now we are at the dividing point between samsara and nirvana. We are ready to know, which is the path of the buddhas. Until now, as a sentient being, we have repeated unknowing, which is ignorance. Instead of remaining in ignorance, we need to recognize the state of knowing.

I am not going to explain these two states in great detail. There are hundreds and hundreds of volumes of texts explaining the impure state of samsara. Besides these, just think of all the books available on subjects like medicine, science, architecture, engineering, cars, airplanes, law, and so on? It is the old story of samsara. The moment you die, none of these books will help you at all. They will provide not even as much as a hair-tip of assistance. To carry around books like that is only to burden yourself. There are also hundreds and hundreds of volumes of scriptures about the nirvana aspect, the *Kangyur* and *Tengyur* and so forth. When you condense all of these, their essential point is this: recognize your own nature. That's it. That is the extract of thousands of words.

If you want to be totally clear about what is in the Tripitaka and all the commentaries, not even a hundred human years would be enough, even if you studied day and night. Nobody could possibly remember all the many details of the pure aspect of nirvana, even if they somehow managed to study that long. Better to 'know the one thing that liberates all', and recognize the essence of your mind. See that it is no thing to see, which is the dharmakaya. That which sees that, the knowing quality, is sambhogakaya. To see that they are indivisible is nirmanakaya. Is there anything easier than that? Can you find anything simpler? This is called knowing one that liberates all. If you know that, that itself is the basis of the path to buddhahood.

In this world, you can scan through all the teachings down to the minutest detail, like sifting flour, and you will not find any instruction superior to this. Carefully examine everything, every single thing, in this world, and you will not find any other advice that is more profound. This is the path that all the buddhas of the past followed. This is the path that all buddhas of the present are journeying. All the buddhas of the future will embark upon this path as well. It is also called the great Dharmakaya Mother. It sounds like an old lady, eh? It is the old mother through whom all buddha-children were born, are being born and will be born in the future. There is also the old father, called Dharmakaya Samantabhadra. The old mother is called Great Dharmakaya Mother. All buddhas and sentient beings are the offspring of this couple, who are not really entities, but unconfined empty cognizance. The empty quality is Samantabhadri, the great Dharmakaya Mother, who is also known as Vajra Varahi, or Jetsün Tara. The cognizant quality is the dharmakaya buddha Samantabhadra, also known as Vajradhara or Vajrasattva, our old dad. Their offspring, their children, are all the sentient beings of the six realms.

Unfortunately, we have not stood by our mom and dad. Instead, we have strayed into the bardo states and the six realms. Right up until now, we have been caught up in the three poisons, floundering around in the three realms of samsara. We have completely lost touch with our old father and mother. If you want to stay with your real father and mother, then enter the path of recognizing empty cognizance. If you want to return back to your original nature, you have at hand the three great views of Mahamudra, Dzogchen, and the Great Middle Way, as well as the view of Prajnaparamita. Those are the paths you need to enter.

People sometimes wonder why is there not only one path, why there have to be several. It's just like approaching Bodhgaya from four different directions — from the west, south, north or east. If you continue your travel from any of these directions, the place you reach is still Bodhgaya, the same destination. There is only one Buddhahood, one awakened state, one ultimate destination. In Tibet you have the Kagyü

School, Sakya School, and so forth, so people may think that there is a Kagyü enlightenment, or Sakya enlightenment, or a Geluk or Nyingma enlightenment. Actually, there isn't. The true essence of buddhahood is undivided empty cognizance, suffused with knowing. This is the basic nature of your own mind. It is the same for a follower of Sakya, Gelug, Nyingma or Kagyü — they all have to enter that path to enlightenment. There are not various types of true enlightenment; it's simply a case of different words, same meaning.

The same meaning is: recognize mind essence. This is so simple, so easy. But sentient beings do not trust it. Instead, they drag themselves around in pointless activities and continuously create their own suffering. In taking birth, there is the suffering of being born. Then we get the suffering of being sick ... the misery of aging ... the pain of dying. After death, we experience the pain of being helplessly lost in the bardo. After that, if we take rebirth in one of the three lower realms, there is not even one single moment of pleasure. We may know this quite well right now, but don't we still fool ourselves?

My teaching is not incomprehensible. What it really comes down to is this: do we actually dare trust the teachings of the Buddha? When we look above, we don't see any buddhafields or celestial realms. Does that mean that they don't exist? And if we look down into the ground, we do not see any of the lower realms. Does that mean that they do not exist? If we use our own ignorant samsaric state as the valid measure for what is real and not real, for what is possible and not possible, it doesn't add up to much. Luckily we have more than that. Did anybody ever come back from buddhafields? Did anybody ever return from lower realms? The answer is yes! The Buddha saw and experienced all of these things very clearly. To be a practitioner on the Buddhist path, we cannot rely only and totally on what we experience with our own eyes and ears right now. We have to rely on the words of the Buddha as well; otherwise, it does not amount to much. Honestly, there is not much other choice.

Yet we still do not fully trust the words of the Buddha. Some people say, "I haven't made up my mind what path to follow, I need to think about this for myself." If we could just think about it a hundred percent ourselves and follow our own conviction, then why wouldn't all sentient beings be enlightened? "I will take my time, I will think about it slowly." The Buddha already thought everything out very clearly. Since the Buddha was both clairvoyant and had unimpeded wisdom, that should be sufficient.

If we, instead of following what the Buddha said, wanted to figure out everything for ourselves, we ought to have the ability to do so. Unfortunately, we don't. The Buddha's teachings have true validity. If we first want to assess everything by scrutinizing, we could spend years doing that. If we finally do arrive at a point of deciding to trust, we then have to find a qualified teacher and start to learn. At that point perhaps half our life is gone. We may find we are already fifty years old.

Supposing we live to be a hundred, half our life will be gone. Half of the remaining portion we will spend sleeping. It gets more difficult as our time runs out. We can make a plea, "Please let me have a slightly longer lifespan, because now I want to practice the Dharma." Add to that the petition for good health: "Please, from now on I would like not to be sick, so I have more time to practice." Unfortunately, our life won't listen. As soon as we start to get sick or suffer from a severe disorder, practice becomes next to impossible and we feel we have no chance. It's like Paltrül Rinpoche says: "When young, we were controlled by others and couldn't practice. As adults, we chased desirable things and couldn't practice. Now that we are old, our strength is gone and we cannot practice. Alas, alas, what to do?"

We are like voyagers who, visiting an island full of jewels, simply stand there with our arms crossed. Our dearly treasured physical body will eventually be left behind. We will depart this life as cleanly as a hair is drawn out of butter, accompanied by nothing. In the bardo, we are totally helpless in choosing where to go. And we will continue to roam around samsara like this. This will happen with a hundred percent certainty. Unless you practice, there is absolutely nothing in the world you can do to avoid being trapped in samsara.

Dualistic mind creates unwholesome karma. Without exception, every thought we have is mixed with the three poisons. Just as poison, when ingested, causes death, the three poisonous emotions, when consented to, take the life of liberation. We may not even notice that our minds are full of the three poisons that produce negative karma. But the lord of the three poisons is our mind, and the servant is our body and voice. Carrying out the command of the three poisons, we continue roaming around in samsara, continuously turning our backs on the three kayas, which are the very basis for all of samsara and nirvana. Instead, we create the causes for the three lower realms.

7

The Highway of the Victorious Ones

❖

STUDENT: How do we engender perseverance?

RINPOCHE: Perseverance, in the context of recognizing mind essence, should be like the unbroken flow of a river. Is there ever any second when the Ganges River does not flow? No, of course not. It's a steady, unbroken flow. Nobody is pushing or pulling it down the riverbed. It simply flows. Of course, there may be a difference in volume and intensity as to how much water is passing through, but the basic flow of the river is never, ever interrupted. Another example is like the constancy of a taut bowstring. Once you bend the bow and make the string taut, it does not sometimes become more tight and sometimes more slack. It stays at an even tension.

This is the kind of perseverance we should have: steady, so that we do not alternate between struggling and pushing ourselves hard and other times totally giving up. How is it possible to exert oneself without fluctuation? It is possible because of training in what we call undistracted nonmeditation. Undistracted means not forgetting. Nonmeditation means not contriving, not imagining. The steadiness or continuity comes from not being distracted, and that is not something that we have to force ourselves to do, because it is nonmeditation. There is no *doing*, in the sense of deliberate meditation taking place. This is the essential point: undistracted nonmeditation, being undistracted while not meditating. Train in that. If you keep at it, at a certain point your training becomes like the steady, unbroken flow of a river.

The word 'recognize' literally means meeting your nature head-on. Recognizing is emphasized quite a lot, because without recognizing your nature you are always caught up in thought, either in the sense of being against it, being for it, or being indifferent to it. There is no break in that involvement for sentient beings; it continues ceaselessly, like a great muddy river. This 'black diffusion' is the incessant pursuit, day and night, when the attention that is ignorant of itself gets caught up in one of the three poisons, either desire, aversion or dullness. This goes on continuously, without any break whatsoever. Yet all the while, that which gets caught up already and *always* is in essence empty cognizance, which naturally is the intrinsic three kayas. However, as long as there is no knowing of our basic nature, the normal state of a sentient being is a constant black diffusion. Luckily, it is possible to recognize it, because the natural face was never lost. One does not have to be permanently caught up in this black diffusion. Without buddha nature, you would have no chance whatsoever.

When the innate nature is not known, we chase the tail of thoughts. In other words, whenever something pops up we are immediately caught up in that, without hesitating for even a second. Another thing comes up, and we chase after that, and the same with a third and a fourth. There is no break in between. This is due to the two big villains, the two types of ignorance. The great demon of coemergent ignorance is simply forgetting our natural state. Conceptualizing ignorance is the moment you forget, when you immediately start to form a thought of what is now experienced. These two nasty demons fool all sentient beings, but in fact, they don't come from anywhere else than one's own lack of knowing. Sentient beings are basically fooling themselves, continuously. It does not have to be like that. When our self-existing wakefulness becomes stable in itself as undistracted nonmeditation, the twofold ignorance no longer has any control over us. Until that happens, try remaining in natural awareness. Isn't it true that after a moment the two ignorances arrive? Again recognize, and they vanish without a trace. This is how to get used to rigpa. This is the root of true meditation training.

In that moment of seeing that mind essence is no 'thing' to see — in that very instant, you no longer need the duality of something seen and someone that sees. This natural unity is called nonmeditation, because it is not created. In addition to nonmeditation we need to train in non-distraction. As we train in this, it gradually becomes easier and easier, and the moments of rigpa last longer and longer. The training remains exactly the same: undistracted nonmeditation. That is the whole purpose of recognizing mind essence. That is the whole idea of the pointing-out instruction.

Here are a few lines from a famous song, a supplication to the great knowledge-holders of the Kagyü lineage which we call *Dorje Chang-chenma*:[4]

> *Nothing whatever, but everything arises from it.*
> *To this meditator who experiences an unceasing play*
> *Grant your blessings so that I realize the inseparability of samsara*
> *and nirvana.*

And:

> *Grant your blessings so that my meditation is free from conception.*

"Nothing whatever" means that mind essence is no concrete thing. The very moment you recognize, it is like a totally pure space. The nature of mind is not made out of any thought or concept whatsoever; it is utterly free of any of that. That is obvious, and it is seen in actuality the very moment you recognize. You see that there is not even as much as a speck of dust of any concept in the essence itself. The song continues, "But everything arises," meaning that all experience takes place because of the quality of cognizance, which is indivisible from the empty essence. Our natural ability to perceive is not blocked in any way whatsoever, it is unobstructed. The essence is not confined to being either empty or some material 'thing' that experiences. There is no split or barrier between being empty and being cognizant. The image often used is that of a bright mirror. The mirror is not obstructed in any way, yet at the same time it has a brightness, a natural capacity to reflect. That is the image for indivisible empty cognizance. It is unimpeded. The empty aspect is dharmakaya. The cognizant aspect is sambhogakaya, and the indivisibility of these two is nirmanakaya. The three kayas are present as the nature of every sentient being's mind. When the master points this out and it is recognized, it is svabhavikakaya. This fact, that the mind is unconfined empty cognizance, is realized the moment we recognize, the moment we simply see it.

In the moment of recognizing that, simply allow it to be, however it is. We don't have to pre-meditate the nature of mind. Don't ever think, "All right, I'll recognize, but it has to look a certain way, and if it doesn't live up to that, then I should correct it a little, improve it." Or "Hmmm, maybe this is not exactly the nature of mind. The nature of mind must be more special than this." Or, "Is this empty now?" Or "Now it is cognizant! Or is it?" Or, "This is the unity, I believe . . . actually, maybe not." That kind of meditation is not necessary at all. The guidance texts mention over and over that the moment you recognize, you must abandon all preconceptions. Mind essence does not require our improvement.

Can we make up mind essence? Is it an entity that can be imagined and then kept in mind? Try to imagine that which is utterly empty; it is impossible, right? Likewise, can you imagine the cognizance? One cannot really do that. If your meditation practice is merely an exercise in imagining mind essence, doesn't that become one's invention? Isn't it repeatedly said that mind essence is not necessarily one's idea of how it actually is? "Uncontrived ordinary mind is the highway of all the victorious ones." That is the essential practice itself.

Do not be like a bird that has been caught in a snare. You know how kids put out a trap, and when the bird comes, they pull and it gets caught in it. It is said in the meditation instructions that once a bird has been caught and escapes, it's always on guard. It lands on the ground, it takes one bite, and it jumps up immediately, out of fear. One's meditation practice might be like that, if you are constantly apprehensive that maybe you are getting it wrong. One thinks, "Oops, this is not it. This ordinary wakefulness couldn't be the buddha mind. There was that fantastic thing called the 'pointing-out instruction' and once I got that, I recognized mind essence. Now I'm recognizing, I see it. But the buddha mind must be totally different from this. This cannot be the buddha mind, it must be more than this." Thinking in this way, there could be a constant impetus to try to create and experience something other than the immediacy of empty cognizance.

When we first receive teachings, we usually get an extensive explanation covering all topics of the Dharma, known as the expedient and definitive meaning. At that point we are introduced to the fact that the definitive meaning is about buddha nature, the essence of mind, which we need to eventually realize. We are given a general layout, an overview, and gradually we hone in on what is of ultimate importance among all the Buddha's teachings. We narrow it down to the 'pointing-out instruction', through which one is introduced to and is able to recognize this nature of mind, the buddha nature. The moment of recognition is like catching the scent. A carnivore out hunting needs to first catch the smell of the deer, then he can hunt it down. The pointing-out instruction is for this little carnivore to get the whiff of buddha nature. Once we smell it, we do not have to speculate so much about it anymore. We are finally on track. Most important is to get the whiff of buddha nature. Before that it is all right to spend a lot of time analyzing. Once you get the scent of it, there is no need to fill up your mind with a lot of intellectual speculation.

What is meant by catching the scent is like this. At some point your guru leans over towards you and says, "Now we need to speak just between the two of us. When you recognize mind essence, what do you see?" A good disciple would say, "Honestly, I don't see a thing." The guru replies, "Well that is true, that is really how it is. Your nature is empty. But in the moment of recognizing that your mind is empty, are you totally blank and unaware at that point? Are you oblivious?" A good disciple would say, "No, I am not. I experience what is present." Then the guru might say, "Isn't it true that this emptiness and cognizance are a unity; that one always occurs in conjunction with the other?" The disciple would again say, "That is true." The guru continues, "Isn't that moment a vivid state of being awake which is at the same time empty, totally without clinging?" In this way, one is gradually introduced to the scent of buddha nature.

After that, the tracking down of the deer does not need to be imagined anymore, because the scent is already there. You don't have to dream up this empty cognizance any longer. You don't have to make up ideas about how it is. You don't have to indulge in fantasies like those I mentioned earlier, imagining how the buddha nature looks and trying to keep that fantasy constantly in mind. Once we receive the pointing-out instruction and recognize buddha nature, the training is not in meditating in the sense of *imagining* buddha nature; the training is in *not losing track of it*, in the sense of not being distracted. We do not have to imagine buddha nature, it is already present. There is no point in trying to make it up. The emptiness that the buddha nature is, is an original emptiness; the cognizance is an original cognizance. The unity of being empty and cognizant is an original unity, isn't it? It is not that we need to create the unity through practice. That fact becomes absolutely clear. Meditation practice is no longer an act of making the mind empty and cognizant, not at all.

Yet what happens is that we do forget it, we do get distracted. This is when the training comes in. The training is to simply recognize again. We need to acknowledge how it already is. Again we forget and are carried away, because of the coemergent and conceptualizing ignorances. Coemergent ignorance is simply losing track or forgetting, getting distracted. Conceptualizing ignorance occurs when, in the moment you are distracted, you start to make thoughts about what you have wandered off towards. This needs to be eliminated. This twofold ignorance is not someone else's doing; it does not come from outside. The twofold ignorance is your own manifestation, just like your own shadow. It is an expression of the essence itself, but directed outwardly.

The training is simply in letting habitual fixation gradually fall away, by recognizing again and again. The more we train in this way, the easier it becomes. It is like memorizing, although not exactly the same as this analogy. When I chant the *Düsum Sangye* supplication a few times, I don't have to think even as much as a hair's tip in order to get from the beginning of it to the end. It comes automatically, because it is already imprinted in the all-ground, the *alaya*. Similarly, once we become more stable in the recognition, it will last for a while, not deliberately but automatically.

Because we have never been separate from it for an instant, the nature of mind is not something to meditate on, but to get used to. Distraction makes the division between these two states. We need the undistracted nonmeditation. If you chant a prayer by heart, do you have to think about it? That is the idea of automatic. Nondistraction should be automatic, not requiring any deliberate thought. You do not need to congratulate yourself every single time, "Wow, now I recognize the unity of empty cognizance. Now I recognize it again." That is a thought, isn't it? If you know this *Düsum Sangye* chant by heart, once you have said the first line, "*Düsum sangye guru rinpoche*," do you need to think, "Now, what is the next line? Oh, it is such-and-such." You don't have to think that at all. When you know a prayer by heart, no thought is necessary to recite it. Rigpa does not require any thought. Once you have grown used to rigpa, it is automatic.

When a master teaches his students the direct knowing of buddha nature, it is the same as introducing a carnivore to the scent of the deer. Once you get the scent, then you have it. The scent is there. You have gotten the scent of dharmakaya; there is no thing to see. You have gotten the scent of sambhogakaya; while there is no thing to see, there is still knowing. Finally, you have gotten the scent of nirmanakaya, that these two are indivisible. Just keep on sniffing it, like tracking down prey in the mountains.

It's quite wonderful, isn't it? It is through this path that we can attain buddhahood. It is called the path of nondoing about which it is said:

This single nondoing outshines all deeds.

Nondoing outshines all involvements in disturbing emotions. All disturbing emotions of the eighty-four thousand kinds require a doer and a deed, subject and object. Here nothing is imagined; it is total nondoing. In one instant, it vanquishes all eighty-four thousand disturbing emotions. When this wakefulness of knowing is recognized, it is like taking an axe and cutting at its very root an immense tree with thousands of branches and tens of thousands of leaves. Once the trunk is cut, everything else comes crashing down in the same instant. How is that possible? Any of the eighty-four thousand disturbing emotions are simply thoughts. The basic wakefulness that knows is free of thought. In the moment of recognizing the moment free of thought, every thought state of the eighty-four thousand kinds is simultaneously vanquished. If the wakefulness of nondual knowing were conceptual, then it could not do away with thought states. You cannot relinquish one thought by grasping onto another. In the moment of recognizing the authentic thoughtfree wakefulness, every type of discursive thought movement is destroyed.

Actually, once you have recognized this genuine state of wakefulness, samsara is no longer the problem it usually is. In the normal state of thinking, we experience joy, we experience sorrow — there are all these thoughts, all our worries and plans. But in the very moment of recognizing this thoughtfree wakefulness, there is no problem at all. At that moment, samsara is quite delightful, with a sense of great equality, expansive and wide open. You may experience happiness, but if you recognize the essence, you don't get too overjoyed and caught up in that. You may experience pain, but if you recognize your essence, you don't get totally depressed and caught up in that. That is why it is called the great equality.

Usually, when everything is going well, people get so overjoyed that their hat falls off their head — they just can't keep it on! But if in that moment you recognize the essence, what's the big deal about being happy about fleeting phenomena? Everything is equalized. At other times people get depressed and weep miserably. But if you recognize your essence, what is the big deal to be depressed about? This recognition is thus your best friend in both joy and sorrow. If you continue the training in this, you will have very good results. If not, well, it is not too much fun in this world. Everything changes; there is nothing we can really rely on. Samsara has a fickle nature, and nothing remains. We need to recognize the unchanging natural state of awareness. Life is not that great if you have to remain as a totally samsaric person. Everything changes; there is no steadiness anywhere in the world, among sentient beings or what is experienced. Second by second, everything changes. In this essence, though, there is no thing that changes.

STUDENT: Could you explain about samayas?

RINPOCHE: The *Yeshe Kuchog* states that one should not drink water in the same valley as a samaya violator.[5] Honestly, though, we do not know who is a samaya corrupter and who is not. Only the Buddha can know that. One cannot fully measure another person. The Buddha said, "Only I and someone like me can know another." There is no way that we can know who is a severe samaya violator, and who is not. And that is not really the point. If we or someone else has broken samaya, we can chant the hundred-syllable mantra and recognize mind essence. Otherwise, there is not much that one can do. One cannot really know who is keeping pure samayas and who is not.

The old masters said, "My best companion is the guru; my worst enemy is the samaya violator." Many realized masters of the past could never be killed by weapons: it would be like cutting in the air. But the moment they came into contact with a samaya violator, they passed away. Nothing else could harm them; however, broken samaya can cut a lama's life short.

The samayas taught in the tantras of Maha, Anu and Ati are incredibly profound. There is immense benefit from being connected to someone who practices the teachings of deity, mantra and samadhi. It is said that anyone who comes into contact with a true practitioner will not go to the lower realms. Conversely, contact with someone who turns against these teachings can take you down. There is definitely an impact in relating to either of these kinds of people.

While samaya can definitely be broken, it can also be mended by Vajrasattva recitation and recognizing mind essence. Chanting the hundred-syllable mantra while recognizing mind essence causes all defilements or negative influences to melt away like snowflakes falling onto a hot stone. Snowflakes cannot in any way cover a hot stone, can they? They just vanish, disappear. But otherwise if one walks around in a normal state, it's like snow falling on cold water: the water freezes solid and slowly becomes a thick layer of ice-encrusted snow.

There is a story from Kham that involves an old guy speaking to a lama. He says, "When you talk about the benefits of the Dharma, it's certain that you have no problem. Even this old sinner will probably be safe from rebirth in hell. But when you speak of the effects of evil deeds, I will surely go to hell. In fact, I wonder if even you might not be in trouble!" Chanting the hundred-syllable mantra with pure attitude and remorse a hundred thousand times will certainly eradicate all one's negative karma without any trace left. On hearing that one feels that there is no problem whatsoever — "Even this old sinner here will have no problem." But when you hear about the negative effects of killing even a small insect, then it is like what the old guy says: "I worry about where you will go after you die — even you, a lama."

There are many details to what 'samaya' fully entails, including the hundred thousand sections of samaya precepts and so on. All of these can be condensed into the basics, which are the samayas of body, speech and mind. The samaya of body means to visualize the yidam deity, remembering that one's own form is the divine form of the yidam. The samaya of speech is to remember to chant mantra. And the samaya of mind is to recognize mind essence. Those are the three basic principles of Vajrayana, known as deity, mantra and samadhi.

Concerning samaya with the guru, do not hurt his physical form. Do not beat him or physically injure him in any other way. To not break his command means to not disobey if he asks you to do something. In regards to the guru's mind, do not do anything that makes him upset or displeased. In addition to keeping the samaya with the guru's body, speech and mind, one has also to keep the samayas with one's own body, speech and mind as deity, mantra and samadhi. This twofold set of samayas of body, speech and mind, with the guru and oneself, includes all other samayas.

It is very important to maintain the link with deity, mantra and samadhi. Where do these instructions come from? We receive them from our personal master. To turn against the master from whom you received the oral instructions of deity, mantra and samadhi is an immense display of ingratitude. One could also damage the samaya with the guru's body, speech and mind by belittling his words, or by attaching only minor importance to his body, or to how he feels.

In terms of Dzogchen, the Great Perfection means that everything that has to be abandoned and everything that has to be realized is fully and completely perfected. That is the king of all the vehicles. The samayas for the Dzogchen teachings has two aspects: primordial purity and spontaneous presence — *kadag* and *lhündrub*. Primordial purity refers to the view of Trekchö, the 'thorough cut'. Spontaneous presence refers to the meditation training called Tögal. Each of these has two samayas. The samayas for Trekchö practice are called nonexistence and pervasiveness. The samayas for Tögal training are oneness and spontaneous presence. So there are four samayas, nonexistence, pervasiveness, oneness and spontaneous presence. Because everything is included within these four, these are known as the king-like samayas. All phenomena of samsara and nirvana are complete in this.

These four aspects of samaya — nonexistence and pervasiveness, oneness and spontaneous presence — are explained in the following way. Nonexistence, or literally 'devoidness', means that the primordial pure essence that is empty is unconstructed, totally devoid of any concrete substance whatsoever. Like space, it is pure from the beginning. The word 'pervasiveness' refers to being uninterrupted in or undistracted from the primordially pure wakefulness. In the moment of recognizing, there is also some sense of ongoingness, of continuity. This pervasive quality implies unbrokenness, a quality of arching over or en-compassing all.

Spontaneous presence is the other samaya for Tögal. From the pri-mordially pure space, spontaneous presence naturally unfolds. It is the apparent aspect (*nangcha*). So, these two — kadag and lhündrub — are actually indivisible, as emptiness and experience. The samaya, then, is to recognize that the essence of your wakefulness is primordial purity free of constructs and that the knowing quality of this wakefulness is the spontaneously present nature. You can also speak of three aspects of wakefulness being empty in essence, spontaneously present by nature and indivisible as empty experience.

Our essence, which we call the basic space of dharmadhatu, is al-ready primordially empty and nonexistent. At the same time, we have a natural cognizance that is spontaneously present: that is the other as-pect. These two are the main qualities. That is to say, in the moment of recognizing how our essence actually is, there is a spontaneously present wakefulness that knows or sees this primordial purity. Therefore, you can say that primordial purity and spontaneous presence are indivisible, or that, in other words, basic space and wakefulness are indivisible. This indivisibility is the meaning of oneness, the fourth samaya. The essence is empty but also cognizant by nature. These two aspects are indivisible. Spontaneous presence is not fabricated in any way whatsoever. Once more, the samaya of oneness is the indivisibility of kadag and lhündrub.

Understand the samayas this way: the awakened state of rigpa is not an act of meditating or fabricating, not at all. Once you grow fully trained in this and it becomes uninterrupted, there is only the awakened state of rigpa. That is the time when you have transcended the division between keeping and breaking any precepts. When going beyond a conceptual frame of mind, there are no more concepts of keeping or breaking. Since at this point experience is an ongoing state of rigpa, the practitioner does not have to hold onto any concept of observing or not observing, of keeping or not keeping, of breaking or not breaking, or recognizing or not recognizing. This is traditionally called 'transcending the borderline between keeping and breaking the samayas'. In short, the meaning of the four samayas of primordial purity and spontaneous presence is that apart from recognizing the nature of mind, there is no 'thing' to do to maintain the bond to or connection with the awakened state of all buddhas.

The moment we are caught up in dualistic mind, there are definitely samayas to keep and samayas that can be broken. But the moment conceptual mind dissolves into the expanse of nondual awareness, there is no samsara left to be rejected and no other nirvana to be accomplished. At that moment you transcend the concepts of keeping and breaking. Until that point, however, there definitely are samayas to keep. Please don't misunderstand this point.

I would like you to be familiar with three Tibetan words — *digpa, dribpa* and *bagchag* — that are connected with our body, speech and mind. The first one, digpa, means misdeed or evil action. It refers to unwholesome, negative, evil behavior, like stealing, lying, or taking another's life. Digpa creates negative karma, and being involved in those actions *does* prevent the realization of buddha nature. The second word, dribpa, means obscuration, veil, or cover. Dribpa can be compared to the walls of this room: they prevent us from seeing what is going on outside. Our vision is obstructed. These obscurations are something more subtle that prevent us from realizing the nature *as it is*. Bagchag means habitual tendency, and is even more subtle yet. The easiest way to understand bagchag is through the example of the dream state. Whatever seemingly takes place while dreaming is the product of habitual tendencies and is nothing that we can take hold of. Nothing is tangible, yet everything can be experienced. That kind of delusion taking place on a very subtle level is called habitual tendency.

However, our basic nature of self-knowing wakefulness cannot be essentially obscured by digpa, dribpa or bagchag. It is primordially pure and remains so. As proof of that, observe a time when you are involved in conceptual thought, being happy or sad, planning the future or remembering the past. The very instant you recognize your own nature, it is again seen as being totally and utterly pure. Our nature remains unobscured and untainted by misdeeds, obscurations and habitual tendencies. After a while, we do again get caught up in thinking in a dualistic way — we get involved with the thinker and what is thought of, subject and object. Being carried away by that, we again create negative karma that obscures ourselves and forms habitual tendencies. There is no point in pretending otherwise!

In order to find our way out of the unaware and mistaken clinging to duality that has gone on endlessly in samsara, we begin with mindfulness. Mindfulness, however, has a definite dualistic connotation. It is like putting a hook in a piece of meat and holding it there. There is a subject keeping an eye on the object. There is a more subtle level called watchfulness, which is a mere noticing, but it also is subtly dualistic. Even more subtle than watchfulness is awakeness. That is the point of separating *sem* and rigpa. Sem, the dualistic frame of mind, means involvement with thoughts of either past, present or future. Rigpa simply means uninvolvement in thoughts of the three times.

The buddha mind, rigpa, is undivided empty cognizance. The moment we recognize that this is so and see this in actuality is called 'undivided empty cognizance suffused with knowing'. 'Empty' here means primordially unformed, not made out of any cause or condition whatsoever, already devoid of any concrete substance. 'Cognizant' means that while being empty, the capacity to know is spontaneously present. 'Undivided' means that these two aspects, primordially unformed emptiness and spontaneously present cognizance, are indivisible. They have always been an indivisible unity, and this is what all the teachings of all the buddhas are about.

There is a saying in Kham, "Swing the hammer around in the air, but hit the spot on the anvil." The anvil is where you put the red-hot iron. You may wave the hammer around here and there, but there is only one place to hit, and that is right where the iron is hot. If you hit any other place, you are not going to be able to shape that piece of iron in any way, which is the whole point of blacksmithing. In the same way, there may be an incredible number of details to all the different teachings of Sutra and Tantra, but ultimately they are only concerned with one point, which is undivided empty cognizance suffused with knowing. Please understand that the empty essence is dharmakaya, the cognizant nature is sambhogakaya, and their indivisible unity is nirmanakaya. To realize this when recognizing one's essence is not an outcome of concentrating or meditating. When simply letting be in this nature, you do not have to unite and fuse together emptiness and cognizance: they are already a unity. There is no 'thing' to do, make or create at that point. This is the key point of all the teachings of the Buddha.

This is the vital point to be understood, and this is also what we should gain experience in. This is exactly what all sentient beings are unaware of. When there is unawareness of this undivided empty cognizance, it is said that it is 'suffused with unknowing', with ignorance. It's just like a man who possesses a wish-fulfilling jewel, but has unknowingly thrown it behind himself, and instead takes a fake gem in his hand. Although you may make all sorts of wishes in front of it, nothing happens.

There is one single essential point that encompasses view, meditation, conduct and fruition — one phrase I have now mentioned quite a few times: 'undivided empty cognizance suffused with knowing'. This is of sole importance. This undivided empty cognizance is our basic nature, which is exactly the same whether we are a buddha or a sentient being. What makes the difference is whether it is suffused with knowing or unknowing. The difference simply lies in recognizing or not recognizing. An ordinary sentient being is unaware of his or her nature. Ordinary sentient beings are 'undivided empty cognizance suffused with unknowing', caught up in the three poisons. A yogi, a true practitioner, is someone who has been introduced to this natural state, and is 'undivided empty cognizance suffused with knowing', the three kayas. A yogi does not take it as enough to merely have recognized. Without training, the strength of that recognition will never be perfected, and there is no stability. A yogi trains in this until perfection, the fruition of the three kayas.

Do not be content with just recognizing the nature of mind — it is essential to also train in that. The way to do so is as Padmasambhava said in these four lines from the *Lamrim Yeshe Nyingpo:*

Empty cognizance of one taste, suffused with knowing, ⸙
Is your unmistaken nature, the uncontrived original state. ⸙
When not altering what is, allow it to be as it is, ⸙
And the awakened state is right now spontaneously present. ⸙

As it is here means in actuality. 'Actuality' means seeing directly how it is, not as an idea or a concept. By recognizing the nature of the thinker, one realizes the fact that emptiness and cognizance are an indivisible unity. This fact is no longer hidden; it is experienced. When this actuality is allowed to be *as it is*, it is not contrived in any way whatsoever. Then the state of a buddha, the awakened state, is, right now, spontaneously perfected. All obscuration has dissolved. These are quite impressive words, these four lines spoken by Padmasambhava himself. They encapsulate the whole meaning of training in the view, meditation, conduct and fruition.

Once more, it is not enough to recognize the nature of mind as being empty and cognizant. We have to train in perfecting its strength. I explained what the training is earlier, recognizing again and again. The moment we recognize undivided empty cognizance, that is rigpa itself. But it is not fully grown— it is not an adult state of rigpa — it's baby rigpa. The level of recognition we are at now is called baby rigpa. It needs to grow up, because at present it is not capable of conducting itself or functioning fully. We need to grow to the level of a human who has 'developed the strength', who has reached the age of seventeen, eighteen or nineteen, and has become independent and can take care of him or herself. That is stability. For that to happen, we need to train repeatedly. That is essential!

The word simplicity is extremely important in Dzogchen. Simplicity means free from mental constructs, free from extraneous concepts. A famous statement says:

See the view of no viewing.
Train in the meditation with nothing meditated upon.
Carry out the conduct of nondoing.

Achieve the fruition in which there is no thing attained.

This statement is incredibly profound, and it is very important to understand exactly what is meant here. It is pointing at simplicity, at nondoing, at nonaction, at the very fact that our innate nature is not a view to be seen as a new orientation that we somehow gain comprehension of. The true view is not like that at all.

Complexity obscures simplicity. In all the other vehicles, starting with the vehicle for shravakas and up to and including Anu Yoga, there are principles to grasp and objects to hold in mind. There are actions to carry out and results to achieve. But the view, meditation, conduct and fruition of Ati Yoga transcend everything other than acknowledging what is originally present as our own nature. This vehicle is simply a matter of acknowledging that our essence is already an undivided empty cognizance. Why imagine being empty what is already empty? There is no need to grasp an emptiness that is anything other than what already is. This is the meaning of 'see the view of no viewing'.

Next, 'train in the meditation with nothing meditated upon'. To meditate means to keep something in mind. Do we have to keep in mind the empty cognizance, or do we rather simply acknowledge what is already present? How can you imagine empty cognizance, anyway? It is not necessary to do anything fancy; simply see how it already is.

About 'carrying out the conduct of nondoing': in all the other vehicles there is something to do to keep oneself busy with, but here the ultimate conduct is to abandon the ninefold activities. It is said, "Don't busy yourself with deeds and doings." Deeds and doings means activity involving subject and object that obscures the state of nonaction. It is also said, "Being free from deeds and doings, you have arrived at nondoing." That is the very key point. In this teaching, we simply need to recognize the original state of empty cognizance. At that point there is no 'thing' to concentrate upon, no struggle to achieve.

All teachings are completed in the Great Perfection. The sutras all start out with, "In the Indian language, the title is such-and-such," and end with, "Hereby the sutra called such-and-such is completed." The word 'completed' means 'finished', 'perfected'. In other words, in the moment of recognizing the nature of mind, all the vehicles are perfected. Great Perfection means that our nature itself is already fully perfect. We don't have to make our empty essence pure; it is primordially pure. We don't have to make our basic nature cognizant; it is already spontaneously perfected as cognizance. Nor does the all-pervasive capacity need to be fabricated. Honestly, how could you possibly create the empty essence or cognizant nature? They are spontaneously present, effortlessly. Train in this effortlessness!

8

Mingling Practice with Daily Life

✧

STUDENT: How do I mingle practice with daily life?

RINPOCHE: In the general Buddhist system, there is usually a difference between the meditation and post-meditation states. In the context of the Sutra system, the meditation state is like space, while post-meditation is like a magical illusion. One, the meditation state, is considered a session: the other is the break from the session. During the session, one practices; during the break from the session, one moves about, talks, eats and sleeps.

In this way the meditation state during the session is to be free of mental constructs, like space. Post-meditation is likened to the eight analogies of illusion. They begin with the metaphor of a magician who can conjure unrealities by the means of mantra and magical substance. He creates people, creatures and buildings that seemingly really exist. Although they do not have any concrete existence whatsoever, they are still experienced by the audience, and the watchers believe these phantoms to be real. In actuality, however, they are nothing other than a magical creation. Everything — all our daily reality — is like that. The other analogies of illusion include an echo, a mirage, a reflection, a city of Gandharvas, a dream, a rainbow, and the moon in water. These illusions are all examples for how sentient beings deludedly believe phenomena to be real.

According to the Sutra system, during post-meditation one should superimpose the idea of magical illusion upon whatever is experienced during the activities of daily life by reminding oneself, "This is nothing but a dream; it is all unreal." One trains in regarding all experience as possessing this sense of insubstantiality. The training in the sessions is to not hold anything in mind whatsoever. It is therefore taught that the meditation state is unconstructed like space, while the post-meditation state is like magical illusion.

In the context of the view of Mahamudra, Dzogchen and the Great Middle Way, you do not make any essential distinction between sessions and breaks. You do not have to divide the practice, making one practice for the meditation state and another for post-meditation. Here, the meditation state lasts up until one is distracted from awareness, and then turns into the post-meditation. Actually, the training is exactly the same, regardless of whether you sit, walk, eat, talk, lie down or move around. The moment you remember to recognize, you see immediately how mind essence is. You see emptiness. Right then, that itself is the view. It does not make any difference if you recognize while you are standing or sitting, while you are eating, talking or moving about. Being undistracted is the session; being distracted is the break.

Do not make any division between recognizing mind essence during session and breaks. Remain in the undistracted view, in rigpa at all times during all activities. The practice, as I state over and over again, is short moments repeated many times. What could last for a long time right now is the fabricating of a space-like meditation state. Do not fabricate anything; remain in naturalness. In this training, it is not necessary to hold any concept about it. It is a training in the natural meditation state, which is simply the original state of unconfined empty cognizance. The view is primordially empty and cognizant; it is the indivisibility of these two. Primordially, the empty quality is the dharmakaya; the cognizant quality is the sambhogakaya, and this unity is called nirmanakaya. Get used to this at all times.

This original state is not of our making. Acknowledging this is the perfect view. I am not saying that this view is good while the views of the lower vehicles are bad; but there is a difference in the extent to which the view is mixed with concept. One could convince oneself that, "This is the meditation state! This is probably emptiness." That is superimposing emptiness upon one's experience. In other words, it is not the natural state *as it is*. Similarly, to remind oneself "This is all a magical illusion," during the activities of daily life is still a concept.

To cling to a particular concept is like a bird that flaps its wings and tries to fly but cannot, because it's bound by a chain. The training in the true view is not a training in holding concepts, even the subtle types. It is a matter of recognizing what already *is*, by itself. Our nature of mind is naturally empty and cognizant; it is not of our making. There is no need to hold a concept about it. In other words, when you remember to recognize, you see immediately that there is no thing to see. That's it. At other times one has forgotten, and it is lost.

First we need to recognize self-existing wakefulness. Slowly, slowly, we need to repeat the instants of uncontrived naturalness, developing the strength of the recognition. Once we reach stability, there is non-distraction day and night; space and awareness have mingled. Our minds have been under the power of dualistic grasping and fixation for so long that we have taken the nondual for a duality. Thus, it's difficult to immediately be used to the awakened state. We have trained for so long in the opposite of recognizing mind essence, which is exactly what samsara has been in all our past lives, up until the present moment. We have this unwholesome and deeply ingrown habit. Now we must change this habit into the habit of recognizing mind essence. Since for a beginner the moment of recognition only lasts a very short time, we have to repeat it many times. To repeat the recognition of mind essence, you don't have to necessarily sit down. Do not make any distinction between the training when sitting and the training when moving around in daily life situations — walking, talking, eating, and lying down. Do not limit the practice to sessions. The view is rigpa, the meditation training is rigpa, and the conduct is rigpa. This is the way to get used to the awakened state.

We need to grow accustomed to rigpa. We need to train in the real thing. The duration of seeing mind essence cannot possibly last for a long time right now, because we are beginners in this recognition of self-existing wakefulness. Any success in keeping a long stretch of meditation state cannot be anything other than an imitation, a fabrication, which is precisely what we don't need to train in. Rather, repeat again and again the short moment of true wakefulness. You know from attending school that you learn because you put your mind to it. In the beginning it was difficult, then it became easier. All training is like that. We, like all sentient beings, have gotten used to negative habits, even though we have the nature of Samantabhadra. Since we do not know this, we are governed by habitual tendencies, just like the example of the experiences in a dream or wandering in the bardo. Habitual tendencies are like covers; they can be removed.

If you want to mingle this practice with daily life, do not differentiate between sessions and breaks. Breaks or post-meditation means to be distracted, to get carried away from the natural state by the power of distraction, like the eight examples of illusion. The eight analogies are insubstantial and pointless to pursue, as is the whole of samsara. The chief characteristic of samsara is distraction.

It is always taught that the view is beyond concepts, that natural awareness is unconstructed. The view of Prajnaparamita, the Great Middle Way, Mahamudra and Dzogchen are all views free of concepts. They are never the conceptual view of an ordinary person, which is the incessant creation of thought, day and night. It is said, "There is no awakening through doing." Your own mind fetters you; conceptual mind attaches concepts to whatever is perceived. But the pure view itself needs to be free from concepts held in mind. This present wakefulness is free of concept.

You need to recognize this present wakefulness in which past has ceased and future has not arrived. Don't cover this present wakefulness up with another thought. Sentient beings do this continuously, one new thought being followed by the next, followed by a third, continuously. Do not reconnect anything to the present wakefulness. Do not accept or reject. Do not affirm or deny. Do not adopt or avoid. Remain without holding anything — that is called mind essence. You can call it rangjung yeshe, self-existing wakefulness, or the view of Mahamudra. The Middle Way names it ultimate truth. While conventional truth means the conceptual frame of mind, ultimate truth means the reality of true meaning. It is also called transcendent knowledge, Prajnaparamita. In Dzogchen it is known as 'the immaculate dharmakaya of empty awareness'. If Dharma teachings did not use words and names, there would be nothing to say, right? The meaning is revealed through words and names. If you just sit and make wordless gestures like a mute, we would not get the point!

As Saraha said, "Abandoning the thinker and what is thought of, experience like a thoughtfree child." A small child does not have many concepts, even though it does not see its own nature, or, if it does, it has no confidence in that. The very root of forming concepts is the holding in mind of what is perceived. Like "This is a cup. There is a lid. There are a lot of designs on it. There is a little tea left." This train of thought is called fixating on the perceived through thinking, through mental movement. A yogi, on the other hand, in the moment of seeing a cup, recognizes the nature of the mind that sees the cup. The production of concepts then ceases, and within his mind there is no holding on to anything whatsoever. When concepts of both subject and object fall apart, samsara has ceased. To experience this in actuality is called resolving the view. The moment you hold no concept of either subject or object, that is enough.

Like a one-year-old child, just learning to walk, we are not yet used to this; we are only slightly accustomed. The child stands up on his own legs, and then he falls over; he stands up again, and topples over. This is how our practice is right now, because the innate stability has not been actualized. When you are two years old, you are more stable, and at three years, even more. When you are eighteen, you have attained stability; you are a young adult. You have the ability to run, or do whatever you want to do. This arrival at maturity in the training is called 'having assumed the natural stability of rigpa'.

When there is no more distraction throughout day and night, you are very close to the dharmakaya throne of nonmeditation. You can sit together with Buddha Samantabhadra in the dharmakaya palace of Akanishtha. The benefit for beings that occurs out of this state is spontaneous and automatic. You do not have to say, "Now *I* want to benefit beings." There is no need for that thought. It's like when the sun shines: you don't have to *make* the sun warm and brilliant, do you? It's naturally like that when it shines. When achieving stability, you can truly benefit an infinite number of sentient beings. Once you have realized the nature of dharmakaya, it is like the sun being free of clouds. Its brilliance, its warmth, its light, radiates spontaneously everywhere, all over the world. When realizing dharmakaya for the benefit of oneself, the benefit for others is effortless. This realization is often described as resplendence, in Sanskrit *shri*, in Tibetan *palden*. The glory for oneself is to realize dharmakaya. To manifest the form body, the rupakaya, is the glory for others. That is why the buddhas are called 'glorious buddhas'.

In the meantime, you will be distracted when you go about your daily affairs — there is no way around this. Dharmakaya is in ourselves, but since we have not stabilized the recognition of it, we get caught up in thoughts. Yet the essence of thoughts, when acknowledged, is dharmakaya. A thought is simply the extroverted expression of knowing, of awareness. In the moment of recognizing the nature of what thinks, there is no way for this expression, the thought, to remain. Your naked essence is then an actuality. In this experience, there is no way for a thought to remain, just as a drop of water cannot remain in mid-air. Once you are familiar with this way of dealing with a thought, you do not need to suppress thinking. You do not need to correct it. You do not need any hope of gaining or fear of losing the awakened state. That is why it is said that 'the confidence of the view is free of hope and fear'. You do not have to hope for freedom or fear having thoughts, because in the moment of seeing the essence, the thought has dissolved. Do you understand this? Is it clear?

Don't ever expect that anything spectacular will be experienced. Honestly, there is nothing more amazing than this recognition of rigpa in which no thought can remain. The five poisons and habitual tendencies lose their power to rigpa. If we do not know this, we become caught up in thought. Most sentient beings do not know how to recognize; they are carried away by thoughts. In the moment you remind yourself to recognize mind nature, you have already seen the essence. "Seeing no thing is the sublime sight." This is so close that it is hard to believe. It is not an act of imagining. It's because it's so easy that it is hard to trust in! There is not even as much as a hair-tip to cultivate by meditating. But we need to grow used to it; we need to grow used to recognizing this nature of empty cognizance.

Train like this for the rest of your life, and you will have no fear of death. A true yogi is someone who is happy when sick and delighted when dying. Why would you be happy to fall sick? Because when you die, you become enlightened. People usually don't die without falling sick first, and without dying, this material body will not pass. Through this practice, at the time of death original wakefulness free of dualistic mind will be like a garuda soaring free. Your mind, as original wakefulness, merges with dharmakaya. You arrive at the royal throne of dharmakaya; you have captured the dharmakaya kingdom.

Right now, sentient beings have captured the kingdom of stupidity! Once this unaware meandering is cleared up, there is nothing other than the kingdom of original wakefulness. Until that happens, King Ignorance has five ministers, the five poisons. Their deputies are the twenty-one unvirtuous mental events and the eighty innate thought states. The subjects are the eighty-four thousand disturbing emotions. This tyrant rules the kingdom of endless samsara. We all live in his realm, and think it is just great!

At death, however, we totally lose control. Whatever we own is lost; whatever we did is wasted and cannot help us in any way at all. The moment we die, mind continues on all alone, like a hair pulled out of butter. It travels on and on without any freedom to choose where to be, where to go. The kingdom of stupidity is really hopeless. Still, even though it's useless, we stick to it. It is impossible to ever be truly happy; we do not have any mastery over our destinies. If we had control, we could stay as we are in the vast palace of stupidity. But since it is utterly without any freedom, the great kingdom of stupidity does not help. If this ignorance is not cleared up, nothing will help — nothing is of any benefit. Of course there is some temporary benefit by doing virtuous good actions, but "unless you know the secret key point of mind, whatever you do is upside down." The key point of mind is to be free of thoughts of the three times — to remain in present wakefulness, uncontrived, wide open. If you don't know that, whatever you do will be upside down. There is a Khampa proverb: "It doesn't help to join your palms in reverence while you are falling over backwards." In other words, if ignorance is not cleared up in our basic ground, we always return into samsaric existence.

There is one thing we always need, and that is the watchman named mindfulness, the guard who is on the lookout for when we get carried away in mindlessness. As you know, "Along the path of distraction, the Mara bandits lie in ambush." We may think that there are evil spirits out to get us, but the real Mara is this mind being distracted. It's like the famous saying, "Obstructers are your own thoughts; obstructers arise out of your own mind." Once you are undistracted throughout day and night, no obstructing force can obtain any hold over you.

In short, to be able to mingle the recognition of mind essence with daily life is entirely the outcome of training, nothing else. Without training, the recognition of mind essence remains a short glimpse that immediately vanishes. We may recognize again, but it always slips away. We always forget; we always get distracted. Our ingrown habit of not recognizing mind essence, reinforced throughout all our past lives, is simply too strong. There is ultimately no other solution than training in the way I constantly mention: short moments repeated many times. Whether one sits or whether one walks, the training is essentially the same: short moments many times. Unless we repeat it many times we never get used to it. It's most important to recognize again and again. As you grow more and more familiar with recognizing mind essence, and therefore more and more stable, these moments naturally last longer and longer. The periods of not recognizing will become shorter and shorter, fewer and fewer. The training in reminding yourself is thus crucial, until finally there is one continuous, unbroken stretch of original wakefulness that is called the state of complete enlightenment. Until that happens, you need to train again and again.

The way to train now is to remember during the daily activities. This mindfulness or 'remindfulness' is the very heart of Dharma practice. As you grow more and more stable in it, and in recognizing mind essence in daily activities, while walking, eating, lying down at night, and so on, you will be able to recognize again and again. Without reminding yourself to recognize, however, there is never any recognition. Without any recognition, you are totally oblivious to what your buddha nature really is. To live in that kind of oblivion is to be like a corpse, an unfeeling zombie. Without the qualities of enlightenment fully perfected we may look like human beings, alive and awake, but as long as we are ignorant of our own nature, we are actually zombies. I'm sorry to say this, but all sentient beings are like walking corpses. *(Rinpoche laughs).*

STUDENT: How do we clear up very forceful negative emotions?

RINPOCHE: If you know how to do it, an emotion can be cleared up in a second. Not forever, of course, but in that very moment it has completely dissolved. Every emotion is a thought, and any thought is the mind moving. When thinking, the attention moves towards one object, then towards another, then a third, right? The very root of emotion is your attention in motion. To cut the root of this movement you must recognize from where the attention is moving. At that very instant, anger or desire immediately dissolves. In the moment of seeing this in actuality, there is no thought, only thoughtfree wakefulness. When recognizing the naturally empty essence, thinking dissolves. Again a thought comes, again recognize, again it vanishes.

For example, you get angry: recognize and the anger dissolves. By applying this training, slowly, slowly, your tendency for anger becomes weaker and weaker. The mirror of your mind becomes clearer and clearer. In the moment of any thought, recognize the thinker. It is like rubbing away the dust from a small portion of a mirror. You can see your reflection clearly in the place where you've rubbed the dust away. Jamgön Kongtrül said of this "Within thought, I discover nonthought. Within nonthought, I discover original wakefulness." When a mirror is covered by dust, you do not see any images. If you take the tip of a needle and you rub just a little bit, you will see a tiny bit of mirror. Our ignorant thinking is like the dust on the mirror. The more you rub the dust off the mirror, the clearer the image becomes.

Once you know how to recognize the essence in one thought, the procedure is the same for any other thought. It's just like chanting a *puja* text: when a certain number of lines are the same at the end of each verse, the text doesn't repeat these each time; it just says 'etcetera'. You do not have to read them every time; you just know them at that point. It's the same with recognizing mind essence. You don't have to go through a laborious process each time; you simply recognize, and that's it. And thinking gradually becomes weaker and weaker, and arises less and less. The gaps between thoughts naturally last longer. Natural stability extends by itself; it becomes one minute, a few minutes, one hour, a couple of hours. All this results gradually from training. At some point the five poisons are perpetually obliterated. "Free of thought, yet everything is clearly known." When we are free of thought, how can any of the five poisons possibly arise?

What is the issue right now? Simply that you need to grow used to the solution through training. When an emotion is very forceful, can you claim that it is totally impossible to recognize original wakefulness? No, of course not. The solution works regardless of the strength of the particular emotion. You are not a hundred percent stable, of course. Who is, at this point? It's like the example I gave earlier — we are like a one-year-old who tries to walk. He stands up and falls over right away. We are not fully trained. We have just recognized; we haven't perfected the strength. We haven't grown up. When a child grows up, he becomes independent. We are like a young child who doesn't have much strength, who is just getting his bearings.

When you recognize mind essence, there is no thing to see. If there was a thing and you could not see it, you could feel sad about it. But it's said that "Seeing no thing is the supreme sight." There is no thing to see: you simply need to see that. Can you agree? This is being in agreement, literally 'touching horns' in Tibetan, which means touching base. If there is only one head, there is no touching horns, right? You do not touch base. When I say, "There is no thing to see, mind is empty," if you recognize your mind essence and you see that it is no 'thing', then you have touched horns with me.

If the Buddha had taught, "Emptiness has form, has smell, has taste, has texture, and so forth," and we look and yet do not see it, then we would certainly be in trouble. We would not have gotten it yet. But he did not say that. He said, "Emptiness has no form, no sound, no smell, no taste, no texture," didn't he? No matter how much we search for mind, do we ever find it as having form, sound, taste, smell, texture? Seeing no thing when you recognize is 'touching base' with the Buddha.

Seeing this in actuality, you are speechless. It's simply beyond thought, word and description. Can you describe how it is? Just train in this; do not give it up. See again and again that it is no thing to see. Leave it as it naturally is. By itself, it will begin to last longer. If you try to deliberately extend it, however, it becomes conceptual. Do not extend it intentionally; do not cut it short either. The view should be free of concept, right? Sitting and speculating does not help you to be free of concepts.

STUDENT: What should we do about the subtle grasping that doesn't disappear when recognizing mind essence?

RINPOCHE: If you genuinely recognize the state of rigpa, at that very moment no thought, disturbing emotion or habitual tendency can remain. Take the memory of a song, for example; this is a habitual tendency or imprint. Rigpa in itself is free of that. When it seems like these imprints do not dissolve, it is because we lack stability in rigpa. When you pour water on dirt, it mingles with the dirt. If you pour mercury on dirt, however, it does not mix with the dirt at all; it remains intact, pristine. Rigpa is like mercury; it is unmixed with habitual tendencies. It is possible to have a resemblance of rigpa that is mixed with dualistic mind. This is like the dust of dualistic mind.

Rigpa is neither caught up in the object perceived nor with the sense organ through which perception takes place. It is not caught up in the perceiving dualistic mind. Rigpa is not caught up in anything whatsoever. Rigpa is therefore described as immaculate dharmakaya, which means flawless. If rigpa were even slightly affected by some habitual tendency, you would not call it flawless. Rigpa means the state that is totally untainted by any obscuration, negative karma or habitual imprints, just like mercury remains unaffected by whatever it touches.

The Dzogchen tantras distinguish between sem and rigpa, teaching that rigpa is like mercury, while dualistic mind is like water. The perceived objects, the sense organs and the perceiving frame of mind are like dirt. Mercury doesn't get stuck, doesn't get caught up in any way whatsoever with these. It remains unmixed, unaffected by them. But the moment the water-like dualistic frame of mind touches dirt, it immediately mingles with it and becomes mud. Rigpa is innately stable; it is not caught up in the subject-object duality. Sem, like water, has no innate stability. The moment you pour water onto earth, it seeps in completely.

In every sentient being there is mind. The essence of this mind, whether known or not, is rigpa. Sentient beings have both mind and rigpa. A true yogi, a practitioner of this path, abandons the dualistic frame of mind while allowing the state of rigpa to remain when sem falls away. At Shukseb nunnery in Central Tibet, the great female master Ani Lochen expressed a single wish whenever someone requested her blessings. With an implement in her hand she would touch people's head, saying, "May you recognize the essence of mind." She repeated this to every person she blessed: "May you recognize the essence of mind." She would always say exactly the same thing. She never said "May you recognize mind," meaning sem. She always said, "May you recognize the *essence* of mind." In other words, may you no longer be caught up in dualistic mind, like water seeping into soil, but may you be innately stable, like mercury.

It is essential to distinguish between sem and rigpa. If you are caught up in *sem*, you are a *semchen*, which means sentient being, but if you master rigpa you are a *rigpa dzinpa*, which means *vidyadhara*, a knowledge-holder. Padmasambhava attained the four vidyadhara levels. The first vidyadhara level is called the vidyadhara level of complete maturation. The second is the vidyadhara level of life mastery. The third one is the vidyadhara of Mahamudra. The fourth one is called the vidyadhara of spontaneous perfection. This is how one progresses on this path.

9

Doubt

❖

STUDENT: What about doubt? How should I deal with it?

RINPOCHE: Regardless of who you are, until you reach the first bhumi, you are still an ordinary person and you will sometimes experience doubt. Almost everyone gets suspicious. However, is there any doubt that is separate from thought? It is simply another thought. And if you gently recognize the nature of the thinker, it's impossible for that thought to remain anywhere. Discover this, and you have conquered your own doubt. You don't need any other antidote. All different types of doubts can arise for anyone; it doesn't matter who you are. Until you have truly established certainty in the natural state, you can easily become involved in doubt. You might think, "Am I mistaking what isn't for what is?" Or, "What I understand is not really ultimate. Maybe there is something better, something unchanging, that I still need to discover."

Clearly understand that doubt is simply another thought. If you recognize its essence, the thought naturally vanishes. Thought cannot remain in the recognition of the essence. All fixating falls away. The absence of fixation, of clinging, naturally reveals this present wakefulness. The thought cannot stay; its character is such that it vanishes the moment you recognize mind essence. Our basic state is one of unconfined empty cognizance. Thought is not an intrinsic part of buddha nature — not in any way whatsoever. In the buddha nature there are no thoughts. If you could somehow pinpoint the empty quality as being here, and the cognizant as being there, you could justifiably say that there is a concrete remedy against a concrete thought. We create thoughts, and we create the remedy. The ultimate remedy is to not fabricate anything at all.

The recognition of mind essence, of the natural empty cognizance, eliminates the basis for any thought to remain. The most effective way for a meditator to deal with doubt, rather than trying to resolve the doubt with intellectual answers, and rather than applying some antidote to counteract that doubt, is to use the doubting itself as its own remedy. Recognize the nature of that which doubts, the identity of that which thinks. The origin of any thought is the same — it comes out of empty cognizance. The moment you recognize the original state, doubt is not capable of remaining as a concrete entity, like some sort of lump suspended in mid-air. It simply vanishes.

Of course doubts arise. You may think, "My guru has been talking about a state of rigpa, and this doesn't seem to be it. I wonder what it is, because this is not the right thing. Maybe my view is wrong." This can go on for days. "Maybe I should go to India, anywhere else but here." We can have all these different thoughts. And why not? Our buddha nature is now entrapped in this body of skandhas and ayatanas, aggregates and sense-bases. Due to this circumstance, we go through changes; we are enmeshed in samsara.

When doubt tries to trap you, understand that it is nothing other than a thought. To reiterate, thoughts originate out of nonconceptual wakefulness. When you recognize this base of nonconceptual wakefulness, the thought dissolves. If we can remain in our unconfined empty cognizance, all thoughts, including doubt, simply disappear. If a doubt arises, recognize the doubter. You will see the essence. Once you are accustomed to this, then you have confidence in yourself. You have conquered doubt. You will know yourself. You do not need to be afraid of doubt. Nor do you need to think, "I don't want to be bothered by doubt." That is merely another thought.

It's like this electric light bulb. When the light shines, there is no darkness. The 'wakefulness of knowing', *rigpey yeshe*, is like the light bulb when it is lit. Is it possible for darkness to remain in front of the bulb? Darkness is the example for unknowing, while light is the example for knowing. You cannot have darkness when there is light. You cannot have unknowing where there is knowing. In the moment of recognizing mind essence, the three poisons or any other thought cannot remain, just as darkness cannot remain when the light is on.

Simply recognize your nature. When there is light, there is no darkness. When there is darkness, there is no light. The darkness is the thinking, while the light is rigpa. You have to recognize the nature of thought, because thinking is *not* rigpa — deluded thinking is *not* the awakened state of all buddhas. In the moment of recognizing the essence, thinking dissolves; it vanishes within rigpa. It is not that you have to throw away the thought and bring forth rigpey yeshe. That would be just another fabrication. Simply recognize rigpa, and the doubt disappears. Do not entertain doubts and suspicions; instead, recognize rigpa. You need to become stable in self-existing wakefulness. Don't be too tight, be loose. It is said:

> *The looser you are, the easier it is to see your nature.*
> *The tighter you are, the more hidden it gets.*

No matter what happens, the practice is still the same. If you walk to Bodhgaya from here, it is uphill, it is downhill, it is level. If you do not give up and continue walking, you'll reach there at some point, won't you? In the same way, your self-existing wakefulness at this present moment lives in a physical body made of the five aggregates and twelve sense-bases and elements. These are in constant flux. Regardless of these temporary changes, just keep on walking towards Bodhgaya — keep on training. Train again and again in undistracted nonmeditation, without even as much as a dust mote to meditate upon, but also not forgetting for even an instant. Once you recognize the nonmeditation, meaning once you remain undistracted while not fabricating anything by meditation, there is no thought. It is only after being distracted that one starts to think. The ultimate instruction by Longchenpa is this:

> Short moments, many times;
> Like collecting water from the eaves of the roof.

(Rinpoche snaps his fingers three times). For a beginner, unfabricated self-existing wakefulness doesn't remain for more than a few seconds. Since beginningless time we have been continually carried away by thought. At the beginning stage it is not a problem that the recognition is so short. This is not like in the Sutra teachings where you have to go into a meditation state a few times a day and keep long sessions. The state of shamatha can last for a long time, flickering between agitation and dullness. Certainly one feels either dull or agitated if one sits for a very long time. *(Finger snaps)* A short moment, a few seconds — within that, the very moment you recognize, just let be *as it is*. It is impossible to find a word to adequately describe how it is, this ineffable, natural face of awareness. You cannot praise it enough; nor can you find any words to criticize it. Rigpa is truly indescribable. Rigpa-awareness is flawless and endowed with all perfect qualities. You cannot find an adequate word for rigpa, a concept that fully covers it, or even a satisfactory analogy for it — it transcends conceptual knowledge. That is the true meaning of prajnaparamita. Even scientists cannot figure it out. Scientists understand what they can grasp, but transcendent knowledge means what lies beyond the grasp of conceptual mind. As is said:

> Transcendent knowledge is beyond thought, word and description.
> It neither arises nor ceases, like the identity of space.
> It is the domain of individual, self-knowing wakefulness.
> To this mother of the buddhas of the three times, I pay homage.

The awakened state, rigpa, is not formed in any way. It does not arise and come into being; it is like the essence of space. Yet it is in the domain of our experience, within each of us individually. We can experience it; it is within our reach. You cannot recognize the nature of somebody else's mind, only your own. It is right here. It is not some other place. It is the domain of your self-cognizant wakefulness. This self-cognizant wakefulness is within your own experience. It can be known by yourself. You can individually experience it.

When you feel doubt about this, recognize that which is beyond thought, word and description. We might possibly become doubtful. After all, we have been doubtful so many times in the past, so of course we can doubt again — why not? I'll tease you a little: it would be easier if buddha nature would talk to you and say "This is what I am, right here; have no doubt about me." But buddha nature doesn't speak to you! You have to be sure yourself. "Now you see me, I am the buddha nature. Don't doubt now!" Buddha nature does not speak like this.

Your buddha nature neither arises nor ceases; so don't regard it in terms of a threat or a promise. Imagine a thing that does not come into being, does not cease, does not remain anywhere, and is totally open like space. Is anything blocked in space? Rigpey yeshe is like space, the essence of space. This openness of rigpa is supremely precious. Thinking may seem incessant, but it is a stream of momentary nature: as a new thought is formed, the previous vanishes. Thoughts do cease. Once you move your attention to the second thought, you forget about the first. Rigpa, on the other hand, is totally unceasing; it is not blocked by any of the three times.

Furthermore, investigate from where does the thinking come? You don't find any place where it comes from; it is 'nonarising'. Next, does the thinking vanish to some place? Does it go anywhere? If somebody completely knocks you out, you can say that the mind is blocked, that the thinking capacity ceases. Dwelling is like putting an object in a place and having it stay there. Does the present thinking dwell anywhere? Where is the thinking from yesterday, or from tomorrow? Try to find where all those thoughts are, and where they went. First, investigate the arising, where the thoughts come from. Keep on examining like this until you discover there is no source. This is an important point in the Dzogchen teachings: spend time looking into the source of the thinking, until you find that there is no source anywhere. To discover that it has no origin is called meeting dharmakaya.

Continue on by searching for where the thinking remains. Investigate where it is: is it outside or inside this body? Is it anywhere in the world? Is there an abode where mind stays? When you realize it is nondwelling, non-abiding, that is called meeting sambhogakaya. Finally, where does the thinking go? When you analyze like this you won't find any place whatsoever. Once you are totally certain that the thinking doesn't go anywhere, that is called meeting the nirmanakaya quality of all buddhas.

This is why the Dzogchen teachings stress the importance of resolving the nonexistence of arising, dwelling and ceasing. This is considered an incredibly important preparation because realizing the lack of origin is to meet the dharmakaya quality of all buddhas. Realizing the absence of abiding place is to meet the sambhogakaya. Realizing that the thinking does not go anywhere is to meet nirmanakaya. In short, understand these three qualities of your mind as unconfined empty cognizance: empty in essence, cognizant by nature and unconfined in its capacity. When you recognize this unconfined empty cognizance as your own nature, at that moment you are face to face with the three kayas.

Emptiness means totally inconcrete, free of all materiality. All that we see, hear, smell, taste or touch, all that is concrete, has some materiality. Mind does not have any of that. Isn't that true? Isn't it true that mind has no visible form? It is not a sound. It does not smell either, does it? Try to eat mind: what does it taste like? Try to touch it — is it smooth or rough to touch? Isn't it empty, like space? We can use space as an analogy, but not completely. Mind can feel happy or sad, whereas space does not have feelings. For a rough example of how mind is, look at space. For the actual meaning, recognize mind essence.

So: exactly where is your doubt, anyway? Please tell me its location. Is there any doubt that mind is empty, or is there any doubt that mind is cognizant? Is there any doubt as to whether or not this empty cognizance is an indivisible unity? You may think something like, "What's wrong is that there should be some entity called mind, maybe a round lump somewhere, and I missed seeing it." Is that your doubt?

Didn't the Buddha teach that mind in itself has no form, no sound, no smell, no taste, no texture, and is not a mental object. He called it emptiness, unlike space, which he called empty, and void. This -*ness* in emptiness refers to cognizance, as does the -*ta* in shunyata. Buddha said, "Mind is empty cognizance." This is how to discriminate between space and mind. Space is empty, while mind is empti*ness*. This '-ness' always refers back to the quality of cognizant wakefulness. You never say that awareness is empty: you always say it is emptiness. It is empty, yet able to know.

What is meant by 'knowing'? Right now in this body, you can see through the eyes, hear through the ears, and smell through the nose. Take the example of a corpse, which is a body with no mind in it. Do those eyes see? Do the ears hear? Does the nose smell? Does the tongue taste? Does the body feel a smooth or rough texture? The five sense organs of the dead body don't perceive anything. Isn't it certain that it is only mind that can know? Mind is empty and cognizant. Some people compare this cognizance to a radiant 'thing' that shines with a light like a 'clear light'. It means a sense of being wakeful, a quality of being vividly wide awake, which is empty of any identity and naturally alert. It is not limited to being one or the other. It is not either/or. This indivisible unity is called capacity: the capacity for wisdom, compassion and the ability to aid others.

Where would all the buddha activities come from, if they were not part of this cognizant emptiness that is continuously present? The qualities cannot manifest if this capacity is blocked. If you want to completely block this capacity, you need to have someone incessantly knock you out by hitting you on the head with an iron bar. Ironically, sentient beings are doing something very similar to that by training in being mindless. In the aspiration of Samantabhadra, you find the line, "Untainted by mindless gloom." Rigpa is not mindless, because dualistic fixation has stopped. Rigpa is a self-existing wakefulness that is unceasing, not sometimes lost and sometimes regained. It is uninterrupted like the flow of a river, like the shining sun. Have you ever heard that the Ganges River stopped? Or, have you ever heard that the sun occasionally shines and at other times stops? Even though the sun is often obscured by clouds and is sometimes even eclipsed, it still shines continually. Similarly, this self-existing wakefulness has never forsaken you for even an instant. While recognizing rigpa, there is no thought, no thinking. When involved in thinking, you are taken over by darkness, and there is no light. So: where is the doubt now? Is there any doubt left? Where is it?

I'll tease you again. If you get involved in doubt again, it would be convenient if your nature would stick its head out and say, "Hey! I'm rigpa! I'm right here," and talk to you, but it doesn't. The distinction has to be made by oneself. One of the six special qualities of Samantabhadra is to distinguish. We have to emulate what took place in Samantabhadra's realization. You don't think of Samantabhadra in the original state as some blue man who lived a long time ago, do you? We have to abide by those same principles of realization in this same moment, right now.

You do not need to fabricate at all. Once you utterly let be, involvement in thoughts of past, present and future subside. By letting be, you are no longer involved in the thoughts of the three times. When utterly letting be, wakefulness is vividly present. The experience is simply seeing that there is no thing to see. This is vividly seen *as it is*. Getting involved in the three times is not utterly letting be, is it? At this moment, there is not even as much as a hair-tip to see. We need to acknowledge this. It would be difficult if there was something to see and we missed it. We simply need to see that there *isn't* anything to see. If we asked a hundred different people what they see when recognizing mind essence, each and every one of them would have to say there is nothing to see. We may think that there is something we need to see, but that is merely a thought. There is no thing. Sometimes, when people see the nature of mind, they get disappointed because they assume that there is something and they missed it. They feel they have not seen it yet. But the innate suchness is like seeing space. The Buddha said, "People say they see space, but tell me, exactly how do they see it?" A shravaka asked the Buddha, "What does suchness look like?" The

Buddha replied, "Look at space." What does it look like? Can you say you see space? When people say they do not see anything, I call that 'seeing space'. Suchness, the nature of mind, looks like space because there is no thing to see, hear, smell, taste or take hold of. It is similar to space, but not identical, as I explained earlier.

While training there is no need to mentally acknowledge empty mind. To think, "Now it is empty, it is empty" — such formulated emptiness is totally useless. It is merely a thought. Emptiness does not mean imagined emptiness. It is *as it is* by itself, naturally self-existing: you do not have to think in order for it to be. To conceive the idea of our essence being empty is to construct a thought. What's the point of creating further thought, since our task is to be uninvolved in thinking? One may be intelligent and still miss it by misconstruing emptiness. Constructing the idea of emptiness is a mistake.

Once you get more used to nonconceptual wakefulness, it is like arriving on an island made entirely of gold. At some point within awareness you may try to find conceptual thinking, but you won't find it anywhere, no matter how much you try. When everywhere you look is made of pure gold, you may look for ordinary stones, but you will not find any. That is how it will be eventually. Until that time, you need to train. Not meditate, but train. When fully accustomed to training in the state of rigpa, you may try to find a normal thought, but you will not find it.

Until then, be diligent and persevere, not in meditating, but in being undistracted. Meditate, meditate — that idea has fooled us from the beginning. When we hear "Don't meditate, don't meditate," we may wonder, "Why did they say meditate to begin with, when there is really no thing upon which to meditate?" It's true that all things *seem* to happen. The eighty-four thousand types of disturbing emotions happen, for example, although these can be boiled down to the fifty-one mental events included within the aggregate of formations. All things that happen can be included within these. We can deal with all of them by recognizing mind essence. It's like "crossing a hundred rivers over one bridge" — if you know that one bridge. All the different streams that flow from the top of the valley converge together under one bridge at the bottom of the valley. These thought states are not simultaneous; they arise one after the other. But in the moment of seeing that the essence of that which thinks is dharmakaya, any of the eighty-four thousand disturbing emotions are vanquished at the same instant.

When we make ourselves a problem, then there is a problem. All sentient beings make their own thoughts, although they may not be aware of that. Only sentient beings make thoughts. Buddhas may look for a thought, but they will not find any. The wisdoms, the compassion, the buddha activities are all perfected — in fact, that is the word for buddha, 'purified and perfected'.

The sun is radiant, warm and bright; we look at it and we see this. Likewise, simply acknowledge the state of rigpa. When sentient beings are caught up in thoughts, they are caught up in their own creation. As we grow increasingly accustomed to recognizing self-existing wakefulness, this fabric of thought diminishes, until it is totally purified, totally perfected.

Awareness wisdom is primordially so. The problem is simply a failing to acknowledge our own nature. Some people think that if we can meditate very hard, then slowly, slowly we can 'milk' the qualities of enlightenment and obtain more and more until finally we get them complete. It is not like that at all. The enlightened qualities are primordially present; we have them already. Do not think that through some kind of macho striving you can make it through the path, and realize rigpa more and more until finally you have it fully established. This is not how the buddhas teach. The enlightened qualities are naturally and spontaneously present from the very beginning. The more we meditate conceptually, the more they are obscured. Our meditating covers up what is spontaneously present.

We do doubt upon occasion, which is perfectly all right. The way to deal with it is to recognize the doubter. Then the fact that there is no thing there to see is clearly seen *as it is*. That in itself clears the doubt. Isn't it a hundred percent sure that there is no thing to see? Or do you sometimes see the doubter?

STUDENT: No, I don't.

RINPOCHE: That which sees itself is awareness. Without this there would be no recognizing: it would be exactly like space — no thing to see. If there were no awareness, natural cognizance, there would be no knowing that there is no thing to see. These two are an original unity, empty cognizance. Then how can we maintain the idea that there is a 'me' as one thing, and there is a separate thing, the nature of mind as an entity to be seen? If emptiness and cognizance are a unity, how can there be two different things? Do not doubt whether this is really so or not. You need to dissolve that doubt. In his *Mahamudra Aspiration*, Karmapa Rangjung Dorje said:

> *When looking again and again into the unseen mind,*
> *The fact that there is nothing to see is vividly seen as it is.*
> *Cutting through doubts about its nature being or not being,*
> *May we unmistakenly recognize our own essence.*

The Buddha also said:

> *When mind looks into mind,*
> *Not seeing is the true seeing.*
> *This is taught in the most profound sutras.*

When directing your attention towards perceived objects, how can you ever see the nature of this attention? Let the perceiving mind recognize itself, its own nature. At that moment, can you truly claim that you can't see it?

At some point you may start to affirm mentally: "Oh yes, this is what being empty means," or "This must be the cognizance," or "Now I got what is meant by unity." We do not have to conceptualize our understanding in this way. Your basic state is already unconfined empty cognizance, all by itself. If, after having this pointed out, you regard this 'understanding' as being the training, you are merely fooling yourself with thought. In the moment of unconfined empty cognizance there is no thought present. If you try to assist this natural emptiness by means of a thought-up emptiness, what happens? The result is only more thought, which is itself the fuel for further samsara. When we are sup-posed to be free of thought, sitting and holding more thoughts only continues samsara. Self-existing wakefulness is already free of thought; we do not have to *make* it free of thought. If we think of something in order to make it so, it is the same as holding hands with samsara. The key point is this: don't meditate; don't get distracted.

Don't be too fond of being in doubt. Don't claim ownership of be-ing in doubt, because doubt is simply another thought. When needing to be free of thought, don't hold on to a thought! Doubt is always only a thought. So, if you do start to have this thought, merely recognize the nature of the doubter. The moment you see this directly, there won't be a doubt like a thing that remains anywhere; there won't be a lump of doubt hanging around. Because it is empty, it vanishes in the moment of recognition. Machig Labdrön said to the demon, "Even I don't see you. Even the buddhas of the three times don't see you." Thinking is a movement that is empty in itself. If you give into this thinking, it throws you right into the three realms of samsara. The moment you acknowledge the nature of that which thinks, the thought vanishes.

STUDENT: Can there be thinking during rigpa?

RINPOCHE: The state of rigpa is not oblivious; there is a natural bright-ness that allows anything to be reflected. This reflecting quality is also called *rang-tsal*, which means natural expression. The natural expression can take two forms: either *sherab* or *namtog*, insight or thought. "The expression moving as sherab is liberated. The expression moving as namtog is confused." That makes an enormous difference. Honestly though, in the state of rigpa itself, there is no real movement. When the expression moves as sherab, in the same moment it *seemingly* moves, it is already liberated. There is no actual arising. That is a very important point. You cannot have both darkness and light at the same time.

It is essential to resolve the fact that there is no namtog whatsoever in the state of rigpa; it is impossible. Darkness cannot remain when the sun rises. A hair cannot remain in a flame. It is only in a moment of distraction that you lose the continuity of rigpa. It is only out of that loss, which is *marigpa*, unknowing, that thinking can possibly start to move. This loss of continuity, in the sense of forgetting and being distracted, is called coemergent ignorance. To reiterate, thinking means to conceptualize out of the state of unknowing. Thinking only begins after marigpa sets in, at the loss of rigpa. During the nondistraction of rigpa, no thought can begin. I cannot emphasize this enough — there is no thought during the state of rigpa!

One's sustaining of the state of rigpa ends at some point, of course, just like the fading sound of a bell that has been rung. The continuity finally ceases. It is at that point, after the loss of rigpa, that thinking reoccurs. At that moment, nonetheless, if you immediately recognize rigpa, almost simultaneously with the thought, there is what we call the *rangshar rangdröl* of the thought, 'arising from yourself and being freed into yourself'. This does not happen while rigpa continues; that is impossible. First, look, and simply let be. The recognition continues for a while, just like when you've sounded the bell. There is a natural continuity of nondistraction, just as the sound of the bell goes on by itself. You do not have to ring the bell again to have the sound continue. For a beginner, this continuity lasts only for a little while, maybe three seconds. There is some innate stability in this that is present all by itself — it is not kept up deliberately. It is not that one thinks, "Now I must make myself undistracted." That is not necessary. There is a natural sense of being undistracted.

(Rinpoche demonstrates recognizing and simply letting be.)

At some point, you get distracted and you start to think. It could become a train of thought. At that moment, you can again recognize. If you recognize right away, that is the rangshar rangdröl of a thought, which would make the state of rigpa seem to be almost continuous. But I will repeat this over and over: in the true state of rigpa, there is no namtog.

10

The Heart of Training

❖

There are four lines by Vairotsana, the great Tibetan master and translator that go like this:

Within the inconceivable naked state of dharmadhatu,
Place ineffable awareness undistractedly.
If a thought arises, it arises out of yourself and dissolves into yourself.
There is no basic view, meditation or instruction superior to this.

These four lines spoken by Vairotsana are the heart of all view, meditation and conduct. My root guru, Samten Gyatso, taught them once when he visited the retreat center above Lachab Gompa, in Nangchen, Eastern Tibet. He was about to give two empowerments that were termas of the first Jamgön Kongtrül by the name *Yabkah* and *Yumkah,* belonging to the *Sangtik* terma cycle of the *Secret Essence.* While he was explaining about the superior qualities of Jamgön Kongtrül, how he was an emanation of Vairotsana, and so on, he became choked with emotion. He simply could not continue. He wept for 20 or 30 minutes. Then he started again, and again he broke down. I had never seen this happen before; he never lost himself in devotion like that. The empowerments took the whole morning; in fact, they were not completed until the middle of the afternoon. He used these four lines by Vairotsana as the basic structure for giving the instruction on how to embody the heart of the practice, the essential point of the training.

You hear about the vital unity of space and awareness, of *ying* and rigpa. Ying is the Tibetan term for *dhatu*, referring to dharmadhatu, the naked state of basic space. Dharmadhatu is not something you can think of, as it is not conceptual. The inconceivable, or literally 'un-imagined', dharmadhatu is not an object of thought. Within this basic state, without distraction, simply leave rigpa, which is ineffable. Leave inexpressible awareness undistractedly within that. A thought may arise out of yourself, but it dissolves into yourself. A thought moves out of your own awareness, but the moment you recognize what thinks, it dissolves within your own essence.

What is meant by basic space, dharmadhatu? It means uncon-structed, with no beginning, no present and no end. It has no name. It is beyond cause or condition, just like physical space. We have never been apart from unconstructed space, not for even one instant. It is the very nature of mind. It is the primordially empty and rootless innate nature, the nature of dharmata. All other things come from somewhere; they have a source, but unconstructed space does not. Failing to simply know that our nature is unconstructed space is called unknowing, ig-norance, marigpa. Knowing this with natural cognizance is called rigpa. Without the cognizant nature, which is indivisible from unconstructed space, there would be no ability to know the *reality of what is*. This in-divisibility is described as the unity of space and awareness, or the unity of space and wakefulness. The unity of these two qualities is also sym-bolized by Samantabhadra with his consort. Basic space is Samantabha-dri, and the wakefulness of knowing is Samantabhadra.

This unity is our true nature. The space quality is dharmakaya, the quality of self-knowing wakefulness is sambhogakaya, and the moment of acknowledging this unity is called nirmanakaya. In reality, the three kayas are our own nature. If you fail to recognize what is real, then con-ditioned experience takes over in an innumerable variety of ways. Ex-perience is then seen as objects perceived by a mind perceiving, giving rise to thoughts, emotions, the creation of karma and the states of samsaric existence which are endlessly produced in all kinds of different ways. This is called 'dharmata getting overtaken by dharmas', reality overtaken by conditioned phenomena. However, in the moment of recognizing your natural face, conditioned dharmas dissolve into dharmata.

Here's an analogy. In this world, you have day and night. Dharmata is like daytime, and conditioned dharmas are like night. During the day, the darkness has subsided, and you cannot find it anywhere. Likewise, the moment of not recognizing rigpa is like the daylight fading into darkness. This is of course a crude example, but the principle is that delusion vanishes the moment you recognize rigpa, just as darkness subsides at the break of day.

All of samsara and all of nirvana, all these states, take place nowhere other than within one single basic space. During all these myriad experiences, you *can* recognize your natural face. When recognizing this basic space, there is no other samsara to abandon, no other nirvana to accomplish. For ordinary sentient beings there is day and night. During the day darkness has subsided; at nighttime daylight has subsided. There are two different terms, day and night — but in actuality, there is only one basic space, which is sometimes dark, sometimes light. During the day, darkness is latent. Likewise, thoughts and confusion subside into latency. At night, it is light that is latent. Like light during the night, the wakefulness of knowing is still latent, potentially present, within the state of ignorance. It does not mean that rigpey yeshe disappears or is irretrievably lost; it is only latent during dualistic mind. After recognizing rigpa, training and attaining some stability, the thoughts vanish, much like the night disappears when the sun rises. For the Primordial Buddha — rigpa — there is no duality of samsara and nirvana. For someone who has not recognized at all, or has only glimpsed this, there is definitely day and night, samsara and nirvana. There is either being caught up in thinking, or there is a moment of rigpa. During either of these two times, the opposite state is latent.

To continue Vairotsana's verse: "If a thought arises, it arises out of yourself and dissolves into yourself." Thoughts do not come from some other place; they arise out of your own mind. If you know your nature, they dissolve into yourself as well, like drawing upon the surface of water. The drawing upon water and the dissolving of this drawing are simultaneous. Like the track left behind by a bird while flying through the sky, it is traceless.

"There is no basic view, meditation or instruction superior to this." The moment you recognize rigpa as the view, *this* is the meditation training, *this* is the conduct, and *this* is the fruition. At that moment, all of samsara and nirvana are subsumed within the state of rigpa, in one sweep. When you are fully stable in the recognition of rigpa, samsara has totally vanished into nirvana and there is neither distraction during day nor confusion during night. There is only one — the oneness of rigpa.

The actual meaning of meditation state in Buddhism, when using the term *nyamshak*, is equality, composure, equanimity. In the moment of recognizing rigpa there is no need to accept or reject, avoid or adopt, hope or fear. There is an evenness, regardless of the situation. The very basis for such equanimity is this present wakefulness, without which we would be corpses, only physical bodies, material forms. Yet now we are alive because of this present wakefulness. Once you recognize this present wakefulness that does not accept or reject, affirm or deny, hope or fear, that in itself is sufficient. It is not your mind from yesterday or from last night, tomorrow or next month. It is this very moment, right now. Where is it? Can you find it? Can you find this instant? Recognize this instantaneous wakefulness. Let your mind recognize itself, and immediately you know that there is no thing to be seen. This is just as Rangjung Dorje, the third Karmapa, sang:

> *When observing objects, they are seen to be the mind, devoid of objects.*
> *When observing the mind, there is no mind, as it is empty of an*
> *   entity.*
> *When observing both, dualistic fixation is spontaneously freed.*
> *May we realize the luminous nature of mind.*

When examining outer objects, you understand that there are no *real* objects — there is only the perceiving mind. Recognizing the nature of this mind, you find no entity. When looking into both subject and object, the fixation on duality dissolves; the existence of a concrete object and a separate concrete subject simply falls away. The duality of perceiver and perceived collapses.

"May we realize the luminous nature of mind." Here, 'luminous' refers to the fact that rigpa is empty and yet cognizant. Physical space cannot be lucid; it has no capacity to know either itself or something else. This is why rigpa is called 'unconfined empty cognizance suffused with knowing'. It is the unerring, original, natural state. If you do not contrive it in any way, but simply let be what it is, then right now the awakened state is spontaneously present. Your immediate, natural, present wakefulness is itself the true Samantabhadra.

In short, giving up doer and deed, rest in nondoing. When you train in giving up doer and deed you will approach nonaction. Doer and deed refers to the subject-object structure. When you recognize mind essence, do you find any place from which your thinking arises, any place where it dwells, any location into which it vanishes? Right then and there you have reached nonaction. Consider this: have you ever been able to find a place where space came out of? A place where it began? A place where it abides and into which it will disappear? This is described as 'devoid of mental constructs', 'beyond arising, dwelling and ceasing'. It is also called 'nonaction'. When something does not arise, dwell and cease, it is one hundred percent certain that it is empty.

So, mind is empty, but if it were *only* empty, it would be impossible to have pleasure and pain or the experiences of buddhafields and hells. Since they are definitely possible, it proves that mind is both empty and cognizant. Because of this there is samsara and nirvana, pleasure and pain, joy and sorrow — the results of virtuous actions, the higher realms and buddhafields, and the results of negative deeds, which are the three lower realms and the suffering that comes with these. There is samsara below, nirvana above; and in between, the path that is the karmic actions of good and evil. All this cannot be denied.

It is all like a dream. We have not yet woken up from the deep sleep of ignorance. Usually we dream while we sleep. The moment we wake up, we do not dream anymore. Buddhas and bodhisattvas are like somebody who has already awakened from sleep. There are all these different dreams — pleasant, unpleasant, fascinating, horrifying — but at the moment we wake up, where are they? Where do they go? Since they are just habitual tendencies, how can they come from anywhere or go anywhere? Similarly, all the different experiences that arise during the day take place within the framework of dualistic mind. The moment dualistic mind is suspended in rigpa — the moment thinking dissolves — the outcome is the wakefulness of knowing, rigpey yeshe, which is essence without thought.

I have told you the 'story of mind'. Now you need to train in the unfabricated present wakefulness that is only possible through recognition. Knowing how to recognize mind essence is similar to turning on the light. It doesn't come on unless you press the switch. When you have pressed the switch, when the light is on, you naturally meet empty cognizance suffused with knowing. This is exactly what sentient beings never do. They don't know how to recognize. They don't switch on their light. If they did, this one taste of empty cognizance suffused with knowing would automatically be present, because our own nature is dharmata; our essence is rigpa. But even if sentient beings do happen to glimpse the natural state, they do not know what it is — they fail to acknowledge it — and it turns into the indifferent state of the all-ground.

When you are face to face with your nature, if you do not begin any striving in terms of shamatha and vipashyana or ordinary confusion, you have already seen the essence of mind. It looks like no thing whatsoever. Because it is no 'thing' whatsoever, there is no thing that you can label or describe, no thing about which you can form concepts. It is beyond thought, word or description. This is *prajnaparamita*, transcendent knowledge, since it transcends any subject and any object to be known. Let me repeat again the famous quote:

Transcendent knowledge is beyond thought, word and description.
It neither arises nor ceases, like the identity of space.
It is the domain of individual self-knowing wakefulness.

To this mother of the buddhas of the three times, I pay homage.

Since it is within the individual domain of cognizant wakefulness, anyone can know it. 'Domain' here means that it is possible to recognize. What is recognized is not something that can be thought of, described, or illustrated through example. This knowing is the mother of the buddhas of the three times, named Prajnaparamita, the Great Mother. The experience quality of this is called the male buddha and the empty quality is the female buddha. Their unity is the primordial Buddha Samantabhadra with consort, also known as Changeless Light. There is a deep significance to his name, Changeless Light. The nature of Tögal is unchanging light. In colloquial terms, it is said that rigpa lives in a house of light, and that this mansion of light is the deities — the manifest aspect. The dharmakaya Samantabhadra lives in the house of the five buddha families, which is a mansion of light.

STUDENT: I know that I should mingle the practice with my daily life, but most people, myself included, seem to waste their lives not doing this. In order to become quickly adept, how should I structure my practice during the course of a day?

RINPOCHE: You must train in the 'three excellences'. First, when you sit down to practice, you need a support, which is to take refuge in the Three Jewels. This is the heart of Hinayana practice. Next, inspire yourself with bodhichitta, forming the resolve "May all sentient beings be free from suffering, may they all find happiness. May they all be brought to complete enlightenment!" This is the heart of Mahayana. In addition to this, remind yourself that your body is the mandala of the awakened ones. It is all right to think of yourself in the form of Buddha Shakyamuni or Guru Rinpoche or whoever your yidam is. Think that your voice is the essence of mantra. This can be OM MANI PADMA HUNG for Chenrezig, the Vajra Guru mantra for Padmasambhava, or TADYA-THA OM MUNI MUNI and so on for Buddha Shakyamuni. If you do not find any particular deity, it is perfectly all right just to chant OM AH HUNG SVAHA, which is the essence of all sugatas. By reciting this mantra, all physical presence becomes meaningful as the deity and the audible voice becomes meaningful as mantra.

To make mind meaningful, recognize your essence. Vividly and clearly see that there is no thing to see. When recognizing mind essence, it is neither hidden nor abstract. It is an actuality, a vivid presence that does not need to be analyzed. In this immediacy, past thought has already vanished and the future thought has not yet arrived. Do not follow up the present thought with a new one. This is what all sentient beings do, endlessly adding a new thought to the present one. When there is no adding of another thought, the link is broken and that moment is free of the three times: there is no past, no future and no following up of the present. When free from the constructs of the three times, that itself is pure awareness, the nature of mind. This is called 'naturally sealing experience during daytime'.

This is actually the first part of an instruction called 'four sessions that equalize buddhahood'. The first, 'sealing experience during daytime', means that you should simply recognize the essence of awareness during the day. When the movements of the prana-mind dissolve into original wakefulness, the process of inhalation and exhalation completely stops. To initiate this, leave the breathing slightly exhaled. The image for this is that of a sitar with the strings broken. Then, leave the mind without any involvement in thoughts of past, present and future, just like a water-wheel from which the water flow has been diverted. Regard whatever you experience, good or bad, just as an old man watches the play of children, in a state free from both hope and fear. Remain in stable awareness.

I will briefly mention the remaining three aspects, then discuss them in detail. Next are the two for nighttime: 'at dusk, spontaneously withdraw the senses' and, 'at night, retain wakefulness in the vase'. The first of these is for the early evening and the other is for nighttime, so, dusk and night. 'At dawn revive the natural awareness' is to propel the letter AH up while shouting HAH into the sky, which is said to clarify awareness.

To go into more detail, one should practice tummo as it grows dark. Tummo is based on the A-HANG and the visualization of fire with the blissful heat. The red element manifesting below the navel in the form of the short A has the nature of heat and is the essence of Vajra Varahi. The white element in the form of the syllable HANG turned upside down at the top of the central channel is the nature of bliss, and the very essence of Chakrasamvara. These two aspects, the red and white *bindu*, are called the 'basic body'. They are Vajra Varahi and Chakrasamvara, and are originally present from the moment the body is formed. Once you have received instructions from a master, you can practice tummo in depth. In short, the practice of blazing and dripping produces the blissful heat.

Through the tummo practice, imagine that all your negative karma created through body, speech, mind and their combination, as well as all your obscurations and habitual tendencies, are completely and utterly purified, completely burned away. An offering of blissful emptiness is given to the dakas and dakinis who dwell inside your body, within the channels, winds and essences. Your body becomes flawless, immaculate like a crystal ball. Practice this form of tummo from dusk throughout the evening. In this context of 'four sessions that equalize buddhahood', although the main part is effortless, you initially need to exert a slight effort to advance the state of effortlessness.

At night, 'retain wakefulness in the vase'. This entails imagining the brilliant syllable AH in a four-petaled lotus flower in the center of the heart, in order to facilitate recognition of the luminosity of sleep. When going to sleep, lie in the posture of the reclining Buddha, the position in which he passed away, which is also called 'the posture of a sleeping lion'. Put the right hand under the right cheek and the left hand on your thigh, and stretch out your legs parallel to each other. You do not have to imagine your body in any particular form at that time; it is as it naturally is. The most important part of your body is your heart; so in your heart center imagine a four-petaled lotus flower. This is not a physical form but a luminous red four-petaled lotus flower within which is the letter AH, one inch in size, symbolizing mind. Just as an electric light bulb lights up the interior of a room, this syllable AH lights up the interior of your body, radiating light through it to the distance of an arrow that has been shot from a bow. While your mind remains in rigpa, it shines further, illuminating the whole area around you — 'the whole valley', as it says in the text. The manifest quality is the form of development stage called 'completion stage with attributes'. In this way, go to sleep while visualizing the brilliant AH in your heart center. While your mind rests in rigpa, within that state, gently fall asleep.

In the beginning, you do fall unconscious for a while, you do sleep. Yet within that sleep there is always the possibility of recognizing the nature of mind. When that happens, it's called 'capturing the luminosity during deep sleep'. Experience is unblocked, wide open. Although you do not visibly see what is around you and your body is still asleep, it's like a wide-awake state occurs from within the deep sleep. With training, it is possible to become used to that. Again, one initially visualizes, then simply rests in the state without any focus.

The fourth instruction is 'at dawn revive the natural awareness'. This is done by sitting up straight the moment you wake up and exclaiming "HAH!" At the same time, you imagine that the letter A at your heart center shoots up and emerges through the crown of your head into the sky above you. It is brilliantly and vividly present in visible form. Until it starts to fade, simply focus your attention on it. At the same time, recognize mind essence, so that space and rigpa become indivisibly mingled. Finally, when it begins to dissolve by itself, imagine that it grows in size to become inseparable from the vastness of space. This is a support for all-pervasive wakefulness. This kind of focus is completely free from fixation. Rest in the unfixated state of awareness. There are two types of focus, with and without fixation. In general, when we practice the development stage that is called focus with fixation. The focus that we have in the Dzogchen system is focus without fixation.

These four instructions, 'sealing experience during daytime', 'gathering the senses within at dusk', 'retaining knowledge in the vase at midnight' and 'reviving natural awareness at dawn', are called 'the four sessions that equalize buddhahood'. These are the four sessions of day and night. Equalizing buddhahood means that if you can practice these four you are never apart from the buddhas. When you train in equalizing buddhahood throughout the four periods of day and night, don't force or push during any of these. Everything is gentle and relaxed. Because mind itself is emptiness, it cannot be forced. To do so does not help, does it?

To conclude the three excellences, remember to always, every day, every evening, every morning, dedicate the outcome, the goodness of the practice and make aspirations. Regardless of whatever yidam practice you have, always remember to dedicate the merit.

STUDENT: I have the feeling that unless I spend time in retreat, I will not be able to gain accomplishment in the Dharma. But in my situation I am unable to remain uninterruptedly in retreat. I regret this, having received such profound instructions. What should I do?

RINPOCHE: It's actually good to feel frustrated. The next thing is to act upon that feeling. If you do not feel regret or a sense of loss, you will never practice in retreat. We hear how the great masters of the past practiced in their lives. They in turn advised their disciples to be a 'child of the mountain' and regard the wild deer as their companions. Be like that if you want to emulate their example.

On the other hand, we do not seem really to be able to do so. There are problems and obstacles to practice in our lives. You should therefore try to meet the ideal half way: for instance, stay six months in and six months out of retreat every year. Or, every three months do a retreat. As you train further and further in the practice, it becomes less difficult. You could also do intensive practice for two months, come out to work and make money, then return to retreat. That may be more practical. It is difficult to give up everything and go live in caves in the mountains.

In particular, it is not so easy if you already have a family and people who depend on you, financially and emotionally. If you abandon them, they will feel sad. If you are in that situation, you cannot leave them for good. Still it is not impossible to do retreat. Do two months of practice then, as I just suggested.

There is a reason why all the buddhas and masters of the past always encouraged practitioners to seek remote places to practice in solitude. The simple reason is that in such places there are fewer distractions. In ordinary life we very easily become caught up in all sorts of pursuits and tasks that consume our attention to such an extent that we do not find any real progress in samadhi. By staying in quiet places, half of the distractions are already cut off. That is the reason why all the buddhas have said, "Stay in mountain solitude, or in the jungle."

The Buddha himself, by his life example, showed the way for future practitioners by leaving behind his kingdom, his palace and all its many luxuries. He did so with no more attachment than if they were a glob of spit. Once we have spat it out, after it is lying there in the dust, we'll never try to take the spit back, will we? That is the traditional example that the Buddha gave for practitioners. If it were not the example to emulate, he would not have acted like that. If there were another way to be, he would have done it in that way. He would have set a different example.

There is a very clear reason for this. For beginningless lifetimes we have been completely ingrown in this habit of incessantly linking three things together: sense organs, sense objects and cognitions. Honestly, there is hardly as much as one instant during twenty-four hours when an ordinary person truly remains in uncontrived naturalness. This is the exact opposite habit of Dharma practice. We need to train in the habit of samadhi. In the beginning it seems very difficult. Unless we give up our normal tasks and distance ourselves somewhat from them, we will have no opportunity to change our mind's deep-rooted negative habits. It simply won't happen.

This is why all the buddhas and great masters encourage people to seek out quiet places to grow stable in the recognition of their buddha nature. The Mahamudra tradition tells us that by practicing the 'three-fold solitude' one grows closer to and realizes the innate three vajras. The Dzogchen tradition tells us to abandon the ninefold activities. This profound and amazing instruction is not easy to follow while involved in ordinary life. That is the reason why all the great masters encourage practitioners to stay in retreat.

STUDENT: How do we structure a Trekchö retreat? How do we divide the day into sessions and establish some structure to that?

RINPOCHE: You need to learn the principles of a *gomdra*, a meditation retreat. A gomdra is not the same as a *drubdra*, which means a sadhana retreat. In meditation retreat, people often sit outside. One should make the retreat moderate, not too strenuous or harsh. That is very important. Sit for up to three hours at a time in one stretch — somewhere in that vicinity. Most people cannot sit from dawn to dusk; they need to have breaks for toilet and for meals. They also need to relax. If you structure a retreat to involve sitting continuously from morning to evening, most people will get fed up and leave that kind of practice behind. It will not be successful. The Buddha said the outer form of the training should be adapted to the time and place of the country. In other words, it should be suited to the people who are in that area.

Even though a practitioner may wish to begin a retreat, not everybody has totally resolved mind essence and 'established the natural state'. If there is no master present there to point it out, you should have received the instruction previously, so that if there is no other teacher, you can be your own teacher. If there is nobody else to guide you, you should think over what your guru taught. Additionally, study the meditation manuals. Find out how the teachings fit with your own experience, until you become totally clear about rigpa. Examine your own experience, until you find that it is completely free from any fixation on subject and object. That is how, from within, you can be your own guide. At a certain point, you should arrive at certainty, so that even if you meet with a hundred panditas and they say you are wrong, you will have no doubt whatsoever. Nobody can give you that certainty from outside. Whether you are with a teacher or by yourself, the real teacher is always yourself and your experience. In the final analysis, you are responsible for, first of all, understanding what is said, and second, being clear about whether or not your experience is the same as what was explained.

The essential point of rigpa training is like this: Without meditating upon something 'over there', rest freely. Without holding tight to 'something here', be all-pervasive. Without dwelling on anything in between, remain in total openness. These three — resting freely, being pervasive and being wide open — are the three essential points of rigpa. Any other meditation training is usually stuck in either thinking that there is an object to keep in mind 'over there' or concentrating on something inwardly. If one is not concentrating on anything here or there, one usually thinks there is a state to be retained in between. That becomes like conventional shamatha practice.

Letting go of these three reference points, there is total transparency, a complete openness that is an essential point of rigpa. In Tibetan it is called *zangtal*, which means unimpededness. It's just like the window here: through it, you can unobstructedly see throughout the whole valley. Another analogy is of a sieve, which allows poured liquid to flow straight through, not kept in any way whatsoever. When training in rigpa, that quality of unimpeded openness should be understood as being the most essential. In other words, do not fixate outwardly, rest freely. Do not focus inwardly. Do not hold a reference point in between. That is zangtal.

Now I will tell a story about a gomdra in Eastern Tibet. Once the second incarnation of Chokgyur Lingpa was invited to Dzogchen monastery, where they also had a drubdra. My father, Chimey Dorje, went together with the Chokling Tulku as his attendant. It is from him that I have the story. In the gomdra were about sixty meditators, who all practiced outside. These sixty meditators would sit outside in groups of five or six in lines with straight backs. Both behind and in front of their heads, at a level just below their necks, were strands of thin thread suspended between two poles. If they fell asleep and their head moved either forward or backward, the thread would break. At that point the gomdra disciplinarian would come and say, "Hey you, you broke the thread!"

In that kind of practice, one should not move the body even one inch during the actual session period. During rigpa, one should completely let be. Moreover one is not supposed to move the eyes. For beginners it is difficult not to blink, but eventually one can remain without moving the eyelids. To ensure that the meditators were actually keeping to that, the disciplinarian at the gomdra would sometimes put red *sindhura* powder below their eyelids. If they blinked, then some red powder would stick on their eyelashes, providing evidence that they had blinked. Even there at the gomdra though, they did not sit in one continuous stretch from morning to evening. They also had sessions. This is an example of the training in totally giving up the ninefold activities.

11

Dining with Indra

❖

Without fixating on anything, leave awareness in unsupported space. Rigpa is unidentifiable. A reference point could be the notion, "This is rigpa being sustained." If there is a reference point, a focus, there is no transparency like the openness of space. When you aim a rifle at a target that is called a reference point. How are you going to aim at the sky? There is no focus to target. If there is an objective like "Now this is rigpa and I am aiming at it", it becomes conceptual, confined. To repeat, there are three characteristics of rigpa: freely resting by not imagining something as being there, the pervasiveness of not focusing on something within, and the unimpededness, the total openness, of not placing yourself in any sort of state in between. Here is a very important statement in the *Bodhicharya Avatara* by Shantideva that expresses the final view of the Middle Way:

> *When concreteness or inconcreteness*
> *Does not remain before the intellect,*
> *At that moment there is no other mental form,*
> *And so, there is utter peace without conceptions.*

In the notes on the commentary to *Lamrim Yeshe Nyingpo,* the illustrious master Ju Jamyang Drakpa explained concreteness and inconcreteness as being the notions of existence and nonexistence. In terms of experience, whether one holds the thought that rigpa is a thing that exists or a thing that is nothing, both are thoughts. When not holding any notion, there is nothing else whatsoever held in mind. In other words, to be totally free of focus, free from fixation, is the real view. Nagarjuna said,

> To hold the idea that it exists is to be as deluded as an animal.
> But to hold the idea that it is nothing is to be even more deluded.

One does not need to hold the thought that rigpa is inconcrete, nor that rigpa is an ongoing entity, because whether one thinks one way or the other, both are concepts. As long as there is some notion or reference point, it covers the nakedness, the original free state of openness, which is rigpa.

We need to be free from ideas of both permanence and nihilism. Permanence means to believe that some entity is forever, while nihilism is to believe that there is nothing at all. If one falls into either of these two extremes, fixation on some concept is occurring. We need to be free from that. That is why Ju Jamyang Drakpa spoke about the state of mind that holds nothing, neither the notion of existence nor of non-existence. When nothing is held, mind is not caught up in thinking. Everything is included within these three statements:

> Freely resting is to not imagine something out there.
> Pervasiveness is to not bind something in here.
> Unimpededness is to not dwell on some state in between.

That is how rigpa is described: not imagining there, not tying down something here, and not dwelling on anything in between. In all three instances, there is an absence of conceptual attitude.

'Freely resting' means that you do not focus or meditate on something as being there. 'Pervasiveness' means to not tie down something as being here within you. 'Unimpededness' or openness is to not dwell on something in between. One could also say: do not project outwardly, do not concentrate inwardly and do not place your attention in some state in between. When not doing any of these, that is the view. That is sufficient. Do not project outwardly. Do not concentrate inwardly. Do not place your mind in between. Then there is nothing to do. You have arrived at nondoing. Isn't that true?

If you tell somebody: "Don't go outside, don't stay inside, and don't remain in between, either!" what is that person going to do? There is absolutely nothing to do, right? The view is nondoing, which means it is not a 'thing' to be done. We need to realize this view of nondoing, and abandon the view of things to be carried out. 'Doing' refers to where there is some doer and some deed. If you give up both doer and deed, then what? Once doer and deed have been abandoned, what is left is the true nature of doer and deed, which is Samantabhadra and Samantabhadri, who have nothing to do at all. There is nothing to be done; there is simply thatness. That is the view we need to realize.

Ultimately, as long as we try to imagine, visualize or meditate, we still tie ourselves down. As beginners we cannot help it. Initially we do need to meditate with some effort in order to approach the state of effortlessness. It is said that "the path of effort leads to effortlessness." In the Middle Way, this deliberate effort to meditate is called mindfulness. Mindfulness is attentive, in that there is a sense of being alert, conscientious and careful. Finally, the mindfulness becomes free from the four limits and eight constructs. According to Mahamudra, this effort is called watchfulness. Watchfulness is like a herdsman who keeps his eye on the cattle, who pays attention to whether they drink water or eat grass. Emphasizing watchfulness entails noticing how the mind is. You need somebody to keep watch on that. In the Dzogchen tradition it is called awakeness, in which mindfulness and awareness are indivisible. At this point mindfulness and rigpa-awareness are not two different things.

Dzogchen training is free of an observer and something observed. Awakeness in Dzogchen is devoid of the subtle subject-object construct that is normally retained in mindfulness. In Dzogchen, mindfulness is rigpa, rigpa is mindfulness. When the light has been switched on, it shines by itself. This is the final outcome of all the different approaches: once the light is switched on, we do not need to do anything. For the light to come on, of course, you seem to need two things: the switch on the wall and the act of pressing it. Awakeness is like the light that is naturally shining. This is the point at which mindfulness becomes effortless, after deliberate mindfulness has faded away. In short, this is the essence of the three great views: mindfulness, watchfulness and awakeness.

Honestly, for a beginner, without the mindfulness of reminding, there is no recognition of mind essence. That is called deliberate mindfulness. It is dualistic mind that reminds you to recognize, but the seeing of no thing to be seen is rigpa, the awakened state free of duality. This becomes clearly discerned through practical experience. In other words, a yogi can distinguish the difference between these two, while a beginner cannot. Therefore, in the beginning it is indispensable to be 'remindful'. After all, rigpa has been caught up in *sem*, dualistic mind, from beginningless lifetimes. The essence has been lost in its expression.

To be lost in the expression, or to fail to make the distinction between essence and expression, is like confusing sunlight for sun. If you ask what the sun is, some people are not quite sure whether it's the sunlight or the sphere up in the sky. Then someone else will have to say, "No, this light here is not the sun itself — look up in the sky." You look and see the sun, and you reply, "Oh yeah, that's the real thing." That is the example for the difference between essence and expression. Ordinary beings are caught up in the expression, the thinking. They mistake the light that shines in the world for the sun. If we examine the situation closely, however, we will come to the conclusion that the light is not the sun itself. The sun itself is in the sky. Even though its manifestation, its expression, may appear simultaneously in hundreds of thousands of different ponds of water, all these appearances are only reflections, not the sun itself.

Can we distinguish between the thing itself and its reflection? To be enlightened, we must see the difference between essence and expression. Sentient beings are caught up in their expression, while their essence is unconfined empty cognizance. The mind of sentient beings is of course always unconfined empty cognizance, but their cognizance grasps at subject and object. Where no duality exists, they apprehend a duality. Samsara goes on endlessly due to this dualistic fixation. Buddhas and bodhisattvas do not grasp at any duality, because they have recognized the essence itself. Therefore, they are not caught up in their expression, and they remain as essence. In short, the difference between the mind of a sentient being and the buddha mind is the difference between being carried away by the expression or being stable in the essence.

Buddha mind is the unity of being empty and cognizant, utterly without fixation. The mind of a sentient being is the unity of being empty and cognizant, with fixation. Isn't the difference thus fixating or not fixating? What is meant by fixating here? Fixation is like believing that the reflection of the sun in the water is the sun itself. Buddhas and bodhisattvas are like someone who understands that the sun in the sky is the actual sun, and therefore are not deceived by its manifestation. If you recognize its source while the expression unfolds, you reach the essence. If you follow after what is being thought of, you get lost in the expression. For the expression to dawn as insight, you have to recognize the essence. It's like acknowledging the sun itself. If you think that the reflection is the sun, you will never see the actual sun, only its reflections.

To reiterate, an ordinary person is someone who thinks that the reflection is the real sun. The sun and its light are indivisible. The identity of any thought is the unity of empty cognizance, but there is no knowing of that. If the attention is focused on the reflection, there is a subject and object. This is how duality occurs, and this is what is meant by the phrase 'appearances deceive'. When there is water, there is the possibility of a reflection occurring. Something reflected and the place of reflection — that is duality. In the moment of recognizing the sun itself, however, there is no duality. The mind of a sentient being pursues and gets caught up in the reflections of his or her own mind. That is samsara: being caught up in the fixation on subject and object.

A true yogi is someone who cuts the movement of attention in this first stage. Instead of mistaking the reflection in water as being the sun, he recognizes the sun itself from the very first. Recognizing the real thing, our empty cognizance, is called recognizing mind essence. If you face away from the sun, following after its reflection in water, you can continue to do this for one billion aeons without ever seeing the real sun. Thoughts become endless, unceasing, through the repeated connection of subject and object, like observing the reflections on the water's clear surface. Buddhas and bodhisattvas cut the mental movement in its initial stage. Before attention moves towards an object, there is recognition. Then there is no need to be caught up in the falsehood, in the illusion. Without straying into mental movement, how can any samsara be created? When there is no duality of perceiver and perceived, what can create samsara?

The empty quality of mind essence is like space; the cognizant quality is like sunlight. The unity of these is like sunlit space, like daytime sky. This kind of sky is the example for what we call basic space; and the knowing of that is rigpa. The indivisible unity of basic space and rigpa is Samantabhadra, the original buddha. Realizing this is called the awakening in the ground, the original state. This is exactly what we sentient beings have failed to realize. We confused the ground of the basic state, and got caught up in believing that the reflection of the sun in water is the sun itself. The water is like the three realms. The subject is the six types of sentient beings who roam around, like the reflection moving on water. In short, we were caught up in falsehood. That has happened to us right up until today.

The bottom line here is knowing how to recognize mind essence. Recognizing is nirvana; not recognizing is samsara. If you do not know where to look for the sun, how will you ever see it? This is how all sentient beings are: they possess buddha nature, but do not acknowledge what they already have. We already have the real sun in ourselves. We slip into holding onto subject and object, perceiver and perceived, just like believing the reflection is the actual sun, which it is not. It will never be the actual sun, ever. A yogi is someone who does not believe that the reflection is the actual truth, and therefore knows how to see the sun. For such a person, there is no duality of perceiver and perceived. Without having to let the attention move towards an object, before his attention moves, its essence is already seen. Sentient beings do not cut the movement in its initial stage; instead, they pursue what is thought of. Apart from seeing its essence, this movement cannot be stopped. Without seeing the essence, thought movement goes on and on, like ripples on water or beads on a string, one after the other, from beginningless time until now — thinking of one thing, thinking of the next, thinking of another, and so forth, endlessly.

The genuine view lies in the manner of looking. If you lost yourself, how would you ever find yourself by looking in another place? If you are lost, where can you run to, and how far, to find yourself? In Dzogchen this is called 'tracking the footprints in the jungle while the elephant is inside your house'.

If you want to condense everything into one point: just recognize your own mind. Exclaiming the syllable PHAT, belonging to the precious word empowerment, can sometimes facilitate this. When the thoughts of the three times have collapsed, nothing other than the essence is left. Everything we can remember, think of, or plan belongs to thoughts of past, present or future. When exclaiming a forceful PHAT, most people become spaced out, go blank, disengaged. If there is no recognition of the essence, just being disengaged becomes a neutral, indifferent state. But the identity of this disengagement, if you recognize it, is free of thoughts of the three times. If you recognize, you are not caught up in feeling spaced out. But if you get absorbed into feeling spaced out or disengaged, you fall into being mindless. This is the unaware aspect of the all-ground, from which nothing but samsara unfolds.

In the moment of exclaiming PHAT, free of thoughts of the three times, the quality of recognizing needs to be present, so that one is not merely unaware or mindless. It's not like somebody knocks you out with an iron bar, in which case there is absolutely no recognition. Being mindless is simply stupidity. In it, there is no like and dislike, which are two of the three poisons. In mindlessness, however, the third poison, stupidity, is present. The opposite of stupidity is the quality of knowing after recognizing rigpa.

When exclaiming PHAT, the yogi recognizes rigpa. Practice this, and you are a true meditator. If someone who is not a meditator shouts PHAT, it does not help a bit. Some charlatan yogis in Kham played the role really well. They had long hair tied up on their heads, and their eyes gazed into space. They would look vacantly at you and say, "Don't you see that everything is merely mind, and whatever is mind is empty. Everything is the magical display of mind! Can't you see that?" Then, saying, "Now I will introduce you to rigpa," they shouted PHAT forcefully. But in order to introduce someone to rigpa, you have to recognize it yourself and be in a state of rigpa. If the master is a fraud and the student is not ready, shouting PHAT is nothing other than taking a snapshot of dualistic mind!

Unless you are stable in the essence, this table is not experienced as being empty. *(Rinpoche knocks on his wooden table)*. If you *are* stable in the essence you do not sink into water; you are not burnt by fire; earth does not impede you. A pretentious yogi who says, "All appearances are mind, everything is empty," is not at this level of realization. That is only an imagined emptiness. If it *is* a reality for you, if it is evident that all appearances are empty, then your mind does not fixate on anything. As proof of that, at death you depart from this body as rainbow light. The body is rainbow and all appearances are transparent. You can move freely through mountains or walls. Although everything is unimpeded in the yogi's own experience, it is not like that at all in the general experience of ordinary people. A realized yogi can do anything — swim through water like a fish, fly in the sky like a bird — because his body is like a rainbow. When Padmasambhava and his twenty-five disciples left Tibet, there was not a single corpse left behind anywhere. At Yerpa, in Central Tibet, he had eighty siddha disciples, and at other places thirty-five realized ones and twenty-five dakinis, all of whom attained rainbow body.

Many of the masters of the four major and eight lesser Kagyü schools could also fly like birds, unfurling their shawls like wings to soar through the sky. Among these masters were three men from Kham who were disciples of Gampopa; one of them was called Seltong Shogom.⁶ Above the residence of the king of Nangchen is a cave where Seltong Shogom became invisible and attained the celestial body. The dakinis created a stupa there made out of sand, according to the *Kadam* proportions. The distance up to the stupa in the cave is equivalent to thirteen stories. People later had to build a fifteen-story temple in order to reach the stupa. This siddha had five hundred disciples who could also fly with him. Today you can still see where they landed: they left a whole cluster of footprints in the rock, fifty or sixty altogether. In the morning, when they flew towards the west, all the footprints faced towards the west. When they flew back in the afternoon, all the footprints faced towards the east. When you see all these footprints, you are amazed. This is not merely a story. There were also many, many accomplished yogi and yoginis in the Drikung and Drukpa Kagyü School. Their accomplishments were possible because they had attained mastery in samadhi.

STUDENT: How do I maintain the state of awareness without losing the view or falling into shamatha?

RINPOCHE: The Buddha was asked by Ananda, "Please tell me how to keep the view of emptiness, I am having a hard time, not only mentally but also physically, in terms of breathing and so on. It is not an easy thing to keep the view of emptiness." Ananda continued, "If I focus, I get really tight, and it becomes very difficult. But if I relax, I forget and start to think of other things. What should I do?"

The Buddha said, "You used to know how to play the sitar; is that correct?"

Ananda answered, "Yes, I knew that very well."

The Buddha continued, "How did you get the perfect sound from each string? Was it by tightening it especially tight, or by leaving it slack?"

Ananda replied "No, neither by tightening it nor by loosening it, but by keeping a perfect balance in between."

The Buddha said, "Well then, you already know. That is exactly how to maintain the view of emptiness."

Ananda said, "I understand."

If we totally let go, we become forgetful, and if we tighten too hard on a focus, we create both physical and mental difficulties. So, just as the Buddha taught is how you should practice! Maybe you know how to play guitar; do you know how to tune it? What is best, to tighten the strings really tight or to leave them slack?

STUDENT: Best is in the middle.

RINPOCHE: Right! That is how the Buddha taught. If we totally relax and let go, the practice slips away into distraction. We need to focus on that which is like space. But how can you concentrate on space? Try to grab hold of space for a long time. Is there any other result than a tired hand? That is the only thing you achieve. So, it is not by tightening. But if you totally let go, you are carried away by distraction, and the practice dissipates. Isn't that true? Instead, do just as Ananda said: "Not by tightening too much, not by leaving it too slack, but in a balanced way." This is how you should train in emptiness.

STUDENT: Are there some tricks practitioners can use to remember to be mindful in-between sessions, like when I'm caught up in my daily life activities, work and so on? Each time I remember to be mindful, I realize it has been such a long time since I was last aware. It's a little embarrassing for me. I wondered are there any tricks to apply for re-membering.

RINPOCHE: Okay, here's a question for you. When you see a little bird eating a piece of grain, it immediately looks up and does like this with its head *(Rinpoche demonstrates a bird looking around while eating)*. It's doing this all the time. Why does it do that?

STUDENT: It's afraid of the hawks flying overhead.

RINPOCHE: Yes. We can easily spend our whole life in the 'black diffusion' of confused thinking, which is much more dangerous than those hawks. There is a much greater loss involved here than a bird's life. Just as the fear reminds the bird to look, look, let the fear of mindlessness remind you. If you dread that hawk of unaware dissipation and keep it acutely in mind, you will remind yourself repeatedly, just like the little bird. When reminding, immediately recognize mind essence. If you don't remind yourself, who else is going to do it? If you don't get yourself onto dry land, who else is going to get you out of the water? What is most important for you: the work you are carried away by in this life, or attaining liberation and enlightenment?

STUDENT: Attaining liberation and enlightenment.

RINPOCHE: What's the actual purpose of the work we do in this life? First, to hoard money; next, to protect it from disappearing; then, to increase the stockpile. Those are the three occupations of a worldly person: to gather wealth, to keep it, and to increase it. Our primary efforts in this life are to make money and to pursue the enjoyments we can buy with the money. People undertake an enormous amount of trouble in order to first gather money. Next, they must protect it from being stolen or otherwise disappearing. And we are never happy with what we have; we need to have more and more and more. Our investment has to grow. Isn't it true that this activity only makes you continue in samsara? How ridiculous! No amount of capital can buy you enlightenment and liberation! Isn't that one hundred percent true?

What is most important to you? Is it more important to get rich, or to realize the innate nature through meditation and be totally free from suffering? Usually we are afraid of suffering and hope for pleasure. All this samsaric pleasure and pain, all this hope and fear — what can they do for us? Pleasure can help in this life, but not in the next life, or in future lives. The state of samadhi, the recognition of your innate nature and stability in that, can eradicate the pain of suffering for all your future lives. You won't even hear the word 'suffering' in future lives; you will go from one happy state to the next. Which of these has the highest value, the greatest benefit?

STUDENT: The latter.

RINPOCHE: Samadhi, that's it! You do not have to hoard samadhi, you do not have to keep the state of samadhi, you do not have to increase it

— you can totally let go of it at the moment of recognition. It's like Paltrül Rinpoche said: "Give up, give up everything; that is to work for the welfare of beings." Don't you have enough food and clothing right now? Your body is healthy, right? Realize that there is nothing more to hoard, nothing more to keep; there is nothing more to increase. Otherwise, you become a slave to your wealth and enjoyments. The outcome of that is more samsara, the three realms and the three miserable states.

Other than giving up hoarding and enlarging your amount of wealth, there is nothing to do, right? There is not much busyness involved in this. When you become stable in the unemployed state of mind essence, you automatically rise above the three realms of samsara, and even above Indra, king of the gods. You are more wide open, more carefree. It's like the famous saying: "Wherever you go, the sun of happiness shines. Whoever you are with, you are totally at ease." Isn't that an advantage, a good outcome? Do you want to take another rebirth in samsara, again die, then again be reborn? Is that what you want?

STUDENT: No.

RINPOCHE: I am teasing you.

STUDENT: That was a true practitioner's trick.

RINPOCHE: You understand — thank you very much! Someone who understands this deserves to be called a practitioner. Such a person will rise above this world. You can sit next to Indra, the king of the gods, and share his meal. Wouldn't that be better than lunching next to the Lord of Death with his ox-headed and goat-headed minions, which is what one faces after death? The only thing you will worry about in that situation is, "Where are they going to take me after this!" It is much better to sit next to Indra and eat happily.

So, we have these two roads, and only one goes upward. I used Indra as an example, but he is still within samsara. There are even better places to go than that, like the nirmanakaya or sambhogakaya buddha-fields. The other road leads downwards. When the ox-headed and goat-headed henchmen of the Lord of Death put their ropes around you and drag you down into the hell of the incessant torment, what will that be like? Right now we are at the dividing point of these two roads. What are you going to choose?

STUDENT: I want to go upwards!

RINPOCHE: You have the choice right now. It is in your power to go up if you want, or to go down. Right now you are at the fork in the road. This is not my invention. This is how all buddhas and bodhisattvas teach it to be. The choice is yours. They also say that, "Alas, there is nothing more foolish than to ignore Dharma practice after having attained the precious human body." That would be like orchestrating one's own defeat, like sponsoring one's own poisoning. It would be like reaching the top of the mountain only to throw oneself into the abyss.

Please practice! As I said earlier, it is much better to dine next to the king of the gods. Yet Indra and the other kings of the gods are still in samsara. To compare Indra to the Buddha is like comparing the little finger with the thumb. There is a difference as wide as the sky. Indra is not enlightened. Through this instruction, we can be enlightened, and go beyond the state of Indra, the king of the gods. Bodhisattvas, like us, should aim at buddhahood. I am teasing you. Yet, while teasing, there is some meaning.

Please practice well! If you train well and become more stable, you will not have much trouble in this life. This life doesn't have to be that difficult. Be carefree. The aims, the tasks and projects in this life are like dreams, like illusions. An ordinary person gets overwhelmed and depressed when things go bad, and totally carried away by excitement when successful. We do not have to be like that. To be like an ordinary person is difficult, definitely. Poor people have the trouble of being poor, wealthy people have the problem of being rich. Nobody is happy. Nobody thinks they have enough, ever. Poor people suffer from not having enough. Rich people cannot stay together without being jealous of one another, they also are not happy. Rich people never feel "Now I have enough."

My uncle, Tersey Tulku, told me, "Never compare yourself with someone above you, because you will never be happy. There will always be someone richer or more powerful, better than you are. Much better to measure yourself against those below you. If you compare yourself with poor people you think, 'I'm well off, I am actually okay'. Otherwise you will never be content." My uncle often said, "Take a lower example. Then you are happier. Don't look at someone higher than yourself, you will never be happy." If you want to be happy in this life, compare yourself with beggars. They walk around with one stick and one backpack begging for their food. If you compare yourself with someone like that, you are always content.

STUDENT: How do we cut the thought upon arising?

RINPOCHE: By recognizing mind essence. At that same moment, the viewer dissolves to reveal the awakened state. The viewer here is the same as sem, the dualistic frame of mind. One disappears; one is left behind. Sem disappears; the three and five poisons vanish, right? The outcome of that is rigpa. When a yogi recognizes mind essence, the thought movement is cut in its initial stage. What else is there to do? Does it help to sit and think, "I'm not going to get involved in any more thoughts. I will not think. I do not like this thinking. I'm going to blow up one hundred thousand nuclear bombs to make an end to the thinking." It just doesn't help. Please understand this very well. Can a hundred thousand nuclear bombs stop the minds of sentient beings from thinking? Luckily you don't have to do that; simply recognize the essence of the thinker, which is empty cognizance. While seeing this empty and cognizant essence, the thinking dissolves. This is the only way. The thinking is the expression of your mind: it does not come from any other place. While seeing the essence, the expression dissolves. That is why it is taught that we are our own best remedy. Your thoughts do not come from any other place; they are an expression of your own essence. While seeing the essence, the expression has dissolved.

The very basis or root of a thought is your essence. Seeing its empti-ness dissolves its expression: the thought has gone, collapsed. If your thinking were not the expression of your essence, you would have to do something else. If it came from some other location, you'd have to stop it at that other place. But where do the three realms of samsara come from? They are an expression of our own essence. Without knowing the essence of this expression, we roam continuously in samsara. There is no other cause.

All the different worlds, all the different experiences, all the differ-ent types of beings, are all expressions of this essence. It is the essence being unstable in itself and straying into the expression that allows all of this to come about. The moment you recognize the identity of that which expresses, you dissolve the three realms of samsara. Instead, unfold the dharmakaya realms, the sambhogakaya realms and the nirmanakaya realms. These most wonderful names are realized through recognizing this essence. Not recognizing the essence unfolds the realms of desire, the realms of form and the formless realms. The pleas-ure and pain, joys and sorrows of sentient beings, all arise because they do not recognize their essence and instead get caught up in their ex-pression.

You know the psychedelic drugs hippies used to take, which gave them all kinds of hallucinations? None of those visions actually exist anywhere. They are only the magical displays of mind. When this magic dissolves, it is like waking up from sleep. When you wake up in the morning, there is nothing left of the dreams you had last night. The Buddha taught that everything is like magic, like a dream. It's difficult to understand the analogy of magic, because nowadays there are no true magicians; they are only these tricksters from India. In the past there were real magicians, as I have told you.

However, you do know dreams, don't you? If you dreamed that you found a lot of money, or that you were enthroned as the king of the whole world, what happens to this the moment you wake up? Is there any reality to any of that? Or maybe you dream you are killed, and your body is thrown in a river. Yet when you wake up, you are still lying in your bed. Why is that? It is because you were only dreaming. We dream because we are asleep; in this state, all the illusory events seem to really happen. Likewise, the waking state unfolds during the 'sleep of deluded thinking'; everything we experience is like a dream. Buddhas are someone for whom deluded experience has been cleared up. They are awakened from this dream. That is why the analogy of magical illusion or dream is used so often. All the pleasure and pain, joy and sorrow, in the three realms and among the six classes of beings is like a magical illusion, like a dream.

If we do not know that 'we are own best remedy' and do not recognize our own nature, of course we will not even notice that what we think of as 'my life' is simply dream and illusion. In the moment of recognizing mind essence, you do not have to think that everything is dream and illusion: it is already cleared up. In actuality, if you are truly awakened, the whole illusion has dissolved. Deluded experiences are like clouds. Once the clouds disperse and dissolve, the qualities of the sun, which are primordially present, can manifest.

12

Dzogchen Terminology

❖

There is no real duality. Seen from the Buddha's perspective, samsara, nirvana and the path are all the single sphere of dharmakaya. When realized, everything is unconstructed original wakefulness. However, out of ignorance, when oneness is apprehended as two, it becomes possible to experience a seeming place into which a seeming 'me' takes birth. From the individual sentient being's point of view, there surely is samsaric life and someone spinning around in it.

The oneness of the single sphere of dharmakaya is not some kind of entity, however. Its unconstructed nature precludes even the concept of oneness. When this unconstructed single sphere of dharmakaya is fully realized, it is impossible for dualistic ideas to be maintained. Therefore, there is no longer a 'someone' taking rebirth in some place. For birth to be possible, there has to be the concept both of a place and of someone who is being born. Taking rebirth is impossible for buddhas, since duality has dissolved.

The mistake of duality comes about through not realizing our natural, nondual state. In the experience of the buddha nature, there is no true existence of subject and object. However, because of fixating on that which is experienced as the object, and that which experiences as the subject, the seeming duality of subject and object occurs. This is reinforced repeatedly, over and over again, until it seems solid and real. In general Dharma terminology, this twoness is called 'experience and emptiness' or 'appearance and emptiness'. In reality, these are a unity. It is said, "As long as duality has not become oneness, there is no enlightenment." The two have to become one. The one is free of constructs. But remember, it is a oneness in which there is nothing to grasp.

Within the all-pervasive space of dharmakaya,
Sambhogakaya manifests distinctly, like the light of the sun,
While nirmanakaya, manifesting like a rainbow, acts for the welfare of
beings.

Trekchö, the practice of the 'thorough cut' or 'cutting through', is to recognize your own nature as primordial purity, the all-pervasive, space-like dharmakaya. Tögal, the 'direct crossing', is to recognize that the natural expression of primordial purity is spontaneously present. To recognize that the spontaneous presence appears with no self-nature — that it is beyond any substantiality or independent entity whatsoever — is the unity of primordial purity and spontaneous presence. In other words, this is the nonduality of Trekchö and Tögal. Realizing this, there is neither someone who is born nor a place of birth. There is no 'other' — there is no samsara — only the state of buddhahood. We sentient beings, however, have failed to know our nature. We do not know the natural unity of appearance and emptiness. By being deluded by the expression of appearances, we fall into grasping and fixating on duality, the perceived and the perceiver. If we do not fixate on duality, samsara is freed into the primordial ground. We no longer need to circle in samsara.

In the specific terminology of the Great Perfection, Dzogchen, this is called 'realizing the natural unity of primordial purity and spontaneous presence'. That is exactly what is meant by 'the unified state of a vajra holder'. Unified means fully comprehending the indivisibility of appearance and emptiness. Sentient beings do not know this. They split everything up into object and subject. Not knowing appearance and emptiness as a unity, the six classes of beings in samsara emerge through grasping one as two.

This is where meditation comes in. In order to bring this natural unity of experience and emptiness into actuality for us, the Buddha introduced meditation. The Tibetan term *nyamshak* (translated as 'composure' or 'equanimity') literally means 'to place in evenness'. In the true state of evenness or equality of *nyamshak*, duality must dissolve. It is not that we retain a duality, one thing that we try to hold and bring into experience and another thing we try to push out. That does not infer equality. Therefore, "As long as duality has not become oneness, there is no enlightenment."

How do we actually let be in great equality? Not by trying to adopt and avoid through accepting and rejecting, affirming and denying. This type of training only becomes an exercise in hope and fear. That is *not* what is meant by the phrase, "bringing the natural unity of experience and emptiness into actuality." This is only possible once we truly practice meditation. You are introduced to the meditation state through the pointing-out instruction. The meditation state only begins the moment you recognize your natural face. Before that there is always an attempt to be in equanimity, trying, for example, to be in rigpa and to avoid conceptual thinking. That adopting and avoiding is definitely not the state of equanimity of all awakened ones, of all buddhas. The equanimity of the true meditation state has not yet begun.

To reiterate: in order to initiate the state of equanimity within our own training, we need to first recognize the state of nondual awareness in which there is nothing to accept or reject. In that moment, conceptual thinking is already dissolved, so there is no need for hope and fear. The view is simply to recognize this as being *what it is,* taking it as the starting point, rather than waiting or searching for something that will slowly dawn upon us after a lot of training. When the view is recognized, the training is simply to continue recognizing the view. That is called the meditation. Even though we use the phrase 'placing in equanimity' for training, it is not that you place some sort of 'thing'. I would like to rephrase this to say 'equanimity beyond placing and not placing'. This equanimity beyond placing and not placing is what we train in. Moreover, the conduct that we live by in everyday situations is none other than the view. Finally, the fruition that is attained is nothing other than stability in this view.

The great master Jamgön Mipham Rinpoche wrote a piece of poetry called the *Aspiration of the Great Perfection of Manjushri*, in which he says that the ground, path and fruition of the Great Perfection, as well as the view, meditation and conduct, are like three lines drawn in the sky, sketched in mid-air. *(Rinpoche imitates drawing in the sky)*. Like this is the view, this is the meditation, and this is the conduct. Once you look afterwards, where are those three lines? There is no separation, no distinction, between them.

Rigpey yeshe is not an object of thought. Self-existing wakefulness, empty in essence and cognizant by nature, does not need to be made at all. This is how it really is, and this is the pre-eminent actuality of the Great Perfection. It is never taught as clearly nor shown as directly in any of the lower vehicles. I am not merely speaking about the words. The actual demonstration of the single sphere of dharmakaya has tremendous blessing. It is brought directly into our own experience, not as a concept of something that we may or may not be able to realize later on, but as something of immense value in the present experience of the person who receives this transmission.

In the past in India, this transmission was kept incredibly secret — so secret that when a phrase like 'single sphere of dharmakaya' was given to a disciple, the master would whisper it through a copper tube directly into the ear of the student. No one else was able to hear it. At that point in history, the spirits and elemental forces could not bear to hear such a term with such a profound impact. They would simply faint. Nowadays, due to the activities of the buddhas and bodhisattvas, the situation is different. Human society has been almost saturated with the Dzogchen teachings. It is no longer a great shock to hear words like 'single sphere of dharmakaya'.

You can ascertain the view, *as it is,* the moment duality has collapsed, when there is not even a hair-tip of fabricating. The true self-existing wakefulness does not mean that some external deity will drop into you. It is when your own subtle thought patterns fall apart, dissolve, are destroyed. Any other state apart from that is a mind-made view. A mind-made view, for instance, is to think, "I wonder, is this the awakened state? This must be it." Do not do that! When training in the meditation state, simply acknowledge what already is — that your nature of mind is empty, cognizant, indivisible. It is not anything other than that. There is no need to imagine a state of emptiness and think, "I hope this is it. Well, I think it is. This *must* be the nature of mind." There is no need to speculate, because you already see what is in actuality. To quote Jamgön Mipham Rinpoche,

> *Within the essence, original wakefulness which is primordially pure,*
> *Manifests the nature, a radiance which is spontaneously present.*

This wakefulness that is primordially pure is the empty quality of the nature of our mind. In the moment when we recognize our nature, we do not see any 'thing' whatsoever. It is already utterly pure and perfect. That is exactly what we call primordial purity. Inseparable from that is a quality of knowing: we are cognizant, at the same time. This is the spontaneous presence. These two aspects are indivisible. In this way, we don't have to seek and try to discover the three kayas as somewhere out there in the future, or in any way separate from this undivided empty cognizance that we can recognize immediately. It is not hidden in any way whatsoever. This, the very essence of the Great Perfection, is what needs to be trained in.

This is exactly what sentient beings do not see. Because of not seeing what their nature is, they grasp at seeming duality and create the causes for endless samsaric existence. On the other hand, when simply recognizing the essence of mind, the creation of causes for further samsara is brought to a halt right there and then.

The moment of seeing the unity of the three kayas is our basic 'working capital'. We have something of tremendous value, and it does not have to be said with many words. Even though we need words to understand, please do not confuse the words with the meaning. When we hear words, we connect a meaning with them. The sound of the words and their meaning becomes mingled as thought. Abhidharma calls it "thought that apprehends the intermingled sound and meaning." But that act of apprehending is not the meaning itself. On the other hand, we do have to depend on words to realize the meaning. Please understand that words like *kadag* and *lhündrub*, primordial purity and spontaneous presence, are extremely important. Please understand how precious it is to realize what even such short words actually entail.

Once I went to see the great master Dzongsar Khyentse Chökyi Lodrö in Gangtok, and asked some questions about the *Dzogchen Desum*, the *Three Sections of the Great Perfection*. Though not a long text, it is incredibly profound. It is only one book, the size from your hand to your elbow. I asked, "Excuse me, Rinpoche, but was the whole terma discovered? Isn't there anything missing?" Khyentse Chökyi Lodrö smiled and said, "When I look at it, I don't see anything missing at all. What do you think is missing? Do you know exactly what is missing?" I said, "No, I am merely a stubborn intellectual, I don't know anything." Dzongsar Khyentse continued, "I don't see that it is incomplete in any way whatsoever. Just because it is short and concise doesn't mean that anything is missing or left out." Some of the instruction manuals in these three sections of the Great Perfection are only a couple of pages. Yet, they are all-inclusive and deeply profound. So, it's not that we need many words to discover the essential meaning. Everything stands and falls with the moment of recognizing mind essence. At that moment, you instantaneously meet the three kayas.

The system of Vajrayana uses incredibly skillful means to introduce the *reality of what is*. This method of introduction is often known as the four empowerments. The four empowerments are symbolic. You use implements and rituals to point out the reality of our actual situation. For instance, the first is the vase empowerment. The master visualizes the vase as being the palace of the deities; the water inside is consecrated as nectar. The vase is touched to the crown of the disciple's head, who is then given a drink from it. That is the superficial part of the ritual. What is actually introduced here is that our five skandhas, our elements and sense-bases, are already of a divine nature. This is the meaning of the 'vajra body being the mandala of deities'. In other words, what we are being empowered to realize is nothing other than what we already are to begin with. That is the true meaning of the vase empowerment.

The next, the secret empowerment, is conferred by means of the sacrament you are given from the skull cup. The third empowerment is to introduce the fact that the sensation of pleasure, the moment of bliss, is by nature empty. To point out this nonduality of bliss and emptiness, you are given the wisdom-knowledge empowerment.

The most important of all empowerments is the fourth, also called the precious word empowerment. The first three may have many details and words, but here, everything can be contained in one word. That is why it is called the precious word empowerment. That word can be constructed out of two syllables: PA and TA. The TA is pronounced without a vowel, so the combination becomes PHAT. This sound is exclaimed by the master in a way in which the disciple can recognize mind essence upon hearing it. It cuts through the flow of conceptual thinking to introduce the innate state of original mind that is empty cognizance. This was never really concealed; it is only seemingly concealed from sentient beings because their attention is occupied with other things. When that is the case, you may hear about the nature of mind, but it feels hidden from you; it is not an actuality. In the moment of recognizing mind essence, it is seen immediately. No longer hidden or far away, it has been brought into actual experience, which is exactly the purpose of the fourth empowerment. This is described in all the tantras of the Great Perfection.

There are also the eight exclamations of wonder and the twelve-vajra jokes that describe exactly how this state is. In the Mahamudra tradition it can also be pointed out with this simple verse:

> *Original wakefulness is extremely subtle.*
> *It is the vajra-like center of space.*
> *You are your own father.*
> *Relax into basic space beyond beginning and end.*

Original wakefulness means our basic state. 'Extremely subtle' means it is not comprised of any ideas. Thought usually occupies the mind of any sentient being, either as a coarse emotion or as subtle thinking. There is additionally, a very subtle conceptual frame of mind called cognitive obscuration, which is the last obscuration to be disbanded on the path to enlightenment. Original wakefulness is even more subtle than that, because it is the undivided empty cognizance that lies at the very foundation for any state of mind. It is not made out of anything whatsoever. That was the first line, "Original wakefulness is extremely subtle."

The second line is, "It is the vajra-like center of space." 'Vajra' here means 'indestructible'. Just like the center of space, the totally wide-open sky, is unchanging and unshakable, your original wakefulness is not made out of any causes and circumstances. The third line, "You are your own father," means that your own nature is yourself. The essence or source of any thought is the state of rigpa itself. The master is addressing the conceptual state and saying that your father is yourself. Recognize the identity of thinker and meet rigpa directly.

The fourth line, "Relax into basic space beyond beginning and end," introduces the nature of mind. Once you recognize it, there is no need to wait for another time in the future. Basic space never began and does not end in any way whatsoever. Rigpa never began and does not end. It is totally endless, utterly beginningless. Mind does not come into being; it never began. It does not cease at some point, so it has no end. It does not remain in any way in between, and therefore has no middle. There is not a present moment to be pin-pointed anywhere. Your basic state has a natural stability, an innate sort of uprightness, but it is not some concrete 'thing' to be identified in any way whatsoever. Of course, we can formulate the idea, "This is how rigpa is." But that is simply our idea. The state of knowing is in itself *as it is*. The natural stability is present when you do not forget it, if you do not get distracted. Once you forget, once you wander, this natural stability seems to be lost.

Innate stability is like a needle, not like a hair. If you hold a hair in the wind it bends, but a needle, no matter how strong the wind is, does not bend. A hair has no natural stability. Rigpa is untainted by fixating on outer objects, and unspoiled by focusing on the knower within. It is totally open. That is natural steadiness. No matter how thick a hair is, it still wavers in the wind. The thinking of a sentient being has no stability. The nature of mind has a natural stability. This natural stability is evident when uninvolved in subject and object, not focusing on something as outside, not concentrating on something within.

In this moment, when past thought has gone and future thought has not yet come, do not reconnect with any thought. To use Dzogchen terminology, it is to be awake, vibrant, crystal-clear, fully present. These incredible words do not need our fabrication, our making. They point at *what is naturally so*, not at what is cultivated through training.

The natural state of Buddha Samantabhadra expresses itself as the Dzogchen tantras, which is where these wonderful words come from:

Amazing, natural awareness is beyond thought.
Vividly clear, there is no obscuration.
Nakedly manifest, there is no delusion.
Wide awake, there is no subject and object.

The thoughtfree innate state is experienced in vividness. We do not have to think of it to discover it. The natural properties of rigpa are not conceptual. This is how it is described in Dzogchen. Who taught these Dzogchen teachings? Samantabhadra did. Samantabhadra is original wakefulness beyond concepts. Some people think Samantabhadra was an old, old man who lived a long time ago. Do not think that. When you recognize your mind essence, what word can you use to describe how it truly is?

STUDENT: Awake.

RINPOCHE: Is it hidden, or is it actuality?

STUDENT: It is an actuality.

RINPOCHE: In that moment, is it possible for any thought to linger on, to stick?

STUDENT: No.

RINPOCHE: It is totally free of fault; the fault is the thinking. It is also full of all qualities, because it is in itself immaculate dharmakaya. When that lasts throughout day and night, is it possible for samsara to remain?

STUDENT: No.

RINPOCHE: That is right. Samsara dissolves. Samsara needs your thoughts to be recreated. Because samsara is already insubstantial, there is nothing to keep. The dissolving of samsara is not a totally blank state of unconsciousness. There is no point in perpetuating samsara once we know that, so why bother? To recreate samsara you need to have birth and death, and for that, you need thought in which the nature is not seen. You need the involvement in thinking that lacks the recognizing of our nature; you need a re-disturbance of your essence. This is the type of thought all sentient beings are involved in. There is a big difference between thought and rigpa!

13

Realization Stories

❖

Do you see the photo on the wall behind me? The lama pictured there is Drubwang Shakya Shri, the Lord of Siddhas. In the latter part of his life he lived in Tibet, in a place named Kyipuk Hermitage. My youngest uncle, Tersey Tulku, was a disciple of Shakya Shri and told me many stories about him. Shakya Shri lived in a small, one-story hut. Nobody had more than one-story houses there. It was a hermitage, so there were not any elaborate structures. Shakya Shri's hut was in the middle of a meadow. There was a small enclosure around it. Below the house there was a flat piece of land. He would walk down to pee at the edge of that spot. There was a sort of covering to the side. It wasn't a real toilet, of course, but it was semi-private. One afternoon he went down there to pee; he finished peeing, and lapsed into the state of samadhi, free of any thought. He remained squatting like that for about half an hour. His attendants noticed this and thought they had better go collect Rinpoche. For a genuine meditator, the holding on to this and that dissolves. He was squatting there with eyes wide open. The attendants said, "Rinpoche, you'd better come up now; it's getting dark." He said "Well, yes, the stars are now bright in the sky." Then he stood up and walked back in.

Shakya Shri was also clairvoyant. One time the Bhutanese king sent some gifts. Special emissaries came up from the Bhutanese border through the district of Lhodrak with thirty carriers and thirty bags of rice. The Bhutanese king was very strict about how presents were handed over. The gifts had to be given in front of everybody. The sacks were unloaded right there on the meadow. In one of the sacks of rice, the Bhutanese king had packed a huge porcelain bowl. Now they could not find in which bag it was. They looked in one, they looked in another. It was buried somewhere in the middle of a rice bag, and they had forgotten which one. It seemed that they were going to have to open all of the bags to find the bowl. But Shakya Shri interrupted them, saying, "No, no, it is in this one," — pointing to one particular sack. They opened it and found the bowl right away. His clairvoyance was unobscured. Once fixation falls apart, clairvoyance is unimpeded.

Here is another story about the previous Sabchu Tulku — not the child who lives nowadays in Swayambhu, but in one of his former lives. The first Sabchu was a disciple of Situ Pema Nyinje, Jamgön Kongtrül and Jamyang Khyentse. Before he died, a horrible disease struck him; his stomach became one big open sore. It started with one sore and slowly it became bigger and bigger. Finally all his intestines were lying out in his lap. The pus, liquids and blood ran out onto the floor, all the way out to the door. There were definitely bodily sensations, and he wanted to scratch at it all the time, so he asked to have his hands tied. They were tied with a white scarf to stop him scratching the wound. His disciples asked, "Oh Rinpoche! This must be so difficult, it must be really painful for you. He said, "I'm not sick at all, there is nothing wrong with me." They said, "How terrible, all the pus and blood is flowing down the floor." He answered, "There is an old monk sitting on this bed, he seems to be moving around, quite uncomfortably. He wants to scratch his belly, but for me there is nothing wrong at all. I am not sick at all. However, there is someone who looks like me sitting right here. He seems to be suffering quite a bit, but I am fine." If you are stable in practice, it is like that: there is no fixation at all.

There was another lama, in Kham, by the name of Tenje, a siddha who contracted the same sickness where all his intestines were hanging out. People asked him, "How are you feeling today?" He said, "I'm fine, nothing wrong at all." They said, "But Rinpoche, look down, you have all these sores and open wounds." He replied, "Yes, it looks like there is something wrong there, but I am quite fine. I am not sick at all." The people asked, "We think you will die soon, so will you please tell us where you will be reborn so we can find the tulku?" He said, "Yes, I can take care of that. Call my disciple Tendar." The lama then told his disciple, "Carry me seven steps to the west". While Tendar was carrying his master those seven steps, the master snapped his fingers and said, "May my realization take birth in your stream of being." Afterwards, he said, while pointing at the student, "This is my tulku, even before I pass away. Will he be okay for this monastery? Tomorrow morning at dawn, I will enact the drama of dying. I am going home to the dharmadhatu buddhafield of Akanishtha." The next morning he died while the sun was rising. His disciple Tendar later said that from that moment when the lama snapped his fingers onwards, he was totally undistracted; he never wandered from the state of rigpa. This disciple later was known as Tendar Tulku, and he had the same state of realization as his master — no difference whatsoever.

STUDENT: Why can't the buddhas do that for all of us?

RINPOCHE: Maybe because the buddhas don't have disciples like Tendar! This master had many other disciples, but for some reason, he chose that particular one. It is probably because the mirror of the other people's minds were not that dust-free.

STUDENT: Does that mean the mirror of mind is so clear it can reflect everything?

RINPOCHE: Of course, all beings have the same basis, the same all-ground. If someone is realized, the mirror of his or her basic state is totally spotless. Whatever arises around them is clearly reflected. When you have a mirror, whatever is in front of it is reflected in it, isn't it? If a yogi has attained stability in rigpa, there is this quality of discriminating wisdom which distinctly and clearly reflects what, for example, all sentient beings in this valley think. This quality is then regarded as clairvoyance.

STUDENT: Is it present all the time?

RINPOCHE: A realized master definitely experiences in an unimpeded way. A great yogi like Jamyang Khyentse Wangpo could see very clearly, though he would rarely admit it. To make him admit he was clairvoyant, his disciples would sometimes have to trick him a little. One disciple by the name of Khenchen Tashi Özer sometimes had to pretend to be clairvoyant also. For instance he would say, "Isn't it troublesome for these people down in the Dzongsar village to be so occupied with all these different thoughts and emotions?" Jamyang Khyentse replied, "Yes, it is so troublesome for them to have all these thoughts." It slipped out.

Once Tashi Özer was sitting at the feet of Jamyang Khyentse. All of a sudden Jamyang Khyentse exclaimed, "Oh no! How terrible!" Tashi Özer said, "What happened?" "Far away in that direction, an old monk is calling my name. His pack animal, a yak, is sliding off the trail and is about to fall into the ravine. But he got stuck on a tree on the way down. The two old monks are not strong enough; they cannot pull up the yak and are calling my name. Oh yes, now a few traders are coming. They have ropes. Now they are pulling the yak up." After that he didn't say anything more. Four or five days later, Tashi Öser was in front of the gompa when two old monks came in with a yak. He had a chat with them. They told him that several days ago, their yak almost fell off the side of the trail, but they prayed to Jamyang Khyentse and it did not fall all the way down. "We were very happy about that," one said, "because all of our food was on its back and we would have had nothing to eat. Luckily some traders soon came with ropes and pulled it back up."[7]

So, to go back to your original question, it would be nice if buddhas took all sentient beings without a single exception and placed them in a buddha field, wouldn't it? When the sun rises in the sky, does its light reach into north-facing caves?

STUDENT: No.

RINPOCHE: The meaning here is that sentient beings need to have the openness to access the compassion of the buddhas. The buddhas will guide anyone, but they need to have devotion. It's as if having devotion creates a ring upon which the compassionate activity of all buddhas can catch, just like a hook. Sentient beings have all sorts of attitudes. If they all had faith and devotion, it would be possible to empty samsara; they could be led to enlightenment without too much trouble. Those who have devotion are guided, for sure. People have so many plans and ideas: it's like the Khampa saying, "Thirty people have thirty ideas, like thirty yaks have sixty horns." If everybody would think in the same way, it would be easier, much more manageable. If you have faith and devotion, the buddhas can help you. If you have no doubts, this is guaranteed.

If there is no doubt, it is like the old woman for whom even a dog's tooth yielded relics. Do you remember the story of how she was cheated by her son? Her son was a trader who went to India quite often. Each time he left she would ask him to bring her back a relic of the Buddha. Every time he forgot, because he was so busy with his trading. Finally, she said, "If you come back without a relic of the Buddha I will kill myself in front of you." And still he managed to forget! When he came back and saw his mother's house in the distance, he suddenly remembered, and said, "Oh no! What to do now? What to do?" He looked around and saw the skull of a long-dead dog, pulled out one of the teeth, and wrapped it in brocade. Then he called ahead to his mother's house for them to send down a welcome party, saying, "I have brought back a tooth of the Buddha." They came out with banners, sounding conch shells, waving flags and carrying incense. His mother believed he had really brought back one of the Buddha's teeth. The procession brought in the tooth and she placed it on the shrine. Every day, she made supplications and offerings to it. She had complete confidence that she had the good karma and fortune to be the custodian of one of the Buddha's teeth. Eventually, through the power of her devotion, small relics began to appear from the tooth, even though it was merely a dog's tooth. When she died, a white ray of light appeared and she went straight to the buddhafields.

Now, a dog's tooth in itself does not yield relics. It was the power of devotion that allowed the blessing of the buddhas to come through.

Although you may not practice much, if you have the sincere devotion of thinking, "May the buddhas look upon me," then when you die you also will go straight to the buddhafields. If your devotion does not change the moment your spirit and body depart, if you completely surrender, even though there may not be a white beam of light, there may be a black one still leading in the right direction. *(Rinpoche laughs)*. At that moment, if you have devotion you can be guided to the pure lands in as little time as it takes to stretch out one arm.

Of course, if you have already attained mastery over the practice of deity, mantra and samadhi, being fully stable in original wakefulness, there is no question about attaining enlightenment at the moment of death. But even through simple devotion to the buddhas, you can be liberated. The compassionate activity of the buddhas is unfailing. Likewise, the profound samadhi is unfailing. I can swear to that on my own forehead. It is as true as the certainty that I will leave this body behind. It is absolutely certain that once one's body is abandoned, one never comes back to life. This is a Tibetan way of swearing: "by my skull." It is that true. To recognize mind essence is not difficult; it is so easy. But even if you are not able to train in that, if you can just have devotion to the buddhas, if it is genuine devotion, then I swear that you will not be deceived.

STUDENT: How does a yogi transcend the experience of solidified reality?

RINPOCHE: That which perceives everything is mind. Mind is empty. Any appearance, any perception, is a personal experience occurring within our own mind. It is not something other out there. Personal perception is empty because mind is empty. But doesn't this seem to be in total contradiction to how we experience things? This thing here, *(Rinpoche knocks on the table)*, doesn't it seem real and solid? We feel it is a real thing that we experience — so much so that the emptiness of personal experience and the actuality of solid matter seem to be in total conflict. That is how it is for an ordinary person, due to the solidifying power of karma.

This karmic experience is shared by others of the same species, but only by deluded sentient beings. The majority of us see that we are in a normal room with walls and a roof and some statues. Everything seems solid. However, it actually is not. For something to be ultimately real it should possess the seven indestructible qualities. The seven vajra-qualities are: being uncuttable, indestructible, true, solid, firm, completely unobstructable and completely undefeatable. No perceivable 'thing' possesses these qualities. At a certain point or another all things will be destroyed. The final proof of this is at the end of an aeon when everything disintegrates with absolutely no remainder whatsoever. That is evidence that all phenomena are empty to begin with. Although phenomena are empty, they do appear. Though they appear, they are still empty. Otherwise, it would be impossible to destroy things. If they were real, they would be indestructible. Nothing is like that.

The way we see things, as being seemingly solid, is not the only way to experience. True yogis and bodhisattvas, not to mention buddhas, do not experience a solid reality. Things appear to them, but they do not cling. Everything is seen as the eight analogies of illusion. 'Yogi' means having some degree of stability in the recognition of rigpa. For such a practitioner, everything looks different. And reality *is* different from how ordinary people believe it to be and experience it. Guru Rinpoche and Milarepa were not obstructed by what we believe to be solid matter. The seeming solidity of their own body and the seeming solidity of matter were totally inter-penetrable. They could walk on water; they were unharmed by fire.

This occurs even on the first bhumi. When Düsum Khyenpa, the first Karmapa, performed a ceremony at his temple and there was nobody else around to help, he made three replicas of himself to complete the ceremony. Not only was he the vajra master, but also shrine master and assistant. He demonstrated that everything is in fact a magical display. A realized yogi does not cling to the solidity of things. Everything is seen *as it is*: visible emptiness, audible emptiness and the play of original wakefulness. At the level of buddhahood, which means having reached the full perfection of this path, everything is experienced in its infinite purity. When totally stable in rigpa, whatever appears, whatever exists is all-encompassing purity, also called *rangnang yeshe kyi khorlo* — the wisdom-wheel of natural experience, the unceasingness of original wakefulness.

Let me illustrate this with a story about Milarepa when he was old. His followers invited him to come up to the top of a mountain. He said, "I'm too old now. This old man cannot walk up to the top of the mountain. It's better if the top of the mountain comes down here!" And the top of the mountain extended all the way down in front of him. He stepped onto it, and it went all the way back up. He was on top of the mountain before any of the other people arrived! That is the way of a truly accomplished yogi.

In any case, all experience is personal experience. All personal experience is emptiness, the unity of being empty and cognizant. Once this is seen in actuality, then the next step, called 'mastering personal experience', is possible. Since all personal experience is empty, it is possible to command your experience. A yogi who has totally realized this, not merely as an idea, but as an actuality, can visibly demonstrate it. Such a practitioner is not necessarily harmed by the four elements. His body is not subject to any change by the four elements, unlike someone whose mind always attaches solidity to what is experienced, who denies the emptiness of appearances. As a normal person, you can be buried under earth; you can drown in water; you can be burned in fire, or blown away by the wind. But for a yogi it is not like that, as you hear in these stories. As a yogi, you are in charge.

STUDENT: How is the rainbow body attained?

RINPOCHE: This attainment is a consequence of what I have just spoken about. Right now the coarse material body comprised of the five elements is a deluded experience created out of fixating dualistic mind. When such 'impure' states of mind start to dissolve into the pure state of mind that is rigpa, the deluded impure experiences of a physical nature equally begin to dissolve. It is said that the impure aspects of reality start to dissolve into the pure essences. In a way, it corresponds to the aspect of the death process called the dissolution stages, where the forces of the five elements begin to dissolve.

Right now the physical body is something made of flesh, blood and bones. The ordinary speech is the voice of intermittent sounds and words. The normal state of mind is the constant diffusing into thought patterns, a restless state that does not remain from one second to the next. These three gradually dissolve through training in mind essence. The physical body dissolves into a form of rainbow light, a body of light. The ordinary speech becomes the voice of the buddhas, which is the king of melodiousness, the unceasing voice of the victorious ones. The deluded continuity of conceptual thinking dissolves into the buddha mind, the realization of the awakened ones.

This realization includes realizing the impure body of the aggregates, elements and sense-bases to be their pure nature. The pure nature of the five aggregates is the five male buddhas. The pure nature of the five elements is the five female buddhas. The pure nature of the sense-bases is the male and female bodhisattvas. When this natural purity is realized, whatever appears and exists is all-encompassing purity. The collapse of delusion is equal to complete stability in mind essence — the attainment of the dharmakaya throne of nonmeditation. Everything is seen as it originally and truly is. The five poisons are transformed into the five wisdoms. From an enlightened point of view, there is no impurity anywhere to be experienced. From that perspective, whatever appears and exists, meaning the world and beings, is seen as all-encompassing purity.

Buddhas and bodhisattvas are synonyms for this pure state of mind. The pure state of mind does not conceive of or see impurity. A pure state of mind means that the impure, deluded frame of mind has dissolved, subsided. 'Sentient being' is a synonym for the impure state of mind that does not see the pure state, the *actuality of what is*. When the pure is realized, the impure subsides; the mistakenness of dualistic mind subsides. For buddhas, siddhas and realized yogis, experience is like having arrived on an island of pure gold. There is no ordinary earth or stone to be found anywhere in such a place. Everything is pure gold.

That is the image for when impure dualistic mind has dissolved. There is no impurity found in any aspect of experience; everything is all-encompassing purity.

Total stability in the state of rigpa is also described as 'capturing the innate stronghold of immortality'. Any sense of birth and death, coming and going only has reality in deluded thinking. When all conceptual thinking dissolves into the state of nondual awareness, one has attained stability in rigpa and mastery over all phenomena. If there is no taking birth, how can there be any death? It is because of birth that there is death. Since mind is not a 'thing' that can die, it is possible for both birth and death to be obliterated. That is the meaning of 'capturing the innate stronghold of immortality'.

Even when someone as simple-minded as me thinks about it, how can there be any death if there is no birth? This removal of the basis for both birth and death is what buddhas and bodhisattvas have achieved. After that, although there is no birth, they act *as if* taking birth. Although there is no death, they act *as if* passing away. They do so because ordinary sentient beings hold on to the idea of permanence. But it is not that you can remain passive, because you need to continue benefiting beings, so again it is necessary to act as if taking birth. If you attain stability in rigpa to some degree, the 'illusory city of the physical body' does still perish, and at the same time, there is liberation into true stability. The very essence of nondual awareness is not something that comes into being, abides or ceases; the superficial appearances of this life are all illusory and insubstantial. When attaining stability in that which is truly unchanging, it is possible to awaken, and it is possible for all mistaken experience to dissolve, to collapse, to fall away, into basic space.

STUDENT: There seem to be forces we have no control over. What are they called?

RINPOCHE: There are experiences called the 'three challenges'. Outer challenges are the magical tricks of gods and demons. Inner challenges are imbalances in the body, like disease. Innermost challenges are of elation and despair, like an unexplainable sadness. Without any reason whatsoever, one gets depressed, acutely and severely. Sometimes one may even be convinced that one is about to suddenly die. The pain can be unbearable: maybe the whole body feels like it is about to be blown into pieces. You know, it seems like if you have clothes, food and a place to stay, you should have nothing to worry about. Yet one can get deeply saddened without any reason whatsoever. So these are the threefold challenges. Challenges are experiences that happen, occurrences.

STUDENT: What about the challenges that come from gods and demons?

RINPOCHE: Those gods, first of all, are not wisdom deities. Being mundane, they are referred to as gods instead of deities. They can be of the *mamo* or *tsen* or some other type, there are usually eight classes. They try to trick or influence practitioners by showing themselves in different forms. Their bodies are not material forms, even though they may be believed to be so by the perceiver. It is more like a film or television. Their speech aspect are heard as sounds or voices. Their mind aspect appear as provocations of attachment, lust or fear — any emotion in the practitioner's mind. In other words, they either try to scare you or seduce you. It is easy to be carried away by these apparitions if one attaches reality to what is perceived. In relating to challenges there are two options: either you are overtaken, or you take charge. To take charge one needs to be a practitioner who is somewhat stable in rigpa: then one overcomes, instead of being overcome. The inexperienced male practitioner can easily be seduced if the gods and demons appear in the form of a beautiful woman; he may think she is a wisdom dakini!

When the Buddha sat under the bodhi tree in Bodhgaya, all the gods and demons, headed by Garab Wangchuk, the chief of the maras, saw that he was about to become fully enlightened. Unable to bear it, they agreed to try their best to distract him, by fear, seduction, or any other means. Huge armies of demons surrounded him and let lose a shower of weapons and thunderbolts. But the Buddha did not flinch:

not even a hair on his body moved. There was nothing they could do. He was utterly invincible. Next, they decided, "Well, if we cannot scare him, let's seduce him." All the maras came in the form of beautiful maidens, with the full array of the five sense pleasures: enticing forms, sweet voices, fragrant smells, delicious tastes and smooth to the touch. Endless parades of the most beautiful goddesses, more beautiful than the daughters of the gods, kept appearing. They approached him in long lines. Again the Buddha was unmoved from his samadhi. The Buddha simply directed his gaze at them and immediately they turned into shriveled old women with tattered clothing. They all became terribly embarrassed and ran off. And that morning, just at dawn, he awakened to true and complete enlightenment. The maras tried their best to prevent this, through both wrathful and peaceful means. That is the most famous example for external challenges; the magical shows by gods and demons.

Here is another story about magical shows. My father, Chimey Dorje, was a practitioner of Chö. Chö practitioners are at some point supposed to train in frightening places. In eastern Tibet, in a place between two cliffs, there was a cemetery where corpses were abandoned. This place was renowned as being extremely frightening, and strange things would often happen to practitioners who stayed there. So my father went there one evening with two attendants. Since a Chö practitioner is not supposed to sit in company when doing his practice, his attendants had to remain at least eighty paces distant. After night had fallen, Chimey Dorje began his practice. All of a sudden, something fell down from the sky right before him. He looked at it and saw it was a human head, looking at him with glaring eyes and moving tongue. Another one fell down, then another one, making a loud thump when they hit the ground. One of them even hit him right on top of his head, and he felt a strong pain. After that the downpour became violent, like a hailstorm of human heads. They all seemed to be alive. Finally, the whole place was full of human heads, complaining and making noises. They coughed and spat up globs of putrid stuff. Some of them were moaning, "I died of rotting lungs."

Still Chimey Dorje did not move. He continued his practice. The heads shrank in size and diminished in number, until they eventually all vanished without a trace left. After a while he stood up and walked over to see what happened to his two attendants who had been lying down in the middle of the hailstorm of human heads. They had not noticed anything; they were still asleep and quite all right. This is an example of what we call 'challenges by magical shows from gods and demons'.

Another incident happened when Chimey Dorje was practicing Chö at Drag Yerpa, a famous cave hermitage near Lhasa. A huge gang of monkeys with grinning teeth and white beards attacked him, coming all the way up to his face, touching him and biting him. When they tried to grab his hands, they felt solid and real. Yet he never lost the confidence that all this is merely a show; it is not real. He continued to practice, and slowly the monkeys shrank in size until they were the size of rats. Then they vanished.

Another time my father saw what are called bone demons, skin demons and hair demons. There is a certain place in Tibet where skeletons would start to dance. Male and female skeletons would dance together before him and behind him. They performed elaborate folk dances, trying to scare him. He later said that the dancing was not such a big deal to cope with — he simply continued his practice. The worst were the skin demons, big sheets of human skin that would slowly move towards him in grotesque shapes. When they got very close he was struck with an intense pain in his gut. Once again, he simply remained in the state of rigpa and the human skins shrank in size and finally vanished. The hair demons were like big bundles of human hair that would swing back and forth in the sky in front of him, jumping up and down. They staged all different sorts of theatrics until they also disappeared. When I was small, I heard quite a few scary stories from my father! This is another example of challenges of gods and demons that have no solid existence.

Here's another story. A meditator in a hermitage saw outside his window a sheep stomach coming down towards him. He didn't do anything. After a while he thought, okay, I will do something, so he took a piece of charcoal and drew a cross on the stomach. The next day, he saw a cross drawn in charcoal on his own stomach! After he had left, a couple of years later another meditator sat in that hut in that same hermitage. He saw the same thing. He got angry at it, saying, "I'm going to get that." So he drew his knife and stabbed the sheep's belly that was coming at him. All of a sudden, he discovered that he had stabbed himself in the belly. He screamed, and one of his friends came and saw the practitioner sitting with the knife with which he had stabbed himself in the stomach. The practitioner's intestines were coming out of the big wound. The friend asked, "What happened?" He answered, "I saw this sheep stomach come down and I got angry and stabbed it. Now it seems like I did this to myself. I will probably die." And in fact he did die.

One lama I knew, who was quite a good practitioner, told me another story. When he was younger, he never liked one protector called Gyalpo Pehar. He would always frown at him and put him down. Once when he was in retreat doing the practice called *Könchok Chidü*, a revelation of Jatsön Nyingpo, he had a vision of Padmasambhava telling him, "You are about to attain great accomplishment. As proof of your attainment, take your bell and throw it against the wall, then you will see what I mean." He thought, "How wonderful: Padmasambhava said that to me in person, so I must do what he says." He took his bell, which was a very precious old bell, and threw it right at the wall. It splintered into many pieces. "Padmasambhava" disappeared and was never seen since!

14

Death Row

❖

In response to a request for teachings for someone on Death Row, Rinpoche gave the following recorded talk:

Translator: What you are going to hear now are the words of Tulku Urgyen Rinpoche. I have explained your situation and asked him to advice you.

RINPOCHE: The most benefit comes from trust in the Three Jewels above you, and compassion for your parents from past lives, which are all sentient beings of the three realms, below you.

It is your mind that experiences pleasure and pain. Your mind is also that which can go to a heavenly realm or to the hells. What is this mind? In essence, it is empty; by nature, it is cognizant. Its capacity is the unity of the two, being empty and cognizant. Once you recognize this, there is knowing. Without recognizing your own nature, there is unknowing, ignorance. This ignorance is the first of the twelve links of dependent origination, followed by formation, dualistic consciousness and so forth. Your present body was formed based on these twelve links. We take birth, we grow older, and finally the body dies, but mind is not some 'thing' that can die. The reason why there can be a succession of lives is because of this mind. If mind could die, there would be no rebirth. Because mind does not die, because it is still ignorant, again it will unfold the twelve links: formation, then dualistic consciousness, and again up to aging and death. Like a wheel incessantly spinning, this is called the wheel of samsara.

The root cause of samsara is unknowing, ignorance. Once you recognize that your mind is empty cognizance, then it is suffused with knowing. Without knowing this nature, which is the basic state of all other beings as well, it is empty cognizance suffused with unknowing. If you meet a master and receive instructions, what can he tell you? He will tell you, "Recognize that your mind is the unity of being empty and cognizant, suffused with knowing. When your attention is extroverted, you fall under the sway of thoughts. Let your attention recognize itself. Recognize that it is empty. That which recognizes is the cognizance. You can trust at that moment that these two — being empty and cognizant — are an original unity. Seeing that your nature is indivisible empty cognizance and acknowledging this is called self-knowing wakefulness.

You need to recognize the identity of that which feels happy, that which feels sad. Unless we know how to see our own nature, we reconnect again with the twelve links of dependent origination and the wheel of samsara spins endlessly. If you first recognize the nature of that which is ignorant, of that which is unknowing, then samsara stops at the first step in this wheel. That is called 'ignorance purified at the very base'. The moment you recognize mind essence, this self-knowing wakefulness interrupts the stream of deluded thinking which is formation, the second link. Once formation is stopped, dualistic consciousness stops, and gradually all the other links are cleared up. In one instant, the very basis for continuing in samsara has been interrupted, because dualistic consciousness has become original wakefulness.

How do you train in this? Let your mind recognize its own nature. When seeing your nature, there is a sense of being empty and yet awake. In actuality, this being empty is called dharmakaya. Along with this, there is a sense of knowing — an awake quality that acknowledges it is empty. That is called sambhogakaya. These two are originally a unity, which is nirmanakaya. This unity is the same as the indivisibility of water and wetness. In short, you are face to face with the three kayas of the awakened state.

But if one does not know how to recognize mind essence, there is unknowing, ignorance. As long as ignorance and formation continue, samsara does not end. That which is ignorant, that which forms new thought constructs, does not die. Therefore, samsara can go on ceaselessly. To recognize mind essence is the opposite of ignorance, of unknowing, and brings ignorance to a halt. The root of samsara collapses, dissolves.

As an ordinary sentient being, we are involved in an incessant stream of thought. For beginningless lifetimes, right up until now, it has been one overarching stretch of deluded thinking. This thinking is not something that we can simply stop. We cannot shake it off, either. You cannot burn your thoughts, flush them away or blow them up. The thinking, however, can be its own antidote. In other words, recognize the nature of the thinker; acknowledge the empty cognizance suffused with knowing. In the moment of seeing this, boundless aeons of negative karma and obscurations are purified. Joy and sorrow are evened out in the great expanse of equanimity.

In this world we go through all types of joys and sorrows. The traditional Tibetan term for world is the 'realm of possibilities'. Nothing is impossible here. Where do all these possibilities unfold? In the realm of one's own mind. Why? Isn't it this mind that experiences all that is pleasant, unpleasant or neutral? There is no other thing than mind that can experience in this world. This experiencer is the thinker. In the moment this thinker dissolves, there is thoughtfree wakefulness. An ordinary person is caught up in this thinking; a buddha is stable in the state of nonthought. Ordinarily, mind is busy thinking of all different possible things: "I want to stay, I want to go, I want to do this, I want to do that." Instead, recognize the nature of that which thinks, and simultaneously the thought vanishes tracelessly. After a while, another thought will occur. Again recognize the identity of that which thinks, and that thought will go as well.

Why is this possible? It is because all thinking is empty. You do not need to try *not* to think. Simply recognize the nature of who is thinking, and the thought disappears by itself. By simply recognizing this, we do not have to imagine that our mind is empty. The Buddha said, "Mind is emptiness; train in that." This is what you should train in. This is true peace.

In actuality, death is only the death of the body; mind does not die. When the time comes, prepare yourself by imagining that you are giving away everything — the entire universe, all your connections to others, your belongings, even your own body. Give away whatever is good to the buddhas. In that way, you can feel confident that you are not attached to anything whatsoever, not even as much as an atom. Think "This mind of mine, which is emptiness, is in essence indivisible from the awakened mind of all buddhas." I will simply let it mingle indivisibly with the buddha mind. So when I die, I will be enlightened. Death is not anything that can cause harm. It is like returning home." In the same moment of thinking this, you will arrive at the 'city of all buddhas'.

The buddha mind is not some distant place. It is like when you hold a mirror towards the sun: doesn't the sun's reflection appear instantly? If you have the openness of trust and confidence, there is no distance at all to the state of enlightenment of all buddhas. You can feel confident that "From today onwards, may the fear and dread of myself and all other beings in a similar situation be totally cleared away by the compassionate blessings of the buddhas. I can be totally without any fear whatsoever." When you open yourself with trust to the buddhas at the instant of passing on, there is no doubt whatsoever that you will be guided to the pure lands of awakened beings. You do not need to have any doubt about this. Please keep this in mind. That is all I have to say.

15

Daytime Stars

❖

Ever since Buddhism arrived in Tibet, its applied teachings have been transmitted through the Eight Chariots of the Practice Lineage. One is the Nyingma School, the 'Old School' of the early translations. The seven others are the Sarma Schools, the 'New Schools' of the later translations. These terms were given relative to when the teachings arrived. It was primarily the three great masters, Vimalamitra, Padmasambhava and Vairotsana, who brought the old school of the early translations to Tibet. Their accomplished disciples are said to have been so numerous that they practically filled the entire Land of Snow. Later, among the followers of the masters of the other seven chariots of the practice lineage there have been innumerable accomplished beings. Because of the way they practiced, they could not help attaining realization. Because of their realization, they could not avoid becoming enlightened. Because of being enlightened, they could not help accomplishing the benefit of beings. The teachings of the Practice Lineage have been tried and proven. Innumerable practitioners reached attainment through them. This is a fact that I would like to talk more about.

Sentient beings, not just human beings in this world, who do not practice the spiritual path are as countless as the stars at nighttime. Those who are interested in practicing the Dharma are as rare as stars in the daytime. All of us here today are daytime stars, very rare, precious people. I am happy for you. Not just because you have come to hear me, to receive teachings from this old man up here at Nagi Gompa — that is not what I am talking about. I am happy about the fact that you are sincerely interested in receiving and practicing the teachings of the enlightened one, the Buddha. That is truly wonderful!

One could divide all people into two groups: those who are wise and those who are foolish. You also know that people can be either successful or unsuccessful, right? If you look around in the world today you see people who are seemingly very smart and successful in hoarding wealth and fame for themselves and in subduing their enemies. There are many individuals like that. But viewed from the perspective of the Dharma, such people are not smart at all, because they are not successful when it comes to the crucial point. An individual may be so powerful, so influential, so famous that everyone knows his name, so that his name is as well-known as the sound of the thunder in the sky. But honestly, a roll of thunder is merely a loud and empty sound. Fame is temporary; it is only for a short while. It may seem useful, but how much can fame help you when you die? It cannot help one bit, not even as much as an atom.

We may take a lot of care of our body, paying special attention to it in various ways. We get anxious about being cold or hungry, and we try our best to avoid these situations. But honestly, this body will become a corpse, which people generally consider to be frightening. Milarepa said, "A scary, awful corpse is nothing other than this present body once you breathe out and don't breathe in." It is no further away than that.

When we try hard to develop a reputation, to build up fame and wealth, we make ourselves a slave to those things. We can become the servants of fame and money. If fame and money could help us after we die, then it would be useful, meaningful, to spend so much time pursuing them. At the moment of death, however, they are of no benefit at all. On the other hand, we can choose to use our time and energy on a true spiritual path that ensures that we ascend above the three realms of samsara. Be content with simply enough money, food and clothes to get by on. If our striving after fame, wealth, power and influence were actually meaningful, it would be fine. But such selfish pursuits only lead straight downward, leading one as far as the 'hell of incessant torment'.

You have heard about Milarepa, the great Tibetan siddha who attained mastery over prana and mind and was able to fly through the skies. Some people saw him and said, "He has been starving himself for so long, now he is being blown away by the wind!" They thought he was a madman who did not know how to take care of himself. These people assumed Milarepa was deluding himself. Milarepa, perceiving their minds, thought, "I am someone who has attained mastery over prana and mind, who has realized that this body is illusory, and I see also that the nature of my mind is the same as all the buddhas. There is nobody who is happier, more content and freer than I am in this world. Look at these people; they are totally deluded!" They thought Milarepa was deluded, and Milarepa felt they were deluded. That is how it is, an interesting irony.

Sentient beings of the six realms are in a state of delusion with no appreciation of what can rescue them, what can bring them to liberation. But I feel that all of you are well aware of this; you know what is of true value. All of you daytime stars know that none of the things you can achieve in this world will ultimately help you in any way. I am simply refreshing your memory. To repeat, if any mundane achievement — fame, wealth, influence, power — would be of ultimate help, then certainly we should pursue them; it would be fine to do so. I feel you understand it is better to be happy with enough to get by on. Instead of striving after material gain, aim whole-heartedly at attaining realization. If you go into retreat, you can reach a level that goes totally beyond this fleeting world.

A famous quote goes, "For the sake of food and clothing, people cast away what is of lasting value." It is often the case that for the sake of temporary benefit, we throw away what is of true value. I do not have to go on and on about this. Any intelligent person can think well about this. How much use is wealth and fame when you are in the bardo state? Simply ask yourselves that. You do not have to think about this for long, agonize in terrible doubt, and struggle to finally resolve this. It is totally obvious such things are futile to pursue. Yet at the same time — I am not putting blame on anyone, but "appearances are seductive and mind is fickle". We are easily carried away by the fleeting, the temporary. But think about it: isn't it true that there is something of lasting value? Isn't it possible to achieve liberation from samsara and attain the state of complete enlightenment? Liberation is not a fleeting moment of happiness, not at all.

If we think in terms of doing good business, we should not get involved in a venture that we will not get any profit from. And we should definitely not get involved in a business situation where we could lose everything. That would be bad business. I am asking you to line this up in your minds: what is most profitable? Is it better to pursue that which disappears quickly, or that which has lasting value? Think clearly about this, because what everybody wants is to be happy. We want comfort and pleasure. Nobody in this world wants pain and suffering. Everybody universally agrees on this. Since this is indisputably the case, wouldn't it be better to accomplish a happiness that lasts?

What is of utmost importance and lasting value? In general, it is practicing the Dharma; in particular, it is recognizing your buddha nature and training in that. To summarize, buddha nature is the identity of the three kayas of the awakened state. The three kayas are dharmakaya, sambhogakaya and nirmanakaya. They are also called the three vajras: vajra body, vajra speech and vajra mind. It is taught that the empty essence is dharmakaya, the cognizant nature is sambhogakaya and the unity of the two, the unconfined capacity, is nirmanakaya. The essence of mind is primordially empty: this is exactly what we call dharmakaya. If you want to use an example, this emptiness is like space. Space is not something that you can see, hear, smell, taste, touch or think of in terms of an entity that is pleasant or unpleasant. Space here is an analogy, not the actual literal meaning. When the Buddha said, "No form, no smell, no taste, no sound, no texture, no mental object," that describes how our mind is. In the true words of the Buddha, our mind has no form to be seen, and no sound, no smell, no taste, and no texture to be experienced; nor is it a mental object.

The essence of mind is primordially empty and rootless. Therefore, the Buddha said, "Realize the emptiness of your mind." To realize emptiness means to understand and see in actuality that our mind is empty, groundless and rootless. That is its essence, its identity — but what is its nature? It is an ability to know. In the case of a buddha, that knowing is called omniscient wisdom. Right now, at this very moment, don't we have the capacity to know and experience? In this world, there is only one thing that can know, experience and comprehend, and that is the mind of a sentient being. Nothing else can do this. In short, the Buddha taught that we should realize the meaning of emptiness.

To reiterate, the empty quality is free from the eight limiting constructs; it is primordially empty, rootless. The analogy used is space, because space cannot be created. Space is not our doing. Sunlight is the metaphor for the cognizant quality; there is also no one who makes the sunshine. It is spontaneously and naturally present. Space and the sun are forever inseparable. The sun can never go to some place outside of space. The meaning to which this analogy points within us is that our essence is empty, and by nature it is cognizant. The capacity of this is the unity of being empty and cognizant. To recognize and realize this is the very heart of all the eighty-four thousand aspects of the Dharma.

According to the traditional method of Tibetan Buddhism, the student begins practice with the four or five times hundred thousand preliminaries in the proper, correct manner. Then he or she proceeds on to the yidam practice with its development stage, recitation and completion stage. After that, the student is introduced to the true view of Mahamudra and Dzogchen. The sequence is conventionally laid out in this order: first you remove what obscures you; next, you suffuse your being with blessings; finally, you are introduced to the natural face of awareness.

These days, however, disciples do not have so much time! Also, masters do not seem to stay in one place and teach continuously. I hear that nowadays several masters first give the pointing-out instruction, introducing people to the main point of the practice, and afterwards teach the preliminaries. The view and the conduct can thus be adapted to the time and circumstances. In the world at this time, there is a growing appreciation of and interest in Buddhism. This is because people are more educated, more intelligent. When masters and disciples do not have a lot of time to spend together, there is no opportunity to go through the whole sequence of instructions. I usually also give the whole set of teachings in completeness, all at once. A proverb from where I come from goes: "The wise may still find truth in the words of a rascal."

This approach, of giving the essence at the beginning and then later teaching ngöndro, development stage, mantra recitation and completion stage, can be compared to opening the door all the way from the start. When you open the door the daylight penetrates all the way in so, while standing at the door, you can see to the innermost part of the shrine room. Some Buddhist teachers may say about me, "How can he possibly try to immediately point out mind essence without having made his students go through the ngöndro of purifying obscurations and gathering the accumulations." Some may raise this objection, but, with all due respect, I feel that it is not incorrect to do that. Why? Because we are now in the Dark Age and there is the prediction that, "At the end of the Dark Age, the teachings of Secret Mantra will blaze forth like wildfire." Secret Mantra here refers to Mahamudra and Dzogchen.

Honestly, if one has received the teachings on mind essence and then practices the preliminaries while remembering to recognize nature of mind, it multiplies the effect tremendously. It is taught that to practice with a pure attitude multiplies the effect one hundred times, while to practice with pure samadhi multiplies the effect one hundred thousand times. Combine the preliminaries with the recognition of mind essence and your practice will be tremendously effective.

You could also practice the preliminaries with simply a good and sincere attitude, and this alone will definitely purify your negative karma. But a good attitude in itself does not suffice as the true path to enlightenment. If you embrace these practices with the correct view of recognizing mind essence, however, the preliminaries become the actual path to enlightenment. If you have a painting of a candle, can it somehow generate light in the room? Wouldn't it be better to have the actual candle flame spreading actual light? In the same way, when we practice taking refuge, the true refuge is to take refuge free from the threefold concepts of subject, object and action. The same goes for the bodhisattva attitude; the true state of awakened mind, ultimate bodhichitta, is free from holding the threefold concepts. It is likewise with Vajrasattva practice, the mandala offering and guru yoga. There is only one way to be free from the threefold concepts, and that is to recognize the true view. I do not feel there is anything inappropriate in giving the pointing-out instruction to people. They can practice the preliminaries afterwards. It is completely fine.

Another point is that when giving a teaching such as this, there needs to be some kind of pure link between master and disciple. I feel that we do have a pure link together. There will not be much chance for anyone to destroy that by impure perception or damaging the vows of the precious samaya, because all of you meeting here will not stay together with me for very long. Therefore, there will not be much chance to break samaya. It is said that a master is like a fire: if you stay too close, you get burned. But if you keep a bit of a distance, you can get the warmth and brightness, and you will not be burned. When everyone goes home to his or her own place, you will have gotten the teaching, and you will not have a chance to break samaya with me. That is a good thing.

Many of you have one foot in the material world; there is no way around that. You have to make money to take care of your own living situation. I am not forcing you to immediately be a renunciate and get in trouble because of that. Renunciation will naturally grow forth from your training in mind essence, all by itself. As you practice this teaching further and further and gain more conviction, your attraction to the fleeting world and pursuits will become less and less, all by itself. From within you will discover the true value of the Buddha's teachings, and you will gradually put more time and energy into this practice. I do not want, or need, to force or push anybody; this development happens all by itself. Intelligent people understand what is valuable all by themselves.

Another point I want to make clear: I did not invent this teaching. I do not feel I am breaking any Buddhist law by speaking freely about the nature of mind. I am simply repeating what enlightened beings in the past have all discovered. Not merely one or two — a countless number of practitioners have realized this teaching, and can all bear witness to its truth. They are all evidence of its worth. If I were to depend only on what I have learned and understood, I would not be able to teach very much. I have not studied a lot, nor have I done any significant amount of meditation practice. If I were to rely on my personal experience, there would not be much to talk about. But since I am repeating the words of enlightened beings, I feel quite confident of the value. I am not lying about this: what I have been teaching here is only the truth.

Some people come to me and say, "Now I have practiced for ten years," or even, "I have practiced for twenty years and stayed a lot in retreat, but I haven't attained special experiences or any special realization. Nothing has happened." Why is that? It is not enough to call oneself a practitioner and let the time fly by. That is not the meaning of practicing the Dharma. We have been in samsara for countless lifetimes. Our minds have been so absorbed in the tendencies for samsaric existence. How can we expect to be totally transformed within a few years' time? It does not happen like that. The habitual patterns, the three poisons and the dualistic fixation are all latent in our minds. They have been there, in continuous recreation, from time without beginning. Whenever a situation presents itself we are caught up again, and this occurs repeatedly, over and over. The preliminary practices are so important precisely because they purify these negative habits and thus enable realization to take place. When these tendencies are purified, our intrinsic three kayas are realized in actuality. Once the three kayas are fully evident, we have reached the level of buddhahood.

Until this point, however, our buddha nature is hidden. The only way to make buddha nature fully manifest is to continue practicing the Dharma in an authentic way. And this does not happen by only practicing off and on for a few years. Of course, sporadic practice does make nice imprints, but it does not generate authentic change to the depths of one's being. To truly bring about realization within a couple of years, you need to practice, not just occasionally, but all the time. The foremost way of practicing is to only sleep one hour each night, and the rest of the time try to be undistracted continuously, throughout day and night. If you practice like this I can guarantee that within fifteen years you will be fully awakened, fully realized. There is no doubt about that! But that means continuous practice, not simply once in a while. The ability for this to happen is in your own hands.

To be discouraged because nothing extraordinary has happened since you began practicing is missing the point. Renunciation is the true sign of accomplishment, blessing and realization. In other words, there is a natural disenchantment with samsaric attainments, with any samsaric state. Unfortunately, people sometimes yearn for the extraordinary. Some expect the divine to come down from above and endow them with special powers. Others think that by forcing a certain experience forth in their minds to intoxicate themselves with, they can be high all the time, drugged on Dharma practice. Such types run around with their eyes turned heavenwards, not looking at the same level as normal people anymore, thinking they are tremendously special. Some people, when they get into an altered state of meditation, think that the very subtle forms of the three poisons, known as the experiences of bliss, clarity and nonthought, are realization. Many people get stuck in their beliefs. When you start having clear dreams, the demons will take advantage of you. They will come and act as if they are messengers of buddhas, bodhisattvas and deities. They can lead you astray in all sorts of different ways.

Do not attach any importance to these temporary experiences, not at all. There is only one thing to be confident in: the true state of realization that is unchanging like space. Understanding this is of utmost importance. What really matters is to increase your devotion to and confidence in the Dharma, so that from within you feel that only the

Dharma matters, that only practice is important. That is a sure sign of accomplishment.

Always nurture the feeling, "For the rest of my life I will never give up the practice of the Dharma!" Otherwise, we can be carried away by misusing the Dharma, or even worse, give up the Dharma. Forsaking Dharma practice can happen when an individual does not feel he or she can get anything out of it *for me, for myself.* "I have practiced the Dharma now for so long, I didn't benefit at all. Maybe I'd better do some business; at least there is profit in that." That, we Khampas call "Giving a bad end to a good beginning." You could be an exemplary practitioner the first half of your life, but later the enthusiasm begins to fade. Finally you turn to business and at the end become totally unspiritual. That type of Dharma career will definitely cause you deep regret at a certain point. It is much better to give a beautiful end to a bad beginning: to be not such an impressive practitioner at first but slowly, slowly let the Dharma take effect as you progress. In Kham we call that "a good child of a good father." Follow that example!

I want to emphasize this: never give up the Dharma! When you travel to Bodhgaya by foot from Kathmandu, there are many ups and downs; it is not always easy. There are mountains, there are valleys, and there are rivers we have to cross. If you stop on the way, you will not get there. Traveling to Bodhgaya without getting sidetracked means to apply the view, meditation and conduct as often as possible. Continue your Dharma practice at a constant pace. Please endeavor again and again to bring spiritual practice into every moment of your life. We often make this prayer, "May I equalize life and practice." Don't practice a little bit just once in a while, living the life of an ordinary person most of the time. Equalize life and practice! Fill every moment of your life with spiritual practice. In whatever you do, try again and again to let be in uncontrived naturalness. If you stop somewhere along the way, you might end up in dusty Raxoul at the Nepali border, and never reach Bodhgaya itself. Train in recognizing your buddha nature, and you will one day arrive at the Bodhgaya of true and complete enlightenment.

Rinpoche gave this talk on the final day of his last public teachings at Nagi Gönpa, October 30, 1995. He passed away three and a half months later.

Notes

[1] The *Ngakso Drubchen* is published as *Ocean of Amrita*. Teachings on the *Lamrim Yeshe Nyingpo* are contained in the *Light of Wisdom* series (Rangjung Yeshe Publications).

[2] This quote is taken from *Calling the Guru from Afar, A Supplication to Pierce your Heart with Devotion*, written by the first Jamgön Kongtrül, Lodrö Thaye. Several English translations exist: one in *Journey Without Goal*, (Shambhala Publ.), one by Michelle Martin with Ringu Tulku, and one from Rangjung Yeshe including extra verses for lineage masters.

[3] Gyalwa Götsangpa Gönpo Dorje (rgod tshang pa mgon po rdo rje) (1189-1258). One of the great masters of the Drukpa Kagyü lineage.

[4] The *Dorje Changchenma* chant is widely used in all Kagyü centers in the West, and an excellent translation was made by Chögyam Trungpa Rinpoche.

[5] The *Yeshe Kuchog* is an apology chant combined with the peaceful and wrathful deities. It belongs to the *Tantra of Immaculate Apology*. A translation is included in the feast offering for *Kunzang Tuktig*.

[6] This story is explained in detail in *Rainbow Painting*.

[7] More stories of this type can be found in Tulku Urgyen Rinpoche's memoirs.